Turning the Tide

Leo McKinstry worked as a researcher for Labour MPs at Westminster, and was a prominent Islington Labour Councillor. Since his resignation from the Labour Party he has been Associate Editor of the *Spectator*. His last book was *Fit to Govern?*, an analysis of the prospects of a new Labour Government.

Also by Leo McKinstry

FIT TO GOVERN?

TURNING THE TIDE

Decadence and Decline in Modern Britain

LEO McKINSTRY

MICHAEL JOSEPH
LONDON

To my family

MICHAEL JOSEPH LTD

Published by the Penguin Group

Penguin Books Ltd, 27 Wrights Lane, London W8 5TZ, England

Viking Penguin Inc., 375 Hudson Street, New York, New York 10014, USA

Penguin Books Australia Ltd, Ringwood, Victoria, Australia

Penguin Books Canada Ltd, 10 Alcorn Avenue, Toronto, Ontario, Canada M4V 3B2

Penguin Books (NZ) Ltd, 182–190 Wairau Road, Auckland 10, New Zealand

Penguin Books Ltd, Registered Offices: Harmondsworth, Middlesex, England

First published 1997

1 3 5 7 9 10 8 6 4 2

Copyright © Leo McKinstry 1997

Set in 10.5/12.5pt Monotype Bembo

Typeset by Rowland Phototypesetting Ltd,
Bury St Edmunds, Suffolk

Printed in England by Clays Ltd, St Ives plc

A CIP catalogue record for this book is available from the British Library

ISBN 0 7181 4230 6

The moral right of the author has been asserted

Contents

Introduction

'Often several couples slept in the same room and might vary their entertainment by changing partners during the night. In hot weather the parasites in their clothes and bedding and the stifling atmosphere made lodgers of both sexes lie on top of the beds, entirely naked – a powerful indication of how far they had abandoned all standards.' – Kellow Chesney, *The Victorian Underworld*, in a passage describing life in the worst inner-city slums.

'Herded into slums where religion, propriety and civilisation were impossible, interspersed with criminals and prostitutes, deprived of light and air, craving for drink and "cheap excitement", "the residuum" was large enough to engulf civilised London.' – Gareth Stedman Jones, *Outcast London*.

Most commentators would argue that our society has made enormous progress since the end of the Victorian era, almost a century ago. Compared to the degradation and abject poverty which scarred parts of late nineteenth-century urban Britain, we now live in an age of unprecedented wealth and individual freedom.

A Victorian social reformer, if he were able to visit the Britain of the nineties, would be astounded at the material prosperity of all social classes, the electricity and running water in almost every home, and the near universal possession of (strange to him) household goods such as washing machines, cookers and telephones. He would be struck by the comforts and accessories which most of the population take for granted, such as heating, an annual holiday (often abroad) or a car. The technological innovations of our age would arouse near disbelief. Reports of space travel, satellites, micro-surgery, the internet, and robotics would be beyond his comprehension, while he would shake his head in wonder when told that virtually every British household, even the very poorest, owns one of the miraculous electrical boxes that emit lifelike pictures and sounds.

Our time-travelling Victorian philanthropist might be almost as impressed to learn that every citizen has the right to receive assistance from the Government in times of hardship, and that the elderly and the unemployed receive extra sums. The right to free schooling and free medical treatment could also be seen as indications of an advancing civilisation, as would the quality and extent of public housing. A keen believer in the importance of education, he is pleased – and amazed – to discover that a third of our young people now attend universities or colleges, with their fees met from the public purse. Indeed, our Victorian is intrigued by the wide range of duties expected of both central government and local authorities in catering for the needs of the populace: providing housing; paying a financial benefit for every child born; subsidising wages; looking after the elderly and the disabled; funding civil legal actions; organising public transport; and running museums, opera houses, art galleries, libraries and sports centres, to name a few.

Yet our Victorian is also profoundly disturbed by his visit to our nineties society. For, in the midst of this apparent prosperity, he finds criminal behaviour and boorishness at levels beyond anything experienced in his own age a century earlier. (In 1900 there were 250 indictable offences per 100,000 of the population. In 1994 the rate had increased dramatically to over 10,000 per 100,000 of the population.) He is appalled at the threat to civil order in many of our cities, reflected in the thuggish antics of gangs of youths, in the lack of respect for the police, and in the resigned acceptance of foul language, vandalism and burglary.

Hailing from an era which regarded the family as the keystone of civilisation, he is shocked at the changing structure of the family, particularly the instability of marriage and the phenomenal number of divorces. He is outraged to hear that more than a fifth of families are now headed by a lone parent, not because of widowhood, but because of marriage breakdown and the toleration of childrearing outside wedlock. To his disgust, he learns that this toleration is now so pervasive that the very word 'illegitimate' has disappeared from modern vocabulary. He finds it incredible that homosexuality and promiscuity should not only be legal but can even be 'celebrated', a usage of the word he cannot grasp. He is stunned at the overt sexual imagery he finds all around him, the absence of any sense of shame.

Perhaps even more troubling for our Victorian is the collapse of organised Christianity as a major force in nineties Britain. He is transported into a secular land, where the established Anglican Church is utterly without influence, where the vast majority of the public neither worships God nor has any understanding of the tenets of Christian faith. To his frustration, even the clerics seem fearful of discussing belief. Poverty, not piety, is their greatest concern. Christianity is nothing more than a minority pursuit, he realises, demonstrated by the fact that there are now more Muslims than Methodists in the new Britain.

Our anxious Victorian, surveying the alien landscape of our modern society, keeps asking himself awkward questions. Why do adolescents appear so ignorant of English and history when they are at school for so many years? Why are there such bitter complaints about poverty when so much is spent by the Government on welfare? What incentive is there to work when public assistance can provide a higher income than many jobs? Do those who receive such assistance have any duties? Why are so many people more willing to believe in astrology than in God? Who disciplines boys in these single-parent homes? Why are there so few expressions of pride in our country? Why are words like 'respectability' and 'honour' heard so little, and 'rights' and 'needs' so much? What is meant by 'multi-culturalism' or 'non-marital parenting' or 'public sex environments' or 'lifestyle choices'? Without waiting for answers, he retreats back to his own age.

Our Victorian is right to be dismayed by what he sees in the structure and attitudes of modern British society. This is not to argue for a return to some mythical Victorian golden age. As the two quotations at the start of the chapter demonstrate, late nineteenth-century Britain contained examples of brutality and squalor which it would be hard to emulate today. The debate about 'the underclass' in the 1990s had its equivalent in the 1890s in the expression of fears about 'the residuum'. 'Moral panics' were perhaps an even stronger feature of Victorian public discourse than they are today.

Yet the Victorian era had two great advantages over our modern age. First, during the last fifty years of the nineteenth century, they could see real progress being made in strengthening the civic order, reflected in lower crime rates, lower illegitimacy, rising standards of education, and the growth of community institutions like working men's clubs. Second, they had a powerful moral code, accepted by all classes, which supported and reinforced the fabric of society by encouraging discipline, restraint, self-help and responsibility. Of course, these 'virtues' (to use the Victorian terminology) were transgressed all the time. But such transgressions were usually carried out in recognition of the existence of the moral code, and therefore led to either shame or defiance on one side, and disapproval on the other. The reference in *The Victorian Underworld* to the nakedness in the doss house would have shocked Victorians precisely because it transgressed 'all standards'. In the Britain of the 1990s, there is precious little moral code to transgress. Any attempt to criticise such demonstrations of doss-house nudity, far from winning approval, would be seen as 'judgemental' or 'restricting personal freedom'. Anyway, the 'real issue' would, of course, be 'lack of government funding' to provide alternative accommodation. Instead of 'attacking the victims of a harsh housing policy', such critics should be 'campaigning for more resources for housing'.

The foundations that the Victorians laid for a cohesive society were built on in the first half of this century. The good manners, discipline, and low levels of crime among the English were commented on by many observers. In 1955, the American anthropologist, Geoffrey Gorer wrote:

'The English are certainly among the most peaceful, gentle, courteous and orderly populations that the civilised world has ever seen. The control of aggression has gone to such remarkable lengths that you hardly ever see a fight in a bar and football crowds are as orderly as church meetings.' – Quoted in Norman Dennis, *Rising Crime and the Dismembered Family*, London 1993.

It would be absurd to write such words about Britain today. Far from behaving like church congregations, our football crowds descended to such levels of hooliganism in the 1980s that British clubs had to be banned from Europe. Even in 1996, after all the changes in police methods and the composition of football crowds (reflecting much higher seat prices), a crowd of England supporters caused serious rioting in Trafalgar Square. Nowadays we hear much about the need to segregate opposing fans at matches to avoid violence. In 1937, a crowd of some 76,000 (more than 30,000 higher than today's largest attendances) saw Arsenal play Chelsea at Stamford Bridge without segregation or trouble.

The incidence of football violence over the last thirty years is just one indicator of the crisis in our civic order. All around us are others: the prevalence of juvenile crime; the vast increase in the prison population; the growth of random violence like the misnamed 'road rage'; the burgeoning social security bill; the dismal standards of education in our schools; the rate of divorces, co-habitation and lone-parenthood; and the spread of drug-taking, particularly among the young.

This is the theme of this book: the threat to civilisation in modern Britain. I will argue that, amidst growing affluence, our nation is losing confidence in its culture, codes of morality and institutions. Universally-held beliefs in right and wrong are disappearing. Personal behaviour, no matter how damaging to the wider public good, must not be judged or condemned. Everyone has the right to his or her own opinion, but no single view is any more valid than another, just as all 'lifestyles' are equally valid. The ethics of personal responsibility and duty are seen as outdated or irrelevant restrictions on personal freedom. Nothing must stop the pursuit of gratification. The right to personal happiness is all. In the lexicon of the new hedonistic culture, words like 'commitment', 'decency', 'thrift' and 'discipline' have lost their place.

This dangerous cultural mood has been fostered by both wings of the political spectrum. Since the late seventies, the Right has promoted rampant individualism, claiming, in Mrs Thatcher's famous dictum, that 'there is no such thing as society'. Under this creed, Britain is no more than a collection of atomised individuals, each pursuing their own economic ends. The traditions and institutions which have long bound people together are meaningless in the face of the free market. Consumerism, not community, is the driving force of this outlook. And it is a consumerism that extends far beyond just goods and services. It now reaches relationships, family life, welfare and religion. This individualistic, consumerist philosophy is reflected in societal changes as diverse as the present willingness to resort to legal action over the slightest misfortune or demands for increasingly sophisticated IVF treatment. The bloated salaries of the privatised utility bosses, the reluctance of public figures to resign from office over wrong-doing, and spiralling welfare claims are part of the same regrettable movement.

In spreading the cult of individualism, the Right has, paradoxically, had an unwitting ally in the political Left. Fixated with warped ideas about 'oppression', 'equality', and 'unmet needs', many Left-wingers have emphasised only the 'rights' of the individual, particularly those who are seen as the victims of economic, racial, or sexual oppression. And just as some on the Right despised those institutions and mores which, they felt, inhibited personal freedom or the role of the free market, so certain Leftists have railed against those elements of the civic order which are supposedly responsible for oppression, like the police, the Church, or the family. So deep-seated has been this concern with alleged discrimination that they can elevate the rights of the criminal above those of his victim, explaining that the crime is the result of poverty or racism or some other injustice. In this inverted Leftist moral universe, any expression of concern about the breakdown of the family becomes 'an attack on the rights of single mothers', any questioning of the welfare budget is seen as 'another assault upon the poor', any attempt to introduce efficient management in the public sector is an affront to 'the working class and trade unions'.

These two political philosophies have heavily influenced the development of public policy over the last twenty years, the Right through Tory dominance at Westminster, the Left through its control of local authorities, state education and parts of the media. It is partly as a result of these twin forces that Britain, at the end of this century, is such a fragmented, amoral and self-absorbed society.

In his great speech of 12 June 1940, on the eve of the Battle of Britain, Winston Churchill warned:

'Upon this battle depends the survival of Christian civilisation. Upon it depends our own British life and the long continuity of our institutions and our Empire. The whole fury and might of the enemy must very soon be turned on us. Hitler knows that he will have to break us in this island or lose the war.'

The tragedy is that, after winning the war, our institutions, traditions and Christian civilisation are now, more than fifty years later, being destroyed from within.

In the multi-cultural, non-patriarchal, secular, do-your-own-thing Britain of the nineties, it is almost impossible to see how a sense of national allegiance could be fostered in times of crisis. Pride in our national symbols, like the Union Flag or the monarchy, is challenged on the grounds of being 'élitist' or 'discriminatory'. Authority is held in contempt. Love of one's country is derided amongst the young as outdated or offensive. Britain's past, when it is discussed at all, is seen as either an antique irrelevance or a shameful tale of imperial conquest, xenophobia and class hatred. Opponents of the relentless march of European integration are condemned by the intelligentsia, both Left and Right, as 'Little Englanders' or 'petty nationalists', simply because they want to maintain the existence of Great Britain as an independent state.

Terrified of accusations of discrimination or traditionalism, we can no longer promulgate Judaeo-Christian values. 'Preaching morality' has become an indefensible activity. In our secular, non-discriminatory age, Christianity is just another religion and English just another language. To argue otherwise is to indulge in a form of 'cultural imperialism'. This growth of the moral-free, judgement-free outlook has led to a crisis of authority in our society. When laws, institutions, language and even morality are under constant challenge, they will have to struggle to survive. Traditional guardians of discipline – the police, teachers, the courts, doctors, priests and, in the home, fathers – are all finding their roles under attack. Without a universally accepted moral code, there can be no concepts of right and wrong. And without such a concept, figures of authority lose their legitimacy. They become, not the upholders of the common good, but the wielders of arbitrary and discredited power.

In a secular age, nothing is sacred any more. There are almost no taboos in the Britain of the nineties. A Channel Four soap, for example, feels no compunction about showing a scene of incest on a Saturday afternoon. At the Royal Court Theatre, a play features cannibalism, defecation, infanticide, and rape, and is interpreted as an allegory about Bosnia. A woman, pregnant with twins, decides to have one of them aborted simply because she feels she 'could not cope' with both of them, though each foetus is perfectly healthy, while a representative of the Birth Control Trust warns against 'moral posturing' on this issue. Prostitutes – or 'sex workers' as politically correct language has it – can receive support-funding from the National Lottery and the European Union. The practice of cottaging by gay men – having sex in a public toilet – is now subsidised by the National Health Service. A health clinic in Bristol hands out condoms to children aged as young as nine, along with an explicit sex-education leaflet. The Chief Constable of West Yorkshire calls for prostitution to be legalised, saying he 'sees no disadvantages except the one that says prostitution is wrong'.

This desire to avoid judgements has infected every area of society. It has created havoc with our schools, preventing both the teaching of the essential subjects and the imposition of discipline. In a judgement-free world, there are no 'wrong answers' or 'poor behaviour', only 'different' answers and 'challenging' behaviour. Instead of listening to teachers 'impose their values', children must be allowed to 'express themselves'. Thirty years of such 'progressive', 'child-centred' methods have led to a catastrophic fall in standards of literacy and numeracy. Armies of ill-educated, semi-literate, disaffected youths now leave school without the equipment or the desire to participate in our society.

The disease of non-judgementalism has swept through the Anglican Church, where tolerance and forgiveness are the only Christian values that seem to matter. In some quarters, theology appears to have been replaced by sub-Marxist sociology. The concept of sin is alien to many of our clerical economic theorisers. After a night of vicious rioting in Leeds last year, when a gang of about thirty youths burned down a pub, threw missiles at the police and set twelve cars on fire, the local vicar, the Reverend Anne Jenkins said: 'There's very little for young people to do round here. They feel forgotten.' No concept of wrong-doing there.

The problem is just as serious in social services, Britain's biggest growth industry of the last two decades. The social work profession is notoriously unwilling to pass judgement on the actions of their 'clients', no matter how feckless or damaging. In a case in Islington in which an astonishing sixty-seven different care professionals were involved, a couple so brutally neglected one of its children that he died in utter squalor, horribly scarred by the acid of his own urine. Despite the neglect and the squalor, welfare agencies felt that the household was 'dirty, smelly but happy'. This culture is exacerbated by social-work training, which is suffused by the doctrine that the service users' problems are caused, not by individual failings, but by societal forces: economic disadvantage, racial prejudice or, that most predictable of mantras, 'Government underfunding'.

No judgements can be made about the recipients of social security, while the welfare budget continues to spiral out of control. A third of all government spending, more than £90 billion, goes on benefits, with single parents taking up to £10 billion of this sum. An ever-increasing tax burden is now met by those in work, while many adolescents regard the DSS as the provider of the first, not last, resort. It is a grotesque perversion of both morality and common sense that an able-bodied young adult might earn less in working a forty-hour week than in drawing social security payments, for which no contribution has been made. Yet, as Shadow Chancellor Gordon Brown has discovered, any attempt to impose duties on such welfare claimants is met with a chorus of ululation about 'rights'.

Non-judgementalism is further reflected in the visual arts in modern Britain, much trumpeted in certain quarters for their vibrancy and originality, but, in reality, displaying no more than the third-rate, sub-rebellious, cliché-mongering of a discredited form that has lost all faith in absolute standards and universal truths. The ability to shock, rather than transcend, is all that appears to matter to the new wave of sculptors, painters and so-called performance artists. If a work is seen to carry some form of political message, especially about AIDS, racism or the evils of capitalism, then it is certain to be awarded that most coveted of all modernist adjectives: 'important'. So craven is the surrender of the art world to the creed of political correctness that the racial origin or sexuality of the artist is often seen as more interesting than their work.

The irony of this obsession with discrimination and victimhood is that it actually encourages divisions within society by promoting the idea that people are defined solely by their skin colour, or gender, or class background,or sexual orientation. Instead of fostering harmony and fair treatment for all, too many equality zealots categorise social groups as 'oppressors' or 'victims', indulging in the most crude forms of prejudice. The consequence can be that a policy designed to establish equality of opportunity achieves the very opposite, with appointments based not on merit but on some form of victim status.

This is the age of the victim. As a result of the constant emphasis on individual 'rights', we are losing the long-standing British virtues of fortitude and stoicism. The stiff upper lip is being replaced by the demand for compensation. 'Grin and bear it' is not a saying observed by our nineties army of litigants and legal aid claimants. Someone else is always responsible for any accident, any difficulty, and they should be made to pay. The moral vacuum at the heart of our society, reflected in this persistent emphasis on 'rights' and 'needs' rather than 'duties' and 'responsibilities', has meant an expanding regulatory, penal and punitive role for our Government. The well-ordered, highly civilised society needs far fewer laws and regulations than the disordered one, for most of its citizens will respect the moral code of their own volition. As W. B. Yeats said, 'Civilisation is the exercise of self-restraint.' Edmund Burke put it thus: 'Men are qualified for civil liberty in exact proportion to their own disposition to put moral chains on their own appetites.' In our age, sadly, where we do not even know what moral chains might look like, never mind how to wear them, it is the Government that has to restrain our appetites.

One of the frequent sayings of modern life reflects this replacement of a moral code by a Governmental one. 'I've broken no law' is usually uttered by a wrong-doer (sometimes a public official or business executive involved in a dubious transaction) who shows not the slightest grasp of any code of personal morality. Again, the frequent demands for more Government action on problems like under-age drinking and sex and teenage drug-taking – only, of course, in the form of 'education and support', not punishment – reflect the difficulties of many parents in imposing discipline on their own children. The state, in such circumstances, is expected to take on the parental, guiding role.

The chapters that follow this introduction will expand the claim that modern Britain is a decadent society, a society without a moral base or confidence in its own heritage. In looking at crime, the family, the welfare system, education, and public services, I will argue that our sense of collective identity is disappearing, that the ties that once bonded us together are weakening. I find it difficult to imagine the nation unifying for a great common cause as we did fifty-six years ago. Terms like 'Christian civilisation' and 'our British way of life' are an anathema to those who have been educating our young since the sixties. A society which has contempt for long-held morals, institutions and traditions is approaching disaster. As the sociologist Philip Rieff argued more than twenty years ago in *Fellow Teachers: Of Culture and Its Second Death*: 'Where there is nothing sacred, everything will be destroyed.'

Surely I am guilty of wild exaggeration? I sometimes think my own fears are unfounded. As I write this sentence, the church clock is tolling in the Essex village where I live, a sound that has been unchanged for centuries. I have just taken our Jack Russell terrier for a walk along the river and watched the ducks paddling below an ancient bridge. Passers-by nodded in a friendly manner. A group of boys fished contentedly and patiently. An elegant 1960s Rover P5 was parked in the forecourt of the nearby White Hart Hotel. England in 1996 was hardly approaching the apocalypse, I said to myself.

Yet, on my return, when I glanced at the local news on BBC TV's *Look East*, a less idyllic picture of life in modern Britain emerged. The first item was an in-depth report on under-age drinking in the region, featuring groups of sneering adolescents swigging from bottles of Thunderbird or vodka, boasting about how early they had started drinking and how many pints they could manage. The local reporter also visited Addenbrooke's Hospital in Cambridge, where a nurse spoke of a large recent increase in the number of dangerously drunk teenagers taken into casualty, and, more disturbingly, of the aggression, even violence, that many display towards hospital staff. Finally, still at Addenbrooke's, we were treated to the sight of an adolescent lying unconscious apparently having been out on a binge, his mother standing by his side. She said she wasn't cross, just anxious about him. Again, the unwillingness to pass judgement.

The second item on *Look East* featured a distraught mother with her boyfriend, appealing for information about her three children who, she feared, had been taken by her estranged husband back to his home in the Middle East. Though a distressing personal story, it was all too indicative of the collapse of the family in modern Britain, of the fragmented nature of relationships, and of the consequently unstable atmosphere in which many children are reared.

I am not arguing in this book, however, that our civic order is beyond repair, far from it. Though the decay is extensive, there are also many signs of health, even improvement: the large amount of voluntary work undertaken by the public (more than a quarter of women and a fifth of men have done some sort of voluntary work for those in need during the last twelve months); the language of Labour leader, Tony Blair, about responsibility, community, and standards in education; the continuing high level of charitable donations, despite the Lottery and the welfare state; the growing concern for the environment and treatment of animals; the widespread popular appeal of institutions like the National Trust, English Heritage, and the Royal Society for the Protection of Birds; the impressive fall in drink driving casualties over the last decade; the patriotic spirit shown this year during the European football championships and, in 1995, during the VE and VJ day celebrations; the absence of extremist political parties (except in Northern Ireland); the world-wide reputation of our ancient universities, our medical profession and the BBC; and the comparative rarity of corruption in public life.

It is my task to show how these strengths can be built upon, how we can reinvigorate the roots of our civilisation, how we can turn back the advance of amorality, irresponsibility and relativism which has become such a threat to the fabric of our society.

CHAPTER ONE

An Amoral Age

'If we feel a child needs a condom and is sexually active we provide them, regardless of age. It's quite possible for a nine-year-old to be sexually active. We would never check the name or age.' – Dr Sharon Boddard, who runs the Amelia Nutt family planning clinic in Bristol, responding to complaints in April 1996 that the clinic was giving out free condoms to children as young as nine.

'At MESMAC Tyneside [a publicly funded sexual health project in the North East for 'Men Who Have Sex With Men'] the environments in which services are provided are pro-sex, pro-gay men, confidential and non-judgemental.' – Background information leaflet on MESMAC, Tyneside, April 1996.

'With low self-worth, little pride in their community, no hope for the future and feelings of rejection, some young people feel they have no option but to turn to violence, drugs, crime and rioting.' – From *Disaffection and Non-Participation in Education, Training and Employment by Individuals aged 18–20*: Report by the Department for Education and Employment, 1996.

'Literacy can be a means of social control. Instead of making children more powerful, it makes them feel less intelligent because they realise some read better than others. We must use literacy as a lever for change.' – Peter Traves, English Adviser at Shropshire County Council speaking at a conference on the teaching of English, held at Ruskin College, Oxford, June 1991.

'Through multi-faith education, children can learn about beliefs and values and start to establish their own code of ethics, enriched and informed by knowing how a range of religions work.' – Lesley Prior, lecturer in Religious Education at St Mary's University College and RE adviser to the London Borough of Hounslow, quoted in the *Independent*, March 1996.

1

The five views expressed above come, not from the marginalised fringes of our society, but from its mainstream, indeed its publicly-funded and state-approved centre. In their different ways, they reflect how far we have descended into a confused and decadent society. As I stated in the introduction, we are living in an age without any universally-accepted moral code, or, as Ms Prior put it so felicitously, one where we can each have our own code of ethics.

Because each individual is encouraged to develop his own ethics, no judgements can be made about them. There can be no reference to the wider values of society. My code might be to elevate the 'rights' of animals above those of humans, and thereby to feel justified in blowing up the car of a scientist who has conducted experiments on rats. Or I might believe in the importance of 'expressing my own sexuality' – which happens to involve a fondness for teenage boys. Or I might be opposed to all forms of state activity, and therefore refuse to pay any taxes. Or I might claim that repression of hedonistic impulses is the greatest sin. Or I might think that ruthless selfishness – 'looking after number one' – must be my creed in a modern competitive world. In an amoral society, all such value systems are equally valid. The only difference between them is their legality.

Paradoxes abound in the amoral society. Abortion has never been more freely available nor more widely practised, with 160,000 cases last year. Yet, amidst this destruction, we now go to the most extreme lengths to provide fertility treatment. In the notorious case of Mandy Allwood, the woman who became pregnant with eight children after taking drugs to increase egg production, then sold her story to the *News of the World*, both fertility treatment and demands for abortion were combined in the same grotesque farce. Language in public, whether on the street or television, has never been more foul and abusive, and such usage is defended on the grounds of 'free expression' or 'honesty'. Yet we have never shown a greater propensity for ugly euphemisms to avoid appearing 'judgemental'. So the prostitute becomes the 'sex worker'. Juvenile crime is described as 'challenging behaviour' and drug addiction is renamed 'substance misuse'.

We spout the benefits of multi-faith education, and create a society with no faith at all. Marriage is derided as 'just a bit of paper' or an outdated traditionalist concept, yet we are bombarded with calls – often from the same 'progressive' critics – for the state to sanction same-sex unions. Sexual imagery has never been more blatant on billboards and television, 'in yer face' to use nineties vernacular, yet the mildest form of banter can become the subject of a sexual harassment charge at an industrial tribunal. AIDS campaigners demand more action to combat the disease, yet no one is allowed to censure the behaviour that caused it in the first place. While Christianity is disparaged, Rastafarianism, astrology, and crystal gazing are treated with an absurd reverence. The pulpiteers of the non-judgemental culture rail against prejudice, then elevate skin colour or sexual orientation into the defining characteristics of an individual's identity. Young people demand 'independence' from their parents by becoming dependent on the welfare system.

It is not pure nostalgia to believe that, until the latter half of this century, there was a collective moral sense in this country. George Orwell, in *The Lion and the Unicorn*, written in 1941, described the English thus:

'Their old-fashioned outlook, their graded snobberies, their mixture of bawdiness and hypocrisy, their extreme gentleness, their deeply moral attitude to life . . . The gentleness of English civilisation is perhaps its most marked characteristic. You notice it the instant you set foot on English soil. It is a land where the bus conductors are good-tempered and the policemen carry no revolvers.'

In the mid-nineties, an increasing number of policemen carry guns, while bus drivers frequently complain about vicious assaults from passengers. More importantly, few would argue that the English people now have a deeply moral attitude. Indeed, some of our cultural leaders would probably welcome the demise of any concept of universal morality, arguing that this is the price to be paid for the loss of the 'graded snobberies' and 'hypocrisies' of Orwell's wartime England.

But the moral relativists would be wrong. In the rush to ditch 'snobbery' and 'hypocrisy' in our egalitarian and candid age, we have embraced with enthusiasm the superficial and the tawdry. In our relationships, our education, our entertainments, we glory in the cheap and the transient, claiming that they reflect 'the real world'. Terrified of accusations of superiority, we are in a state of constant downward mobility. We dress down, speak down, think down. The E-taking, jungle-music loving, foul-mouthed, micro-skirted public schoolgirl is one symbol of this trend. So is the screeching, giggling 'wacky' children's TV presenter. Or the bejeaned, trainer-shod, non-dog-collar-wearing Anglican priest. Or the creative advertising executive desperate to appeal to 'uncouth' youth. Or the 'fun-loving' politician who appears to be 'one of the lads' because of his twin appetites for football and female company.

The society without snobbery or hypocrisy is the society without values. They are the negative, unattractive, handmaidens of a powerful code of morality. There is no contradiction in Orwell's view that the English of the forties could be both moralists and snobbish hypocrites: just the opposite. Precisely because of their moral attitudes, they were willing to judge others. Fifty years later, in a society which says there is no qualitative difference between Chopin and Crowded House, which claims that 'honesty' is always better than 'guilt', which refuses to make a moral distinction between the one-family man and the serial father, there is little room for the snob or the hypocrite. And there is certainly no room for morality.

No moral code can be built on an entirely secular basis. Without religion, without the belief in a higher being, ethics become no more than a system for organising society. They can have no claim on a higher authority. They carry no imperative. In a society without any understanding of faith, the injunction to do good is meaningless: there is no sense of punishment for vice or reward for virtue, nor is there any concept of transcendence beyond the self. In such a world, individuals have no need to think beyond the gratification of their immediate wants. Secular ethics have to fall back on utilitarianism, that good should be done in the interests of efficiency or the happiness of the greater number. But such demands have no real resonance with the individual. Moreover, they depend on the hope that all members of society are rational and concerned with the wider needs of society, an optimistic fallacy. As Owen Chadwick wrote in *The Secularisation of the European Mind in the Nineteenth Century* (1975):

'Except in the case of a small number of exceptional groups or people, morality never has been separated from religion in the entire history of the human race; and therefore those who undertook to provide a system of morality which should have no links with religion, because they were convinced that the prevailing system of religion was in ruins, had a task of exceptional difficulty, a task which was perhaps beyond their power if they were to make their system of morality no mere theory but a system which would touch the conscience of a large number of ordinary men and women.'

Religion is certainly in ruins in nineties Britain, and devising a new secular morality has proved far beyond the skills of those cultural thinkers who have tried to do so. Indeed, some modern attempts to propound a new code of ethics, free of Christianity, have only emphasised the hegemony of non-judgementalism in our society. As the authors of a 1996 discussion paper from the Schools Curriculum and Assessment Authority (SCAA), *The Spiritual and Moral Development of Young People*, point out: 'Some school mission statements seem to promote "tolerance" and "respect" without qualification, but it can be argued that it is not appropriate to respect the views of those who believe that, for example, mugging and robbery are acceptable.' Quite, but even the SCAA appears to have fallen into the moral relativist trap. When the SCAA's advisory group, the National Forum for Values in Education and the Community, published its draft new moral code for schools in October 1996 it specifically avoided any reference to 'the need for heterosexual, life-long marriage' as an aim of moral teaching, as a minority in the forum had wanted. The majority apparently felt that they 'could not prescribe on family structures'. One of the advisory body's members, Anthony O'Hear, dismissed the code as 'the usual mish-mash of soft-centred waffle about respect for persons, equality, environmental awareness and political correctness.' He had a point. A central principle of the new code was for our society 'to accept diversity and respect people's right to religious and cultural differences.' Relativism triumphs even in the camp of its avowed enemies.

The decline, even collapse, of Christianity as a force in our society is probably the most damaging change of our late-twentieth-century Britain. The famous religious census of mid-Victorian Britain, conducted on the morning of Sunday 30 March 1851, found that, out of a population of 17.9 million, 7.3 million had attended some religious service. When allowance was made for the sick, the very young and those employed in vital services, it was estimated that 5.3 million had deliberately failed to go to church. The Victorians were alarmed at these figures. As G. Kitson Clark wrote in *The Making of Victorian England*: 'To realise how shocking it was it is necessary to remember how generally it was assumed that at least one visit to some place of worship every Sunday was the normal custom of anyone who claimed to be a respectable Christian.' Today the Archbishop of Canterbury would declare a day of national rejoicing if church attendance reached a third of that 1851 total. In 1996, out of a population of 58 million, just 6.5 million claim to be active members of Christian churches – and a small minority of those, just 1.8 million, are Anglicans, compared to 2 million Roman Catholics. In some of our inner cities, like Birmingham and Sheffield, just 2 per cent of the population attend church for Christmas. The statistics for baptism are even more graphic. In 1900, almost 70 per cent of children were baptised in an Anglican church. In 1995, less than a quarter of newborn children had a Church of England christening. In London, the figure was just one in ten. Moreover, since 1986 the number of children under sixteen attending Sunday services has fallen by a fifth. The number of Anglican confirmations fell by 4,000 from 1994 to 1995. We have the lowest church attendance of any country in Europe.

The decline in church attendance would not be so disastrous if Britain had remained a Christian country in its ethical foundations. But even they are now disappearing. Children growing up today know nothing of the central tenets of Christianity: the Ten Commandments, the four gospels, the Sermon on the Mount, or the unique gift of Christ's 'once complete and all-sufficient sacrifice' on the Cross. We are living in a religiously illiterate society, where young people are not even given the opportunity to decide for themselves whether they believe in God or not because they are so ill-informed about the religion which built our civilisation. In earlier generations, an atheist could only reach his position after an intellectual debate. Now he arrives at non-belief from the opposite direction: sheer ignorance.

Mr Blobby is a more widely recognised figure in nineties Britain than George Carey or Cardinal Basil Hume. 'Love Thy Neighbour' is more likely to be remembered as a monstrously unamusing TV sitcom than as one of Christ's commandments. In the BBC soap opera, *EastEnders*, the devout Christians are treated almost as if they were members of an obscure cult. The Radio 4 *Today* programme's so-called religious slot, *Thought for the Day*, repeatedly degenerates into half-baked denunciations of the Government's social or spending policies. After one *Thought for the Day* broadcast, in which a vicar's wife criticised a service held in Southwark Cathedral to celebrate twenty years of the Lesbian and Gay Christian movement, the Church of England demanded an apology from the BBC, something they had never previously done over the most irreligious contributions. When Tony Blair explained to the *Sunday Telegraph* last year how his social democratic outlook was based on his religious beliefs, he was widely, and ridiculously, condemned for trying to make political capital out of his faith. Christianity no longer underpins our society but has been relegated to the status of a mere 'leisure interest', like Latin American dancing or roller-blading or DIY.

Even when only half the population attended church on a given Sunday in 1851, no one would dispute the claim that Victorian England was a Christian country. The same could be said of the first half of this century when church attendances began the long decline which has accelerated so rapidly in the last twenty years. As A.J.P. Taylor put it, writing of the inter-war years:

'Despite a widespread belief to the contrary, England remained a Christian country in morality, though not in faith . . . Standards of honesty and public duty were astonishingly high. The commercial and financial system rested securely on sanctity of contract. England was one of the few countries where those liable to income tax could be relied on to reveal their correct incomes . . . The gravest handicap was avowed atheism and few ventured to avow it.'

This is a world that is rapidly disappearing. Why has this transformation in our society occurred? Why have the ethics of Christianity so lost their resonance? The decline of the Church in Britain has, of course, been going on for more than a century. Rationalism since the Enlightenment of the eighteenth century has played a part, encouraging the idea that religious belief is no more than superstition, that the world is purely mechanistic and therefore anything not seen can have no credible existence. The advance of scientific knowledge has shaken elements of Christian faith since Galileo was first excommunicated. The belief that the Bible is the literal, rather than the metaphorical, word of God has been especially undermined. Christians of mid-Victorian Britain were outraged over Darwin's *On the Origin of Species* because it appeared to contradict the book of Genesis. The theory of evolution is still not accepted among fundamentalists in North

America. Yet today, for some scientists, the growing understanding of quantum physics only reinforces the idea of a creative, guiding force behind the universe.

The established Church has often been its own worst enemy. In the face of attacks on faith, it has shown the most abject lack of conviction or confidence. Instead of defending their own religious beliefs, many clerics seem only too anxious to apologise for them. Some even appear to feel guilty about holding to Christianity at all. This characteristic was highlighted by the call from leading churchmen in April 1996 that Christians should mark the Millennium by saying sorry to other faiths for persecuting them. In a paper entitled *A Chance To Start Again*, setting out ideas on the way the Millennium should be celebrated, the group Churches Together in England argued: 'In our present multi-faith society, any celebration of Christian heritage must be accompanied by repentance.' Commenting on the report, Gavin Reid, the Anglican Bishop of Maidstone said: 'Organised Christianity has hurt people as well as helped people. If we are to be positive, we must also be penitent.' It is impossible to imagine leaders of other faiths being so equivocal about their own religious festivals.

Another item in the report from Churches Together called for 'credible new proposals' to cut Third World debt and attack inequality. This sort of impossibilist demand is typical of the modern Church in Britain, which too often seems to regard the Gospels as little more than a crib sheet for Leftist political campaigning. Bishops can become passionate about inner-city deprivation or welfare benefits for refugees or the size of the jackpot for the National Lottery but rarely about the lack of faith and Christian morality in this country. When I first moved to Essex from north London, I visited one of my local churches on a Sunday morning, hoping that rural Anglicanism had not yet descended to the half-baked, sociological hand-wringing which, in places, passes for Christianity. I was disappointed. The sermon was given by a spokeswoman from the Colchester Centre for the Homeless, while the prayers were entirely devoted to a tour of the trouble spots of the globe: 'Let us pray for the people of Northern Ireland/ Palestine/ Rwanda/Burundi/ Sri Lanka/East Timor/Somalia.' I felt as if I were being mentally dragged through the international news pages of the *Guardian*. Even when Church leaders deign to refer to Christianity rather than Government housing policy or prison over-crowding, they are afflicted by the disease of relativism. George

Carey, in a speech in the House of Lords in June 1996, made a high profile condemnation of the growing fashion for, as he put it, 'Do-It-Yourself morality' and non-judgementalism. Yet in a radio interview preceding the speech, when asked to comment on the impending Royal divorce, he refused to say anything beyond the usual platitudinous expressions of regret.

In nineties Britain, the parish priest has become, not the promulgator of the Christian doctrine, but a kind of community counsellor, dispensing sympathy rather than theology. Indeed, so keen is the Church of England to reduce the role of the priest as a religious leader, that it is introducing new psychological tests to the selection procedures for candidates for the priesthood, which, it is hoped, will end 'the current bias towards the articulate and academic'. Do the anti-élitists of the Church feel that articulacy and intellect are no longer required in the clergy? Probably. After all, 'caring' is more important than believing.

Because our religious leaders have almost abandoned their role in providing spiritual guidance, the Anglican Church is now preoccupied with the fashionable issues of current public discourse like gay rights. It is telling that the Roman Catholic Church has much firmer, some would say reactionary, positions on women's ordination, the recruitment of gay clergy, same-sex marriages, birth control, and pre-marital sex, yet has not only retained its membership much more successfully than the Church of England but has also avoided being embroiled in the pointless, self-indulgent debates that now dominate the General Synod. The ideals of the Roman Catholic Church are clear, even if its followers cannot always adhere to them. The ideals of the Anglican Church are as clear as the water in a stagnant pond.

This problem reflects one of the fatal weaknesses of the Church of England: the desire to be relevant, 'with-it' or 'in-touch'. Again we see the terror of appearing to be superior or judgemental. But religious faith should be about transcendence, not relevance. It should aspire to bring higher values to humanity, not sink to the passing whims of each generation.

Passing whims come no lower than a collection of Christian liturgies for homosexuals, called *We Were Baptised Too*, published in April 1996, written by two American Methodists and endorsed by Dr Desmond Tutu, then Anglican Archbishop of Cape Town. The book includes a *Celebration of Coming Out* and a *Ritual for Self-Renewal*, the introduction for which explains:

'This ritual is for anyone who seeks to replenish one's spiritual storehouse. The struggle for Queer justice is an ongoing journey. We recognise that coming out, acting-up or facing homophobia (internally or externally) or any other major milestone along the liberating pathway depletes our spiritual resources.'

In *The Declaration of Coming Out* the respondent is required to say: 'I praise God for I am fearfully and wonderfully made – that I know very well. Therefore, I am proud to say, "I am a (lesbian/gay/bisexual/transgender) child of God."' What next? *A Celebration of the Loss of Virginity* or *Ritual for Accepting First E-tab*? The absurdity of these liturgies is that they define individuals by their so-called 'sexual identities', the very contradiction of spirituality.

The Anglicans' desperate quest for relevance has also been demonstrated in other recent events, like the laughable service of thanksgiving in Coventry Cathedral held to celebrate the centenary of the motor car. Alan Ayckbourn could hardly have bettered the farcical scenes into which the service descended, with an old Daimler rolling up the aisle, the Bishop of Birmingham making the predictable fudging 'on the one hand, on the other' speech, and, to cap it all, a naked woman leaping before the congregation, her body daubed in protest slogans about road deaths. The 'Nine O'Clock Rave' services in Leeds organised by the 'fun-loving' Reverend Chris Brain, seen by some in the Church hierarchy as an 'innovative' and 'exciting' way to reach young people, are another example.

Other forces, largely beyond the control of the main Churches, have helped to weaken the roots of Christianity and Christian morality in our society. The more brutalised versions of free-market economics have elevated consumerism into the sole principle of governance. Dressed up in the cloak of pseudo-democracy – 'giving the people what they want' – this outlook allows no space for spirituality, no respect for actions or attitudes to which a price tag cannot be attached. In the culture of consumerism, there are no values, only products. And the only judgement to be determined is whether a product will sell. In the consumerist society, individuals are encouraged to focus only on their immediate, sensual demands, not on any higher goals.

The kingdom of heaven on earth can be found in the out-of-town shopping centre.

While the Church has railed against the shallow consumerism of our era, its attempts at 'relevance' are another sign that it has succumbed to the dominant mood. Pandering to 'gay rights' activists and adolescent ravers, or making the Prayer Book more 'in tune with current thinking' is nothing more than a craven wish to 'give the people what they want'. The IVF clinic, *The Good Sex Guide* on ITV, the *Daily Sport*, the fashion for 'media studies' at university, 'liberal' divorce legislation, and the transformation of libraries into entertainment centres are other signs of this mood.

By its concentration on self-gratification, consumerism has also undermined the Christian ethics of personal responsibility and concern for others. So has Freudianism and the other psychoanalytical movements it has spawned. Through years of intensive therapy, patients are submerged in a darkened well of self-analysis, urged to think about every gradation of their needs, wants, and fears. Apart from inciting the most puerile self-absorption, the Freudian approach has two other regrettable consequences. First, it leads to the 'victim-mentality', where patients are the products of their upbringing and therefore cannot be held responsible for their behaviour. 'I have the most vicious temper but that's because I was not breastfed as a one-year-old', or 'I am compelled to steal credit cards because I was not potty-trained' goes the reasoning. The thug and the neurotic need not feel any shame over what they do. The second problem is the belief that we should not 'repress' our emotions. In the inverted world of Freudianism, self-control is a vice, and lack of restraint a virtue. Repression is allegedly more destructive than expression. We should give vent to feelings like anger, hatred and lust, or, in the more casual phrase of sixties hippiedom, 'let it all hang out'. Self-indulgence has its own Freudian justification. The irony is that therapy usually works – in the sense of relieving deep unhappiness – only when patients start to take responsibility for their lives, not when they are given an armful of excuses for acting as they do.

Marxist ideas have been equally damaging to the acceptance of Christian morals. Indeed, Marx believed that 'Communists preach no morality at all'. In Marxist philosophy, morality reflects, not universal truths, but 'the values of the ruling class'. The ethics or 'cultural norms' of a Christian society are therefore instruments of oppression. In the creation of the workers' state, they must be challenged and overthrown. Even the family is little more than an oppressive bourgeois institution. As Marx and Engels argued in *The Communist Manifesto*: 'The bourgeois sees in his wife a mere instrument of production.' Equally, for the Marxist the Church is one of the pillars of the established capitalist order while the priesthood is an agency of social control.

It was this philosophy that led to the notorious suppression of religious worship in the Soviet Union and other Eastern Bloc Marxist states. In the place of God, the state and its institutions were transformed into national deities. In Britain, fortunately, Communism has never been a serious political force, confined mainly to radical university departments, certain Left-wing local authorities and a few trade union bureaucracies. Yet the ideas of Marx about class, equality and oppression have heavily influenced, not only the Labour movement, but also vital public professions like teaching and social work. Indeed, the nineties neurosis about 'discrimination', which runs through everything from the pressure groups to police work, from corporate recruitment to college admissions, owes much to Marx. What could be more Marxist than this *Equal Opportunities Policy Statement* from Mainliners, a publicly funded HIV and AIDS support body?

'Mainliners accepts that in this society individuals and groups are discriminated against on the grounds of their race, colour, culture, religion, gender, HIV status, past and present use of drugs, domestic circumstances, disability, age, class and sexual preference.'

(Note that in the non-judgemental culture even drug-abusers are members of an 'oppressed group'.) The statement continues:

'We recognise and distinguish between individuals knowingly and unwittingly acting in prejudicial ways and structures and institutions which are organised on, or in effect act on, the principle that one group is superior to another. Thus racism, sexism, ableism and so on are prejudice and power combined. Our policy is designed to counter oppression on both a personal and institutional level.'

Like Freudianism, Marxism clings to the dangerous belief that we are entirely the products of our backgrounds. This social determinism both undermines personal responsibility and promotes the victim mentality. So, when it comes to criminal activity, we should not condemn the behaviour of an individual but only look at the economic or social deprivation which might lie behind the crime. After rioting in Brixton in December 1995, during which a gang dragged a policeman from his bike and proceeded to stamp all over him, we heard the predictable complaints of police brutality and the neglect of young people in the area.

Marxist ideas about discrimination can be clearly seen in the radical feminist movement, with its contempt for the 'patriarchal' structures of bourgeois society, of which the family is the unfortunate centrepiece. What was once an agreed principle of our society – that children should be brought up by a married couple – is now regarded as if it were a means of oppressing women. So motherhood creates a whole new set of societal 'victims'. In a *Guardian* article in October 1996, radical thinker Tariq Ali described as 'grotesque' the idea that morality required marriage and quoted with approval the words of his partner who, when asked why she had not married, explained that 'she did not want to give up any of her rights'.

The same mentality dominates gay and lesbian rights campaigning, throwing up the most outlandish claims of discrimination and demands for equality. Calls are made for statutory equality with married couples in the provision of state housing, in company benefits, pension rights, welfare benefits, even parenthood. A recent report called *Partnership With Parents: An Anti-Discriminatory Approach*, from the Early Years Trainers Anti-Racist Network, set out guidance for nursery and teaching staff on dealing with 'gay and lesbian parents'. The advice urged staff 'to be empathetic not judgemental' (of course), that 'visible and explicit statements and pictures should make it quite clear that the staff are committed to anti-discriminatory practice and equal opportunities' and that 'the resources and curriculum should reflect the variety of cultures and lifestyles in Britain with parental skills encouraged and appreciated. They should also reflect the variety of families in which children are growing up.' A senior policy officer of Islington Council once complained to me that the regulation in the staff code, allowing an employee to have special leave on his or her wedding day, was 'discriminatory' because gays cannot officially get married. She should not have worried too much. This is the council that now has 'paternity leave' for lesbian partners.

What is particularly repulsive about the shrill gay egalitarians is their wilful disregard for any concept of the innocence of childhood. In their determination to fight supposed prejudice, they are willing to dragoon children on to the battlefield. In March 1996, Camden and Islington Health Authority, at a cost of £40,000, produced a booklet entitled *Colours of the Rainbow* for children aged five to sixteen, designed to 'counter homophobia' and 'affirm young gay men and lesbians within our society'. The booklet included plans for lessons such as one where pupils choose 'captions for T-shirts which are positive about being gay' and another 'to give pupils an understanding of homophobia and strategies to cope with it'. One of the book's researchers, Liz Swinden, announced proudly on its publication: 'Teaching materials have assumed that everyone is heterosexual. This is the first time that homosexuality and bisexuality have been put on the agenda as acceptable alternative ways of life.' Is it surprising that the family is in crisis when the likes of Ms Swinden are paid by the Government to spread their radical message of diversity? And why should young children have an 'agenda' about sexuality? Can't they play with their Corgi cars and dolls rather than 'celebrating gay lifestyles'?

Peter Tatchell, the publicity-seeking spokesman for the extremist 'Queer rights' group Outrage, has been campaigning for the age of consent for gay or straight sex to be lowered to fourteen. Indeed, he goes even further, proposing that 'people under the age of fourteen should not be prosecuted, provided both partners have consented and there is no more than three years' difference in their ages.' This amounts to a charter for child abuse, where a tough thirteen-year-old boy could, without any comeback, persuade a ten-year-old girl into having sex. Tatchell justifies his vile campaign with the usual sub-Marxist language about oppression and liberation. 'The restriction of lawful sex to a prescribed age reinforces the idea that people under that age have no sexual rights . . . The sexual health and happiness of young people is best ensured by education and empowerment, not by obfuscation and repression.' Perhaps Tatchell has not noticed that most of them have no sexual feelings either – precisely the reason why they need the protection of the law.

It would be easy to dismiss Tatchell's words as the irrelevant rantings of an extremist, were it not for the fact that this depraved ideology of 'sexual emancipation' has caused such damage in the child protection services of this country. It has provided a cover for child abusers to operate in residential homes, allowing them to escape disciplinary action because of fears by management of appearing 'homophobic' or 'judgemental'. The notorious Islington child abuse scandal was a striking illustration of this. An independent inquiry conducted by Ian White CBE, Director of Oxfordshire Social Services, into the running of the borough's children's homes reported, in May 1995, that social services officers 'believed they would not be supported if they triggered disciplinary investigations involving staff who may be from ethnic minorities or members of the gay community.' The White inquiry also found that 'positive discrimination in Islington has had serious unintended consequences in allowing some staff to exploit children.' One case highlighted in the annex of the White report was of a fourteen-year-old boy who was introduced to a gay lifestyle by his care worker. This professional had a conviction for indecency and no qualifications. Through him, the boy received counselling from a gay group, was encouraged to wear women's clothing and bondage gear, and was taken to gay clubs, all at an age when he could not possibly have been clear about his sexual identity.

Islington may be an extreme example but it is hardly unique. Many of the other children's homes scandals of recent years have featured a horrific level of abuse, usually against young boys. Frank Beck, the senior care manager at Leicestershire, conducted a thirteen-year-long reign of terror. In 1991, he was given five life sentences for abusing more than 100 children. Reports from the several inquiries into homes in North Wales indicate that more than 200 children may have been abused over a period of twenty years. One report into the protection of children by Clwyd County Council found that, as in Islington, paedophiles were able to use an equal opportunities policy for their own degraded ends. The report stated: 'The rights of employees and those of children need to be equally balanced and managed by senior officers and elected members. This does not seem to have been the case in Clwyd, with employees' rights taking precedence while children were sexually exploited under the guise of homosexual equality.'

In the warped climate of sexual explicitness, where all moral boundaries have dissolved, where every lifestyle should be 'celebrated', it is not difficult for paedophiles to develop an internal self-justification for their actions. After all, what are they doing but expressing their own sexuality? When ideologues encourage little boys to play at condoms rather than cowboys, when five-year-olds are told to think up 'positive images' of gays, why should abusers be worried about violating innocence? When even the word 'pervert' is seen as 'discriminatory', why need paedophiles feel any guilt? Once again, we see the paradox of the amoral society, where a desire to counter 'sexual prejudice' results in the most horrific and real, rather than pseudo, oppression of innocent children.

The hysteria over 'oppression', as manifested by the antics of the gay and lesbian activists, has been damaging enough to Christian morality. But even more disastrous has been the direct assault on Christianity made by the zealots of the anti-racist, multi-cultural movement who have argued, with spectacular success, that any attempt to promulgate Christian teaching or portray Britain as a Christian country amounts to a form of discrimination. Since the first waves of Commonwealth immigration thirty years ago, they have been claiming that Christianity is just one religion amongst many and should be given no greater importance than any other faith.

This is arrant nonsense. In the first place, it is an offensive denial of our Christian cultural heritage, of the very foundations on which our civilisation is built, of the Christian influence on our language (the King James Bible and Cranmer's *Book of Common Prayer*), our architecture (St Paul's Cathedral), our music (Handel's *Messiah*), and our literature (Milton and T.S.Eliot).

In the second place, this attitude ignores the role that Christian ethics plays in shaping a citizenry who are concerned about more than their own immediate needs. Far from being a tool of oppression – as some of the more enthusiastic anti-racists would claim – Christianity provides the means to liberty by helping to build a stable civic order in which the values of responsibility, moderation and respect for others and for authority ('Render unto Caesar what is Caesar's . . .') are paramount. Christianity inspires the individual to help his fellow citizen, to be tolerant and patient, and to protect and maintain his family. Value-free multi-culturalism inspires nothing. As the Islington child-abuse scandal demonstrates, where there is moral anarchy, there can be no freedom for the truly oppressed.

The irony of the multi-culturalists' denigration of Christianity as an integral part of British life is that Christians are likely to be the least racist people in this country. The very thrust of Christianity is towards benevolence and 'goodwill to all men'. 'So always treat others as you would like them to treat you' (Matthew, Chapter 7, verse 12) should surely be the creed of all those opposed to racism. It is this intrinsic benevolence that the amoralists have exploited, demanding tolerance of other faiths – and no faiths at all. The disposition of Christianity to accept, to welcome and to forgive has left it vulnerable to the attacks of those who believe in no morality whatsoever. Yet instead of harping on about the undoubted crimes of the Crusades or the cultural imperialism of nineteenth-century missionaries, the race obsessives should recognise that a strong code of Christian ethics could be the greatest bulwark against the abuse of minorities.

A third problem with the multi-faith campaigning is that it does not reflect the reality of British society. We are constantly told that we live in a 'multi-cultural', 'multi-racial' society. This is simply untrue. We live in a society where more than 94 per cent of the population is White European, 52.8 million out of a total population in Great Britain of 56 million. Of the ethnic minority groups, 870,000 are black (including Afro-Caribbean and African), 850,000 are Indian, 730,000 are Pakistani/Bangladeshi and 773,000 come from a range of other groups, including Chinese, making a total of 3.2 million. Indeed, we are one of the more homogeneous societies in the West, far more so than, say, the USA, Canada or France. In the context of religion, even with the appalling decline it has suffered in the last half of this century, Christianity still heavily predominates. There are 6.5 million people who are active members of the main Trinitarian churches, compared to 600,000 Muslims, 300,000 Sikhs, and 100,000 Hindus (roughly the same as the number of Jews, whom the more dogmatic multi-culturalists seem strangely to ignore). Furthermore, a large number of blacks from the Caribbean and Africa are Christians. To destroy the teaching and celebration of the religion on which our moral system is based, just because such an exercise might offend certain minorities in certain cities, is the logic of the madhouse. Do we ban cars because some don't drive or close pubs because some are teetotal? Do we give up teaching English because some don't speak it?

Far from arguing a special case for those genuinely multi-racial parts of the country like inner-city Bradford or Leicester, or the London boroughs of Brent and Lambeth, the race campaigners actually claim that in mainly white areas – 'the white highlands' in their determinedly aggressive terminology – it is all the more important to have a 'multi-cultural agenda' precisely because people may be insulated from the attitudes and needs of the non-white population. 'If we fail to provide an anti-racist, multi-cultural education to white children, we are miseducating them,' says one. For some, even the current flaccid multi-cultural curriculum is too biased towards Christianity. Here is Claude Moraes of the Joint Council for the Welfare of Immigrants, speaking in July 1995: 'If there is a problem in our schools, it is the lack of teaching about cultures like Islam and Hindu.' While they bleat about 'awareness' and 'respecting all traditions', some of the more extreme anti-racists show little awareness or respect for the Christian tradition of this country. In 1996, the Race Relations Unit of Birmingham City Council produced a multi-cultural calendar which, it was claimed, recorded all the major religious festivals during the year, including those of the Muslim and Rastafarian faiths. But, incredibly, no mention was made of Easter, the most important of all Christian festivals.

In practice, multi-faith, multi-culturalism is literally meaningless. Rather than providing a real understanding of a variety of faiths, it only creates confusion and ignorance. An Easter egg here, or a Diwali light there, is no way to imbue people with a grasp of any religion. As one seventeen-year-old from Leeds said in 1995, during the row over the call by Dr Nick Tate, Chief Executive of the Schools Curriculum Assessment Authority, for the development of a British cultural identity in schools: 'We're too multi-cultural now for anyone to come up with a simple way of unifying us all as British people. We learned a bit about other cultures in RE before GCSEs, but the result for most of us was knowing very little about a lot of things.' And here is an A-level student whose Sikh parents came from Kenya and Uganda: 'I was at a Church of England primary and they were cool about not stressing Christian values.' It makes you wonder why it is allowed to call itself a 'Church of England' school.

Multi-faith education is actually a contradiction in terms. It really means the education of no faith whatsoever. Tolerance of other faiths has descended into ignorance of them all. All of the great religions of the world believe that they hold the only route to salvation, that they are the sole possessors of the sacred truth. It is therefore impossible to pretend that, in one curriculum, they can all be given equal value, that all their unique claims to divine revelation can somehow be reconciled. Indeed, for many believers, to do so is a denigration of their own particular faith. Nor can religious worship be taught, as seems to be the case in so many RE classes, as if it were no more than some sort of cultural phenomenon, like sport or music. Culture reflects the values of a particular society. Religion helps to create them.

Many of the people for whom multi-faith education was so noisily established do not actually want it. Tired of the festival-oriented slush which passes for multi-faith teaching, Muslim parents in Kirklees and Birmingham have been withdrawing their children from RE classes and demanding that they be provided with their own Muslim education. In one move, these parents had exposed the hollowness of the disastrous experiment in multi-faithism which has been foisted on our schools for more than three decades. It is time it was brought to a halt. For while the inverted racists of the multi-cultural movement chant their mantras about 'valuing diversity' and 'combating Euro-centric attitudes', many parents, both black and white, are seeking a return to a sense of morality and discipline in our society. There is no better way to achieve this than through clear-sighted religious and moral education. And in Britain, this must be based on Christianity.

Christianity is a tough religion, imposing the most exacting standards of integrity, honesty, generosity, and faithfulness on its followers. Because they are accountable to God, Christians must be responsible for their actions. Unlike Marxists and multi-culturalists, Christians cannot blame 'society' for their sins. They must show repentance, admit their wrong-doing and strive constantly to improve. In our non-judgemental age, sadly, this central aspect of Christianity seems to have been entirely lost. Indeed, a stern, demanding religion has been grotesquely transmuted into a sort of handwringers' code of exoneration for the most reprehensible behaviour. The ethos of forgiveness (The Prodigal Son), mercy ('Slow to chide and swift to bless') and tolerance ('Love your enemies') appears to be all that matters about Christianity to our modern cultural leaders, with the resulting reluctance to condemn crime, promiscuity, or idleness. Many people are unable or unwilling to make the essential distinction between hating the sin and loving the sinner. They consider they have no business to judge, yet such an attitude actually lessens the hope of reform for the wrong-doer. When the Anglican priest, Father

Christopher Gray, was murdered in his Liverpool parish in August 1996, one ten-year-old girl left a card of sympathy outside his church with this message: 'Dear Father Christopher, I am very sad of your murder. You were loved in St Margaret's School. God is with you, I know, and protecting you, and He will forgive the person who killed you.' Touching in one way, but also disturbing. Is this all a young girl has absorbed from Christianity, that forgiveness from God is automatic, without any repentance or remorse, even in the case of a brutal murder?

Because we live in a triumphantly secular society, where Christianity is treated as either a hobby or a 'mission statement' for a social services department, we have not only lost the concept of right and wrong, but also of good and evil. In a Godless age, therefore, we have to seek alternative explanations for the violence and destruction that increasingly lies in our midst. Some we have already heard, like the Marxists blaming slavery and exploitation of the working class, the Freudians warning of emotionally deprived childhoods and feminists attacking the macho-values of a patriarchal society. Another diagnosis made with mounting frequency is the scientific or rationalist one, which claims that brutality and criminality are the result of some chemical, biological or genetic defect in the wrong-doer. So we no longer have the bad man but only the mad man, who needs to be supported and cured rather than condemned and punished. Under this thesis, the more outrageous the deed, the more insane must be the perpetrator. The very act of committing a monstrous crime is proof of an unbalanced mind. Thomas Hamilton, after the Dunblane massacre, was almost universally reviled in the press as a maniac. Yet, as the Cullen inquiry showed, the detailed planning that lay behind the killings was the work of a meticulous, not deranged, mind. None of Britain's most notorious serial killers, Dennis Nielsen, Peter Sutcliffe, Colin Ireland, Reginald Christie, or Frederick West appeared to be mentally disordered in the eyes of either neighbours or colleagues at work. Nielsen was able to hold down respectable jobs in the army, the police and the civil service – how much more normal can you get? – while even Sutcliffe's wife knew nothing of his crimes.

Far from reflecting scientific progress, the replacement of the concept of conscious evil with the pseudo-rationalist one of insanity actually harks back to a primitive, pagan era when the malefactor was said to be 'possessed by spirits' which drove him to his crimes. And where once a witch-doctor was used to cast out the demons now we use counselling and drugs. Tribal chanting and ritual dancing now have their parallel in the therapy courses for multiple-rapists. Again, this thinking promotes the victim-mentality, with the individual no longer responsible for his actions. He is as much a victim as those who suffer from his behaviour. We often hear it said, in either the courtroom or the media, that the most brutal criminals had an 'uncontrollable' urge to kill, maim or rape. But their instincts rarely appear so uncontrollable that they do not take every step to avoid detection.

On a less gruesome level, our society is riddled with attempts to create new scientific or medical conditions which can absolve anyone from responsibility for anti-social actions. 'Road rage' is one of the worst examples. What used to be considered bad manners or loutishness is now dressed up as if it were some ailment requiring counselling and sympathy. The RAC have even given credibility to this notion by introducing road-side 'stress counselling' centres. 'Attention Deficit Disorder' (ADD) is another mysterious late twentieth-century disease whose symptoms include aggression, inability to concentrate, abusive language, and hyperactivity. Most of the sufferers of this tragic affliction appear to be young males and boys, which somewhat weakens the claims from the ADD pressure groups' activists that the syndrome is connected to food additives. For parents and offenders, it is much easier to blame diet than discipline for anti-social behaviour, though it cannot be a coincidence that ADD is growing in popularity as family breakdown and non-judgementalism increase.

This sub-rationalist movement has encouraged the modern climate of irresponsibility in our society. The diagnosis serves as an explanation and then becomes an excuse for the crime or misdemeanour. Committed adultery? Must be suffering from sex addiction. Attacked a motorist with a piece of lead piping? That'll be road rage. Kicked your teacher on the shins? That'll be ADD. Murdered an elderly couple on the Underground? That'll be schizophrenia. Raped a fifteen-year-old girl? That'll be too much testosterone.

Scientists are now said to be on the verge of discovering the so-called 'criminal gene', the biological indicator which will show if an individual is disposed to criminal behaviour. What will happen when they discover it? Will foetuses with this dangerous element be aborted? If born, will they be segregated from the rest of society? Will they receive special medical treatment and education during their childhood? Such ideas might sound nightmarish, but they are only the logical consequence of claiming that genes dictate our actions. Nor are they very different from astrology, the more puerile of whose followers believe their lives are governed by the movement of the planets, a belief without the remotest scientific, never mind moral, basis.

From Marxism to medicine, from Freudianism to feminism, from astrology to ADD, what all these theories ignore is the role of free will. As Shakespeare put it in *Julius Caesar*, 'Men at some time are masters of their fates. The fault is not in our stars but in ourselves.' In Christianity the theme of free will is paramount. The whole of the (metaphorical) Creation story depends upon it. Without free will, where is the virtue in choosing good – or the vice in choosing bad? If all our actions are decided by forces beyond our control, whether it be stars or sugar intake, then we cannot be condemned or praised. We may all grow up in differing economic and social environments, have differing intellects and physical attributes, which may guide us in certain directions, but none of us are prisoners of our backgrounds or our brain cells.

The amoral, non-judgemental society is degenerating into the irresponsible society. Its cast are all around us: the employer who pays his staff less than £2 an hour, expecting the social security system to subsidise their wages through Family Credit and Income Support. Or the social services manager who rewards a young offender with a skiing holiday in Austria in an attempt 'to break the cycle of alienation'. Or the alternative practitioner who convinces little Johnny's parents that his foul-mouthed abuse and tantrums are a result of an allergy to dairy products. Or the mother who has four children by three different men and then complains that the local authority is not transferring her quickly enough to a larger property. Or the film executive who talks blithely of 'freedom of speech' and the 'cutting edge of creativity' while refusing to discuss the effect of his studio's latest violent production.

Such characters are flourishing in nineties Britain because of our loss of moral boundaries. Below I set out some ideas on how they might be rebuilt.

What needs to change

Many would argue that it would be impossible to re-establish a moral code in our 'multi-racial' secular society. Christianity, such pessimists would claim, is utterly marginalised and ideas about 'not imposing values' and 'not preaching' are widely held. In a 1996 Gallup survey on the nation's morality, interviewees were asked which moral subjects schools should teach. The two with the highest rate, both with 95 per cent of people favouring them, were 'Not to drink and drive' and 'Tolerance for the opinions of others' – hardly likely to be the twin engines of a reinvigorated, morally secure society. Meanwhile, only 46 per cent wanted to see the teaching of the Christian doctrines.

Yet this apparently dismal survey also contained some seeds for hope, for 72 per cent of respondents felt that 'we leave it too much up to individuals to behave in terms of their own moral code' and 75 per cent felt that 'society as a whole is less moral today than it was fifty years ago.' The sense that people are yearning for a stronger sense of right and wrong in modern Britain has been backed up by other opinion polls, including one in August 1996 which showed that just 15 per cent of eleven- to sixteen-year-olds thought that pop stars were good role models, and the majority felt they were growing up in a 'dishonest society'. The widespread support for the manifesto of Frances Lawrence, the wife of the murdered headteacher Philip Lawrence, is also indicative of the public mood of anxiety about the moral crisis in our society.

The aim is to channel this yearning into a recognition of a concrete set of values, a code that proclaims ideals of behaviour and does not eschew judgements. Too much of what currently passes for 'moral teaching' is no more than anti-racist sloganising. Here is the feminist Yasmin Alibhai Brown, writing in *Everywoman* magazine in March 1996: 'What is morality but political correctness? What is morality if it is not about respecting colours, races and religions? And is it not teaching morality when you try and ensure that they learn about equal rights for disabled people, women and gay people?' Peter Tatchell as a moral crusader? The idea has as much credibility as an abstinence pledge from Oliver Reed. If morality were based on Ms Alibhai Brown's precepts, Islington Council's Women's Unit would have surpassed the Dalai Lama in moral stature.

It is exactly this sort of thinking that has so badly distorted the promulgation of a powerful moral code in the last thirty years. We must, therefore, move in a different direction. In attempting to rebuild a moral culture, we must have the courage to ignore the relativists and the multi-racists, the individualist libertarians and the gay rights libertines.

The starting point must be education. We have to instil in our schools a renewed moral ethos, where pupils learn that right and wrong consist of more than respecting other people's opinions. The ethos should reflect the tenets of Christianity, not only because it is the basis of our European civilisation, but also because it already contains its own coherent code of morality. School authorities would not have to spend months agonising over the creation of their own form of secular code, which would be doomed to failure in any case since it would be based on the views of the loudest members of the governing body rather than some higher authority.

Lessons in religious education and acts of collective worship are two important ways to inculcate schools with moral values. Both should concentrate on Christianity. Children should learn about the stories of the Bible, the development of Christianity, and the meaning of the ceremonies. Much of what claims to be 'Religious Studies' is little more than a cocktail of sociology, international studies and humanist agonising. One GCSE 'Religious Studies' textbook I have seen is divided into three parts: 'Personal Issues', 'Social Issues' and 'Global Issues'. Of the ninety-three chapter headings, just six relate specifically to an understanding of God or Christianity (or indeed any other religion). The other eighty-seven cover a frightening range of issues: 'Smoking'; 'How does racial prejudice develop?'; 'The football hooligan'; 'Children's rights'; 'Non-violent direct action' and 'Leisure'. No doubt students are encouraged to develop their own moral thinking, except, of course, on race and homosexuality. Instead of the current attempts at 'relevance', readings at acts of worship should contain a spiritual theme. In one school I visited when I was a local councillor, pupils listened to a recital of the vapid lyrics of a much-loved rock album.

There is a genuine problem in schools where a sizeable number of pupils (occasionally even the large majority) are from households of other faiths, but this should not be exaggerated. As I stated earlier, nearly 95 per cent of Britain's population is white European. The absurdity of the current position is that the exceptions have been allowed to set the rules. We are so deferential to other faiths that we are failing to teach our own. The difficulty of other religions has been blown out of all proportion, partly to suit the agenda of the multi-racists who feel guilt-ridden about the 'imperialist' past of their own culture. Arrangements could be made for separate worship or RE classes where parents of other faiths feel strongly. In the tiny number of schools where Hindus, Sikhs or Muslims comprise more than, say, 30 per cent of the school population, there could be dual or trinal acts of worship. What should not be done, in the face of such difficulties, is to abandon religious teaching and lapse into the value-free morass of multi-culturalism. This is not to argue, though, that pupils should learn nothing of other faiths. To do so would be as blinkered as following the dogma of the multi-racists. I am only saying that we should concentrate on the religion of our own culture, hardly a revolutionary idea. The very fact that it could arouse such opposition is a reflection of the overweening secularisation of our society.

Another, perhaps more serious, objection is that we no longer have in our schools enough teachers who believe in the Christian faith to carry out this task, particularly in primary schools where there is much less subject specialisation. How could headteachers lead acts of collective worship if they themselves are not believers? To our forefathers, such problems would seem extraordinary. Before the 1870 Education Act, almost all education in England had been on a religious basis, largely in schools set up by the Anglican or the Nonconformist churches; to many, education was the teaching of Christianity and its ethics. Thomas Arnold, for instance, the great nineteenth-century headmaster of Rugby School, felt it necessary that his 'should be a school of Christian gentlemen'. One solution would be to use priests or prominent lay members of local churches to lead in RE lessons or acts of worship, or occasionally students who are training for ordination. In schools with a large number of Muslims on the roll, local imams could carry out the same tasks. Given the importance that all major faiths attach to their involvement with their communities, churches and mosques would probably welcome such a development.

Attempts to re-introduce religion in schools would no doubt be met with a barrage of criticism. Too costly, not enough time in the curriculum, not enough space for collective worship, teachers already over-worked, not relevant to examination results, too traditionalist, too dated, too offensive to minorities, too presumptuous, not wanted by parents, not in touch with the aspirations of children today, too authoritarian, and too controversial are just some of the dissenting voices that would be raised. Yet, in one respect, I am only talking about enforcing the law of the land, the 1944 Education Act, which stipulates that a Christian, non-denominational act of collective worship should be held at the beginning of each school day. There can be few existing laws which are more widely breached than this Act. It may be time to follow the example of the race relations industry, which has proved so assiduous in enforcing the parts of the 1989 Children Act relating to the registration of childminders and childcare groups. The *Guidance* to this Act states, in uncompromising terms, that registration officers must consider, when deciding whether a person 'is fit to be in the proximity of children aged under eight', their 'knowledge of and attitude to multi-cultural issues and people of different origins.' What scope for the zealots lies in those words. Last year, a vicar in Gloucestershire was warned by the local Social Services Department that his after-school club might have to close because it did not have enough multi-cultural toys, despite the fact that all the children at the club were white. In the same spirit, perhaps the Department for Education and Employment could make a test case of some schools by threatening to withdraw their grant aid if they do not abide by the terms of the 1944 Act. Monitoring the implementation of this measure could be as vigorous as the ethnic monitoring carried out under the 1976 Race Equality Act and the 1989 Children Act.

Atheists and agnostics would no doubt see such moves as a form of indoctrination. Yet how can young people decide whether they believe in God or not, if they are taught nothing about faith? Is an atheistic approach to schooling any more balanced than a spiritual one? No, it is both dogmatic and negligent to deprive pupils of any coherent instruction in the religion which has been, until recently, the binding fabric of our society. The tragedy of our age is our extreme religious illiteracy, not just about belief but ethics and traditions as well. When Christianity is treated as mumbo-jumbo, is it surprising that so few have any understanding or respect for spirituality?

Some educationalists would argue that the need for moral teaching is already covered within most schools by lessons in 'Personal and

Social Education' (PSE). In our secular society, they would claim, PSE does not carry all the offensive, racist or irrelevant baggage of Christian teaching and assemblies. But the problem is that, like many RE lessons, much PSE, through its concern for all the fashionable issues of the day and its terror of any apparent 'cultural bias', only reinforces the amoral society. Last year, several business leaders complained that 'the content of PSE is too often dominated by the rather random promotion of good causes'. Nick Tate, the Chief Executive of the Schools Curriculum Authority, has recognised this failing and has called for more rigorous lessons on 'moral and spiritual development' to be incorporated within the curriculum. He has also put forward the concept of lessons in 'responsible citizenship' as a way of instilling moral values.

Such efforts, though commendable, are doomed to failure until we have a change in the culture of our schooling system. 'Citizenship' education is likely to go the same way as PSE, hijacked by the multi-culturalists and moral relativists who predominate in our education establishment. The only criterion for 'good citizenship' would be a commitment to challenging prejudice and oppression. The ideas propounded would be those of 'gender and racial equality', the encouragement of students 'to clarify their own values system' and 'empowerment to take responsible social action', to quote from *Education for Citizenship in a Multi-Cultural Society* by James Lynch. An initiative aimed at promoting a code of morality would achieve the very opposite. We have often seen how the educationalists capture reforms and use them for their own ends. The Children Act, for instance, designed to protect the interests of children, has become a charter for anti-racist interventionists and local government regulatory bureaucrats, while child abuse and paedophilia are still rife.

What we need in schools is not more anodyne PSE or Citizenship education but an ethos of morality throughout all their work. RE classes and acts of worship cannot take place in a vacuum. They have to reflect the values that are promoted in other aspects of school life: teaching, records of achievement, discipline, music and sport, uniforms, and involvement with the local community. Just as we should not be afraid of teaching Christianity because of the complaints of the multi-faith brigade, so we should not shy away from instruction in moral values in other subjects. Our English literary heritage provides unnumbered opportunities for studying moral questions, from the nature of free will in *Paradise Lost* to corrupting ambition in *Macbeth*. We no longer have absolutes, just 'different' approaches. This lack of rigour, of a willingness to explain what is right and wrong, extends to the feebly uncompetitive sports field and to the third-rate daubs, claiming to be paintings, which hang proudly from the walls of most state primary schools. The absence of graded punishments for wrong-doing, the reluctance to impose order on a class, and the disappearance of the school uniform in most primaries are all characteristics of the same value-free movement in education which has to be reversed.

To do so will require a major change in the teaching profession with better salaries to attract a higher calibre of recruit. The dominant 'progressive' ideal of the teacher as a 'facilitator' rather than an instructor will have to disappear, as will the whole flawed concept of 'child-centred learning'. Teacher training will have to be transformed so staff understand their subjects and are equipped to make moral judgements. According to a study last year by Cambridge University, most trainee teachers in Britain now regard moral and spiritual teaching as 'indoctrination' and are reluctant 'to impose ethnocentric values'. Such attitudes should have no place in a morally secure education system. Teachers and their schools must be agents of moral authority, not cheerleaders for the new anarchy.

Impossible, say the pessimists, the clock cannot be turned back. If that is the case, why are so many parents anxious to send their children to church schools in the state sector, both Roman Catholic and Anglican? Even non-believers have been known to start attending church in the hope of meeting the admission criteria for their children. The answer is simple. Because of their Christian ethos, no matter how much it is downplayed, these schools are generally able to offer higher standards and better discipline, along with a degree of instruction in right and wrong. Even more telling is the number of parents who are willing to make heavy sacrifices to send their children to those private schools where 'ethnocentric' Christian values and traditions are still manifest. The task is to bring this culture from the few of the private and voluntary church sectors to the many of the state.

Without changing our education system, we cannot instill future generations with a powerful sense of moral values. But the work of moral rebuilding cannot be confined to schools. It must also include other institutions which serve the public but which should also act as agents of moral authority. Morality cannot be successfully fostered in the education system if it does not exist in the home and elsewhere. Doctors should not feel inhibited in making judgements about their patients – or 'playing God' as they sometimes call it. Decisions about when to provide fertility treatment or carry out an abortion or prescribe certain drugs or validate a sick note should not be made in a moral vacuum, as if the patients' demands were all that mattered. Probation officers, too, should be able to detach themselves from current determinist notions about the causes of crime to concentrate on reforming the criminal. By doing so they would be returning to the ethics on which the service was founded in the 1870s. Social workers are in a better position than most to exercise moral judgements. Yet no profession is more gripped by non-judgementalism and the fear of cultural bias than social services. Indeed, 'anti-discrimination' is now its guiding principle. Any problems that they encounter – alcoholism, poverty, drug-addiction, child abuse – are always reflections of failings by society, never of their 'clients'. This culture has to change. Helping the individual rather than changing society must be their professional task.

Employers have their role in moral regeneration, encouraging the values of honesty and integrity rather than solely the will to win at any cost. 'Dirty tricks' can never be justified by the need to 'beat the competition'. Business leaders can also set an example by not awarding themselves bloated pay increases while demanding pay cuts from their workforce. Politicians could enhance their public offices by restraint and dignity rather than degrading them through self-seeking pay deals and consultancy contracts. Parts of the media could exercise responsibility instead of constantly forcing back the boundaries of taste and glorying in the breaking of taboos. The welfare state and the tax system could reward thrift and discourage idleness rather than the opposite, as happens at present. Housing policy could support the family rather than exacerbate its disintegration.

Above all, the Christian churches, especially the Church of England, need to reassert their roles as spiritual leaders and teachers of doctrinal faith. Contrary to the view of some bishops, it is precisely the job of the Church to 'preach morality'. If the Anglican Church in this country is unwilling to provide a moral lead, who else can be expected to do so? The desire to give no offence, to be 'in touch', 'down-to-earth', 'up-to-date', has wreaked great havoc. On occasions the General Synod has resembled the Equal Opportunities Committee of Haringey Council, such has been the dominance of gender and gay issues. The road to spiritual enlightenment does not begin on the dance floor of Madam Jo-Jo's nightclub. The fixation with political campaigning is equally misplaced. The only time I have heard a senior Anglican figure talk recently in clear, absolutist moral terms has been about a Tory campaign poster. The Church should show more concern about the Gospels than the latest report of the Child Poverty Action Group. Instead of encouraging the marginalisation of Christianity through its anxiety about temporal 'relevance', the Church of England can find inspiration from the religious traditions of our land: quiet, undogmatic Anglicanism and Catholicism, as opposed to raucous fundamentalism.

In further chapters, I will examine in more detail the changes that some of these institutions could make to end the moral drift. The point I wish to make here is that we should believe in the possibility of *change*. One of the most astonishing features of the last half century is the speed with which the Christian moral tradition has lost its hold on our society. The creed of secular, multi-cultural non-judgementalism has swept all before it like an Australian bush-fire. It would be beyond the comprehension of a Lambeth resident in 1946 that, fifty years later, her local health authority could be funding an event called: 'Come Play With Us: An Afternoon of videos, toys, games and fantasy for Black gay and bisexual men.' Yet if this societal transformation could occur so rapidly, is there not some hope that its influence is more shallow than our cultural pulpiteers pretend?

The descent into the amoral society has been hastened by changes in legislation and taxation, by extensions of welfare and public support, by new approaches and policies from our national institutions and public servants, by the demands of academics and intellectuals, and, perhaps most importantly, the craven unwillingness of our moral guardians to mount a defence of the civic order. Indeed, in some cases, they have enthusiastically abandoned their posts and welcomed the onward march of the enemy. Yet, given the will of Government, public services and opinion formers, the forces of civilisation could still be rallied. And the task has to start with Christian morality, the foundation stone of our civic order.

CHAPTER TWO

Rights, Not Wrongs, in an Infantilised Society

The following items are all taken from the news pages of a single issue (8 August 1996) of the weekly magazine for the social work profession, *Community Care*:

'The closure of the Benefits helpline will add to social services' workload, welfare rights officers have warned. Don Barton, welfare rights adviser to the Association of County Councils, said people in rural areas who did not have a local benefit office would suffer.'

'What is being legitimised is the return and acceptance of public begging and the erosion of people's economic and social rights. We need to challenge the assertion that people's rights to food should be subject to their relationship to the labour market.' – Graham Riches, Canadian academic, at the Conference of the International Council on Social Welfare.

'An advice and advocacy service for families from ethnic minorities has been established by the Family Rights Group and the East Birmingham Family Service Unit.'

'Rural areas have a dearth of alcohol advice centres, says an advice pack from Alcohol Concern.'

'The tendency to overlook the needs of older people with HIV is widespread, but the neglect of those from ethnic minority communities is especially marked.'

'Campaign Groups such as Rights for Women believe that the slow process of judicial enlightenment (towards women who kill their partners) still has far to go.'

As these comments from *Community Care* demonstrate, the demand for 'rights' to be met and 'needs' to be fulfilled – almost always by the Government and its agencies – has rarely been louder.

Adolescents have never behaved more like adults than in the Britain of the nineties, with their pseudo-sophistication over sex and money. But, more importantly, adults have never behaved more like adolescents in their constant expectation that someone else will provide.

Without any concept of transcendence, the needs of the individual are all. We live in an infantilised age, where too many people cannot think beyond their own personal gratification, whether it be in consumer goods or relationships or work. 'If I want something, I go out and get it', or, 'You only get one chance at life, so you've got to grab at anything that comes your way', or, 'If someone gets hurt in the process, that's tough', are three so-called 'personal philosophies' that have been aired recently in the media, justifying adultery. The over-riding characteristic of this new culture is the persistent emphasis on rights and needs at the expense of wider social and personal responsibility.

The American Declaration of Independence of 1776 never claimed that men had a 'right to happiness', only to 'the pursuit of happiness', a very different idea. Sadly, in our infantilised age, the former is demanded all too often. The defiant father at the front of a march against the Child Support Act, holding hands with his third wife and moaning about the injustice of his maintenance payments, is one representative of this spirit. So is the health worker who talks blithely of the 'sexual rights' of a severely handicapped teenage girl with a mental age of two. Or the neurotic who calls out a doctor at three in the morning because of a headache. Or the parents of the boy expelled from school for persistent disobedience, angrily enquiring about their rights of appeal and threatening legal action. Or the young vandal who explains to an arresting police officer that he 'knows his rights'. This conversation in Colchester between an unmarried mother and a young friend was recounted to me last year: 'And you know what the Council did? They gave me a cheque for just £750 to buy some furniture. I mean, you can't even get a three-piece suite for that much. What do they expect me to sit on?' The mother, by the way, had just been given a new flat by the borough council. When I was a Labour activist and councillor I regularly heard the complaint from inner-city residents: 'The Council ain't done nothing for me.'

This from people who lived in a Council flat, had their rent paid by housing benefit, had received income support and child benefit, and had been awarded a decoration allowance. I even had a case of a woman who had been given a large house with a garden by her local authority, and then wanted a transfer to another home because her present place 'was not near enough to the Roman Catholic school' for her boys. Apparently, they had to suffer the hardship of taking a bus there.

In the infantilised society, we simultaneously want both independence and total security from the Government. We seek ever-greater personal freedom yet become ever more dependent on the Government, another paradox of the modern era. The New Age traveller is a perfect example of this contradiction, complaining of threats to his social security payments yet trumpeting his rejection of the civic order. In nineties Britain, like spoilt children, we want freedom without its consequences. We can leave marriages, father children, take drugs or fail examinations without having to worry unduly. Someone else will ensure it is 'sorted'. We wish to live life as a series of gratifying moments. If we make mistakes, or act foolishly or maliciously, we should be absolved from responsibility, allowed to go on as before.

The development of the infantilised state was predicted more than a century ago by the French politician and writer, Alexis de Tocqueville, in his celebrated study *Democracy in America* (1835):

'Over this kind of men stands an immense protective power which is alone responsible for securing their enjoyment and watching over their fate. That power is absolute, thoughtful of detail, orderly, provident and gentle. It would resemble parental authority if, father-like, it tried to prepare its charges for a man's life, but, on the contrary, it only tries to keep them in perpetual childhood.'

De Tocqueville further warned that such a state, where all the necessities of life are provided, would rob the individual of the ability and inclination to exercise his free will, the very essence of liberty. Just as a child cannot be free because of its dependence on its parents, so the freedom of the adult is inhibited by his belief that someone else must provide. George Bernard Shaw put it thus in *Man and Superman*: 'Liberty means responsibility. That is why most men dread it.'

As I stated in the last chapter, the concept of free will – and hence personal responsibility – has been undermined by the determinist forces of Marxism and Freudianism. Socialist attempts to enhance equality and psychoanalytic efforts to lessen individual unhappiness have exacerbated infantilism by encouraging individuals to blame others ('society' or parents) for their predicaments. The alcoholic drinks too much because of a 'dearth of advice centres'. The gay man has unprotected sex because of his mother's obsession with cleanliness. The black child is excluded from school because of racism.

In the last twenty years, the infantilisation of society has further been encouraged by the political movements of both the Left and the Right. For all its rhetoric about responsibility, the long-serving Tory Government has achieved the opposite by its consumerist emphasis on the needs and wants of the individual. Thatcherism may not have deliberately paraded selfishness as a virtue, but that is certainly the impression that the Government created. 'Gain all you can, save all you can, give all you can,' was the creed of John Wesley which Mrs Thatcher claimed underlay her political philosophy. Unfortunately, the last two clauses of that saying were ignored by many of her most enthusiastic followers for whom personal gratification is all. The Armani-suited estate agent in his BMW might be the most potent symbol of the Thatcher era but he had an army of supporters, like the privatised utility boss with his bulging share options and his half-baked jargon about the 'market-place'. The television executive who becomes self-employed as a tax dodge and the Conservative MP who is caught accepting money to ask Parliamentary questions and then whines about press intrusion, are following the new individualistic, amoral creed. And why should the welfare claimant miss out on this festival of money-grabbing?

Under the Conservatives, we have been frequently lectured about the 'freedom of the individual'. But, too often, this freedom is of a narrow, infantilised kind, the freedom to do 'what I want', rather than to meet responsibilities. And, by focusing all energies on individual desires, wider freedoms are thereby destroyed, like stable home environments for children or care and support for the elderly.

From the Left, still stained by the residue of Marxism for all Blair's modernisation, the querulous agenda of 'rights' has been paraded in a different form, with demands that the Government meet every social and economic need of the individual, no matter how idle or irresponsible. If such needs are not fulfilled, the dissatisfied (or 'disadvantaged') are justified in venting their anger. The whole thrust of the Labour movement – indeed one might say its very *raison d'être* – is to extend the scope for government action and cocoon the citizen from any responsibility. In Labour's health policy document *Renewing the NHS*, the party even criticises the Government for 'putting the responsibility on individuals' for health promotion. So Labour is proposing an absurd raft of bureaucratic changes, such as 'local awareness campaigns', 'health audits', a 'senior minister with specific responsibility for public health', 'co-ordinated health promotion programmes', 'healthy alliances between voluntary groups, local government, businesses and health authorities', an 'expanded Health Education Authority', a strategy to ensure the 'maintenance of oral health', a new AIDS strategy to educate and inform the public about HIV/AIDS, a ban on tobacco advertising, new 'joint public health units', and a remit on occupational health services 'actively to seek out health hazards in the workplace.' The idea that runs through this document is that the Government is responsible for every bad tooth, sore back, large paunch, or fat thigh.

In our new irresponsible age, we are becoming a nation of graspers and whingers. We ask for more from the Government and then complain when we have to pay for it. The property boom of the late eighties is another example. Thousands of people felt they had discovered the easy way to make money, just by trading up their homes on a regular basis. But the merry-go-round of price rises was unsustainable. When the market collapsed, some of those in negative equity screamed of 'betrayal' and 'being let down by the Government'. Action was demanded 'to revive the market'. But no one forced them to keep moving house or trading upwards. We heard some even more unjustifiable complaints after the huge losses at Lloyds Insurance. Those who had enjoyed a substantial income from Lloyds for years were suddenly demanding Government help in their newly straitened circumstances. Did no one tell them that there is no such thing as a risk-free investment? It is a sign of the depths to which the Labour Party had sunk in its pursuit of the 'rights' agenda that one of their financial spokesmen initially backed these demands for Government support.

I was recently interviewing voters in Basildon, Essex, about the way they would vote at the next election. Most were opposed to the

Tories, though often for indefinable reasons. One woman, in her answer, encapsulated the worst of this infantilised mentality.

'What would you like out of a new Government?' I asked her.

'Well, er, more on the health service, and more on the schools.'

'You mean more spending?'

'Course, and on jobs and housing as well. And benefits, they've got to go up.'

'Taxes?' I asked.

'Yeah, them too,' she replied.

'What, up?' I asked, slightly puzzled.

'No, down, of course, silly.'

It was not in my remit to enquire how she might reconcile lower taxes with her lavish demands on the Exchequer. A survey by *British Social Attitudes* shows the strength of the public view of the need for yet more Government spending. In this survey, 87 per cent of respondents said they wanted more spent on health, 74 per cent wanted more on pensions and on education, 72 per cent felt more should go on policing and law enforcement. Even on unemployment benefits, usually a source of controversy, only 17 per cent wanted less spent than at present. Previous surveys over the last decade have shown similar demands for higher Government spending. Yet, for all these oft-professed sentiments, the large majority of the public has consistently refused to vote for the party most loudly committed to increases in public spending, preferring to believe that their income taxes will be lowered by the Conservatives. Indeed, one of the most keenly voiced accusations against the current Government is that Ministers have failed to abide by their 1992 election promise to reduce taxation. In this context, it was amusing to read the findings of a 1996 survey of potential Liberal Democrat voters. The party often boasts of public support for its plan to impose 'a penny on the income tax' to provide more funds for education. This opinion poll showed that many Liberal Democrat voters must have interpreted the policy quite literally. Only three per cent of them were willing to pay the additional £12.50 a month that would result from a penny in the pound increase. Had they believed that Paddy meant only 1p on their annual tax bill?

The reason the Government has been forced to raise taxes – largely through extensions of VAT – was because of record levels of public spending. In 1912 Government expenditure stood at 12 per cent of GDP. It has now reached 42 per cent, £290 billion. Spending has heavily increased in almost every field since the seventies. The budget for the health service has risen by two thirds in real terms (i.e., taking out inflation) since 1977, rising to £39 billion last year. The social security budget has more than doubled in real terms since 1977. It is the same story in local government, the police, legal aid, schools, universities, even the arts – the Arts Council grant has increased by 45 per cent in real terms under the Conservatives. Ironically for a Conservative Government, the only area that has seen real reductions is defence. Yet we constantly hear talk of 'underfunding' in the NHS, of local authorities being 'starved of resources', of 'cuts' to schools, of 'straitened budgets' for social work, of 'under-investment' in higher education, of 'inadequate finance' for community care, of 'harsh limits' on welfare claims.

This climate of despair is exacerbated by a host of pressure groups and trade unions who have a vested interest in claiming that every service is underfunded, that the 'disadvantaged' are suffering because of cruel Tory policies. Shelter, the housing campaign group, repeatedly attacks the inadequacy of support for the homeless. You are hardly likely to hear the Child Poverty Action Group say that the welfare system is in cracking shape. Too often the media plays an unfortunate role in highlighting the self-serving claims of pressure groups, who, after all, are unelected and unaccountable. Statements about 'under-resourcing' are regarded as impartial facts. Demands for more cash are treated with a sympathy which is rarely accorded to the Government ministers who refuse them.

Almost every problem raised in the media brings forth a rash of calls for more public money. Failure at the Olympics? More resources for the Sports Council must be the answer. Murder of a headteacher outside his school gates? More spending on security in schools. Fire on a ferry at Harwich? More cash for safety measures. BSE crisis? More compensation for farmers. A fascinating report in 1995 from the Social Market Foundation, *Costing the Public Policy Agenda*, exposed the possible financial consequences of this tidal wave of funding demands aired through the media. Researchers at the Foundation selected a week at random – Monday 20 February to Saturday 25 February 1995 – and analysed all the interviews on the BBC Radio *Today* programme, putting cost estimates against the numerous calls for government action or changes in public policy. By the time Messrs Naughtie and Humphreys laid down their headsets at the end of the week, the total sum of demands made on the public purse during those six days had reached an astonishing £15 billion – enough to add 10p to the standard rate of income tax, a 40 per cent rise on current levels, all in one week. The range of items included: another £270 million for the teachers' pay settlement; more grants for local authorities; higher expenditure on street cleaning; more money for British Rail to refurbish trains; a call from the International Labour Organisation for 'international action to assist the developing nations', 'wage subsidies' and 'easy credit terms for new enterprises'; and a condemnation, by Shelter, of plans to remove mortgage support for the unemployed. Some items, like the Church Action on Poverty's demand for 'a decent standard of living for all', were so Utopian in their extravagance that they could not be included in the SMF report.

Given the statist nature of socialism, it is hardly surprising that so many Labour MPs and activists believe that every problem can only be solved by Government action. The outstretched palm is an integral part of Leftist physiology. But, despite their reputation for fiscal prudence, many Tories are just as bad. They believe in cutting public spending in theory. In practice, they are loath to see this particular hospital close or that particular benefit withdrawn. They have, after all, their expectant electors to look after. In our discredited political system, the criteria for judging the success of a politician are too often based on his ability to gain more Government spending for his constituents, or 'bringing home the federal bacon' as it is described in the USA. As a former local councillor in Islington, I used to share this outlook. I argued the special case for priority to be given to major housing improvements in my locality. An advocate of economic efficiency elsewhere, I was suddenly the most enthusiastic of Keynesians if these were any rumours of budget cuts affecting any local amenities in my ward, such as an adventure playground or a city farm. I would always take up any constituent's problem whether it be a wish to be rehoused or to receive a discretionary education grant or an invalidity allowance.

Our entire political system has become a sort of national giant car boot sale, where almost the only job of MPs and councillors is to weigh up competing demands on the public purse and argue over where the money should be spent. Select committees, questions to ministers, the passage of legislation, adjournment debates and constituency problems are all dominated by the question of cash. In the infantilised nineties, the definition of a 'caring' Government refers only to its eagerness to spend public money. 'Caring' about a budget deficit or the burden of taxation does not come into it. The supposedly 'caring' local authority is the one which has the most lavish services and facilities and hence the highest taxes. 'Islington cares, care for Islington', the slogan of my former local authority, was a cue for profligacy. The 'caring' MP is the one who supports the most demands on the Exchequer. The 'caring' Minister is the one who most vigorously defends his Departmental budget. Few politicians today have the courage to say 'no' to a call for greater 'resources', especially if it emanates from their constituency. Equally, few MPs or councillors dare to risk losing the votes of a constituent by refusing to support demands for alternative housing/a home help/a social fund loan/ a student grant/priority hospital treatment.

This dangerous racket is supported by the media, pressure groups, lobbyists, and public agencies. Social workers, probation officers, health visitors, lawyers, even doctors, are just as skilled as politicians at playing this game. Every inner city MP is familiar with the copy of the GP's letter which begins, 'To whom it may concern', and then argues that X patient needs urgent rehousing because of 'ME', or 'damp', or 'too many stairs', or 'heavy traffic outside', or 'difficulties with neighbours', or 'distance from relatives', or 'lack of a garden for her two-year-old', or a combination of these. Everyone is only doing their job but the result of this prodigal professional chorus is an ever-increasing burden on the public finances and ever-higher tax bills.

Our infantilised age has created a vast new bureaucracy of public professionals, dedicated to 'addressing needs' and 'promoting rights'. These New Public Servants, as I call them, cover a wide range of functions and job titles – welfare rights advisers, community development workers, sexual health promoters, addiction counsellors, equal opportunities officers, race project co-ordinators, youth team leaders, discrimination policy analysts, AIDS awareness campaigners, needs assessors, housing assistants, and alcohol support staff. New Public Servants encourage the idea that no one is responsible for their own behaviour, that the 'needs' of the disadvantaged and the 'rights' of the oppressed can only be met by action from central or local government.

No profession holds this view more completely than social work, the Pilgrim Fatherhood, as it were, of the New Public Service movement. When the modern social services departments were first created after the Seebohm report in 1971, there were hopes they could reduce the incidence of child abuse, alcoholism, domestic violence, under-age sex, drug-taking, family breakdown, neglect of the elderly, racial harassment and mental illness. Yet the worsening of these problems, rather than their reduction, is now used to underwrite demands for further expansion by social work departments. And so we have a vicious – and expensive – equation: the greater the failure by social work departments to reduce the social evils, the greater their demands for funding.

Few public services have grown faster than social work in the last decade. In 1984, total social work spending stood at £2.6 billion. It has now reached £7.5 billion. We are employing 53,000 more personal social services staff than we did fifteen years ago. There are now 238,000 social work employees in local authorities, though you would hardly think it from all the moans about 'underfunding' and 'lack of basic resources'. Yet not only have social work departments failed completely to repair the damage to the fabric of our society, they have also, in many cases, worsened it with their myopia over deprivation and discrimination, which allows them to excuse the most feckless and irresponsible behaviour. Indeed, there must be a suspicion that some social workers never wanted to resolve social problems in the first place, since they are tangible evidence of the failings of a capitalist, patriarchal society. The greater the collapse in the civic order, the more justified they feel in their views.

As the Islington child abuse case demonstrated, the social services' concern with 'rights' rather than duties can have disastrous consequences. So twisted were the values of that social services culture that the supposed 'rights' of paedophiles were in effect elevated above the needs of children in care. On a much larger scale, the same approach of putting theoretical rights before real needs can be seen in the worst extremes of the policy of 'care in the community'. Long-stay hospitals for the mentally ill and mentally handicapped continue to be closed because of the theory that patients will be better off in the 'community'. Their 'rights' to lead as normal lives as possible will be thereby enhanced. For many, this may be true, but, as so often happens in the 'caring' professions, the idea is now applied with dogmatic rigidity. 'Independence' in the community for some severely mentally handicapped people can actually mean being trapped in a small inner-city hostel, unable to leave because the streets are too dangerous, looked after by a few ill-trained staff. The alternative, so despised by the proponents of the new 'rights' orthodoxy because of its 'institutionalised' nature, could be in a large hospital or residential home in scenic grounds in the countryside, with modern facilities like a hydrotherapy pool and a range of specialist staff. The irony is that the resident locked in the city hostel and watching TV all day is far more 'institutionalised' than the one who is able to move around the grounds of a rural centre. As Professor Ben Sacks of the Charing Cross Hospital recently commented: 'You cannot make people who have things fundamentally wrong with their brains into normal people by putting them in a terraced house.' Even worse, the 'care in the community' policy has had literally murderous results for some paranoid schizophrenics and the victims of their actions. Only the most perverted ideology could place the 'rights' of such dangerous individuals above both their own needs and those of society. But such an ideology is another result of the non-judgemental age, where even the twisted instinct to kill is no more than 'challenging behaviour'.

The 'care in the community' policy is the result of a rights-led culture that runs through social services, the NHS and most of the work of the New Public Servants, from gay men's health advisers to race equality officers. Where once they might have had to hawk newspapers on street corners or take boring low-paid clerical jobs, ideologues and 'rights' activists can now earn lucrative salaries from the taxpayer in the public and voluntary sector. At Newham Council, for instance, the staff of the Anti-Poverty and Welfare Rights Unit comprises a grandly titled Anti-Poverty Co-ordinator, a Welfare Rights Adviser (Appeals), Welfare Rights Adviser (Training), Welfare Rights Adviser (Take-Up), Senior Administrative Officer and Administrative Assistant. At Hounslow Council, staff from the £622,000-a-year Equal Opportunities Office perform such vital tasks as organising conferences on 'employment rights, racism and homo-phobia' and developing services to 'meet the drug use needs' of young gay men. In its annual report last year, the Ethnic Minorities Welfare Rights Team at Newcastle City Council – part of a seventeen-strong municipal Welfare Rights service – complained that the 'rules of entitlement to social security are based on a Euro-Ethnocentric base'.

Wouldn't it be extraordinary if our welfare system did not have a Euro-centric base?

Employment opportunities abound for the ideologically correct. At Bath City Council, the 'youth services division' claims that the 'primary purpose of youth work is to challenge and where possible to redress all forms of inequality'. A black Woman Researcher has recently been recruited by the Women's Aid Federation, while Brighton and Hove Health Authority has a Black and Ethnic Community Needs Assessment Worker. A Black Women Project Worker at the Bridges Project in the north-east is currently conducting a 'community-based needs assessment of the HIV Prevention and related sexual health promotion needs of Black Women in Newcastle and North Tyneside'. You can be sure that any assessment of needs will result in a report which says that more resources – and more research – are needed. If the Government fails to meet these demands, our New Public Servants will then launch their barrage of indignation about 'underfunding' or a 'refusal to address the needs of the black community'.

The campaigning organisation Lesbian and Gay Employment Rights last year appointed a Lesbian Caseworker to fight for the rights of lesbians 'who are having trouble at work'. Redditch Council has a Single Parent Project Worker whose job is to 'challenge the negative stereotyping of single parents', while Hammersmith and Fulham has an Asian Women's Mental Health Worker at The Bridge, 'The Centre for Women's Emotional Well-being'. The National Lottery has been another catalyst in the growth of this new salariat. When the first tranche of grants was announced last autumn, the largest, £600,000, went to the Strathclyde Anti-Poverty Alliance, not to relieve poverty, but to provide information and training for its workers. In November 1995, the awards included £100,500 for a project in Nottingham to employ 'three prostitute outreach workers'. Last year a grant of £95,000 was made to the Black Arts Alliance in Manchester 'to pay for a youth worker, travel and training'. The Lottery has also been sustaining the 'rights' agenda. The West Midlands Anti-Deportation Campaign received a grant of £66,000 'to produce a pack for asylum-seekers advising them of their rights, how to appeal against deportation orders, how to find a lawyer and what social security benefits they are entitled to'. Entitlement to legal advice, social security and other welfare rights is, of course, not dependent on any reciprocal contribution to society. In some parts of the NHS, a medical qualification and a good bedside manner appear no more important than a sociology degree and a willingness to 'confront prejudice'. Camden and Islington Health Authority spends more than £50,000 a year on a trio of politically correct crusaders in its health promotion section. One Female Community Development Worker is employed 'to encourage women to take a holistic approach to their own health'. A Male Project Worker encourages 'men in local Asian communities to be more aware of traditional health diets'. A third worker has the task of 'increasing awareness of the health risks of smoking in the Turkish-speaking communities'.

The response to the AIDS crisis by the NHS and other public institutions could almost serve as a case study for the growth of the amoral, infantilised society. We have been constantly urged to address the 'rights' and 'needs' of those most at risk from the HIV/AIDS virus – gay men and drug users – but never to question their personal behaviour, as long as they wear a condom or use a clean needle. If an individual refuses to listen to such mild advice, this is seen as a consequence of our failure 'to get the safe-sex message across', not of his lack of self-restraint or personal responsibility. The greater the promiscuity or drug use, the louder the demands for public support.

The Government is currently spending £270 million a year on campaigning, research and treatment on HIV/AIDS. In order to justify this sum, the AIDS lobby has had to exaggerate the threat of HIV/AIDS and make the most lurid projections for its future incidence. But AIDS is the epidemic that never happened. Contrary to all the grim predictions of the eighties, since 1982 just 9,148 people have died of AIDS, while in total there have been 27,000 HIV infections. The Department of Health estimates that by 1999 there will be only 4,000 cases of full-blown AIDS. Compare this to the 80,000 people in this country who suffer from multiple sclerosis, a condition which receives just £500,000 a year from the Government. Or the fact that 1 in 3 Britons die of cancer, yet the amount spent on cancer research by the NHS, charities and drug companies is £245 million, far less than Government support for HIV/AIDS. So lavish has been Government funding that in some parts of the country there are more HIV/AIDS workers than patients. The full grotesque nature of the spending figures is revealed when they are broken down on a local basis. In the Northern and Yorkshire region, for example, the sum allocated to the district health authorities for AIDS prevention and treatment last year was £13.07 million. With just fifty-nine cases in the region over the previous twelve months, that is the equivalent of an astonishing £221,508 per case. In parts of London, the imbalance is even more extreme. In Kensington, Chelsea and Westminster, where last year 135 residents were diagnosed as having AIDS, the Government allocation amounted to £45 million, a phenomenal £333,259 per case. I recently visited the HIV Network in Coventry which receives £305,000 a year from the taxpayer and employs a staff of twenty, including 'Cottaging and Cruising Project' workers and 'street-based' youth action workers. The total number of new HIV/AIDS cases in the Coventry and Warwickshire area in 1995 was just twelve. In September 1994, when it was announced that the Camden and Islington health authority budget for AIDS was to be above £20 million, one research doctor complained: 'The figures for cancer and heart disease dwarf those of AIDS. The fact is that, whatever the politically correct may argue, AIDS is still, mercifully, confined to a very small section of the population.'

Just as wrong-headed as this disproportionate spending has been the idea that 'we are all at risk', that AIDS is 'not prejudiced'. There has rarely been a more discriminating disease. Over 70 per cent of AIDS cases in this country were acquired as a result of sexual intercourse between men. Other modes of transmission include blood transfusion, and drug use. Heterosexual intercourse between partners from low-risk groups has accounted for just 166 cases since 1982 – little more than ten a year.

The policy of portraying AIDS as an 'equal opportunities disease' was part of a deliberate strategy in the eighties to avoid accusations that the disease was confined to one narrow section of society. If it were seen as a threat to all, the public would be more willing to pay for prevention and treatment. Since the early nineties, however, many leading AIDS campaigners have questioned this strategy, arguing that its message was failing to reach those most vulnerable to AIDS. This has led to the movement called the 'Regaying of AIDS', with demands that most AIDS funding be concentrated on work with gay men. At the forefront of this movement have been pressure groups, like Gay Men Fighting AIDS and Act-Up (AIDS Coalition to Unleash Power).

But why do we need this debate at all? If some gay men have still not got the message about safe sex after fifteen years, they never will. How is more funding, more publicity, more campaigning to make any difference – apart from serving as a means to justify the existence of a myriad of gay rights groups? As one manager of an HIV prevention project admitted to me, 'gay men have been bombarded' with information about AIDS. Every pub, club, and gay event carries the safe sex message. Gays cannot even go on to Hampstead Heath without meeting some publicly-funded condomaniac preaching the gospel of rubber. East Berkshire Community Health Trust has employed staff to nail condoms, capsules of gel and advice leaflets to trees at a secluded woodland spot near Ascot frequented by gays. Barnet Healthcare Trust caused controversy in the summer of 1996 by advertising for 'two gay or bisexual men' to work in its Cottaging and Cruising Project. 'Cottaging' is the ideologically correct term for gay sex in a gents' toilet, also known to aficionados as a 'Public Sex Environment' (PSE). Defending the appointments, Suzy Malhotra, an HIV information officer, said the work 'involves an understanding of the practices of men who go to public places for sex. It is not voyeuristic. It is similar to watching patients in a hospital.' I'm not sure the ward patient recovering from a coronary by-pass would agree.

The Barnet row highlights the way AIDS provision in the nineties has become a vast industry for gay men, providing them with the most outlandish employment opportunities. What was once seen as the bizarre or sordid has now become part of a job description. Knowledge of the 'gay scene' or 'gay lifestyles' has become a vital asset for recruitment. Experience of 'cruising' is seen as a useful skill, like the ability to drive or speak a foreign language. As one disillusioned therapist, who works largely with AIDS patients, said to me: 'In the AIDS field, if you're straight, they don't want to know. There is real discrimination. You don't have to be good at what you do, you just have to be gay.'

Gay Men Fighting AIDS is a gay community organisation which receives more than £250,000 a year in public funds. Among the GMFA's activities has been the production of 'Tuffaware Party Packs' which, in the organisation's own words, deliver 'large numbers of condoms and lube to gay men organising sex parties'. The packs include 'legal advice on sex at parties and top tips on running a successful orgy'. GMFA also runs courses on 'Bondage for Beginners', workshops on 'cruising skills', and 'Sado-Masochism Sex Days', which includes advice for those 'new to the SM scene'. Other material from GMFA features a 'holiday shag bag', postcards carrying messages such as 'My Friend is Positive – Fuck Him', and a 'Wank Mag', an 'erotic and comprehensive safer sex booklet aimed at the fetish market'. This is the decadent, amoral, 'liberated' Britain of the nineties, where NHS funds are used to provide advice sessions on bondage, cruising and orgies.

Gay Men Fighting AIDS may be extreme but it is hardly unique. Rubberstuffers is another publicly-funded London-based project which, according to its literature, 'informs and supports gay men in selecting the right kind of condoms and lubricant for anal sex, through targeted condom information campaigns'. Work by Rubberstuffers' employees includes 'running Condom Skills courses to assist gay men who find difficulty in using or introducing condoms into their sex lives'. The Men Who Have Sex With Men in the Community (MESMAC) project in Tyneside, which receives £140,000 a year from local health authorities, employs gay workers 'to support the needs of gay and bisexual men' by handing out condoms in gay pubs. Healthy Gay Manchester boasts that it has 'an expanding outreach programme providing sensitive and appropriate services direct to men who have sex with men in the cruising grounds and cottages of Manchester'. In a similar vein, Lambeth Southwark and Lewisham Health Authority funds a group called BIG UP, 'Black Men Delivering HIV/AIDS Information to Black Gay and Bisexual Men'. One of the recent events organised by BIG UP has been: *Give Him Something He Can Feel*, 'a safer sex extravaganza for black gay and bisexual men'.

What is missing from all this frantic activity is any concept of morality or self-control. Indeed, for the New Public Servants in the AIDS field, such ideas are not just alien but positively reactionary. No condemnation of any form of behaviour can be made, no judgement can be exercised. Any attempt to discourage the gratification of the wildest hedonistic impulse is seen as an infringement of the 'rights' of gay men. Indeed, Rubberstuffers boasts, in its public advertisements, that its work is 'giving you the freedom to have sex'. As Wes Webb of the Coventry HIV Network put it to me, defending the local 'cottaging and cruising project', 'My job is HIV prevention. It is not to issue moral judgements.' This refusal to criticise enables every sexual practice to be seen as just another 'lifestyle choice'. As

Peter Tatchell says in his brutally explicit book, *Safer Sexy* – featuring photographs that, had they not been considered educational, would have led to immediate prosecution under the Obscene Publications Act – 'the only perversion is unsafe sex'.

This starkly amoral attitude is summed up in an article entitled *Aids: The Language of Oppression* by Peter Randall, Co-Founder of Body Positive, in that organisation's annual report. Randall attacks the Government's initial AIDS campaign in the eighties as 'a blatant example of blame, prejudice and moral judgement. The concentration on the avoidance of sex, and the advocacy of monogamy said a great deal about the moral stance of the authors but very little about how people live their lives.' 'Relating to how people live their lives' is the defence constantly used today by the New Public Servants, whether it be liberalising divorce or increasing welfare payments to single parents. Such attitudes have an element of self-fulfilment. If the state subsidises 'cottaging' by the provision of free condoms and lube, then more gay men are likely to do it because it has received official approval. Continuing his rant against moralism, Randall says that 'for many individuals the pageant of the single, faithful partner is unrealistic and therefore inappropriate and judgemental'. Again, if the ideal of fidelity is seen in such negative terms, it is hardly likely that many will strive to attain it. Then Peter Randall concludes: 'Collectively, the problem for us all is how to accept the advent of AIDS into our society and culture, but not to allow such projections to impose moral judgements.'

These words go to the heart of the problem of dealing with AIDS in our amoral, self-gratifying age. While the numbers of people living with AIDS may be small, the influence of the disease has been enormous, not just in financial terms but also in social attitudes. The assertion of 'sexual rights' and 'sexual freedom' has reinforced the breakdown of fidelity and moderation in our civic order. 'Do your own thing', whether it be in a lavatory or a lay-by, with two a week or ten a week, as long as you 'have fun' and take one small rubberised precaution. When our New Public Servants actually subsidise and encourage such activities, how can the state any longer act as a moral agent? 'The advent of AIDS into our society and culture' (to quote Peter Randall again) has enabled the libertines and liberals to revel in their destruction of every sexual taboo. Using the defence that 'lives may be saved', the most explicit language and imagery is dragged into the public arena, while 'family values' are portrayed as nothing more than dangerous prejudice. Personal self-gratification is almost treated as a civic duty.

Young people are now burdened with amoral so-called sex education to raise their 'awareness' of AIDS, through events like the play from the SNAP Theatre Trust, entitled *Sex, Lies and Tricky Bits*, which is 'targeted at 11- to 15-year-olds and aims to confront them with their own prejudices', or the *Workshop in Kissing With Confidence* for 10- to 12-year-olds from the Caught In The Act Theatre Company. The Catalyst Theatre in Health Education runs a *Sexuality Project* for Birmingham schoolchildren. Amongst the Catalyst's other activities is a *Safer Sex Cabaret* which features 'strippers and drag artists touring gay pubs and clubs'. Peter Tatchell argues that the way to protect young people is not 'to deny them their sexual rights and treat them as criminals if they have under-age sex'. Once again, the self-fulfilling prophecy takes effect. Demands for fulfilment of the supposed 'sexual rights' of the young can only lead to adolescent experimentation.

In our infantilised age, those clamouring for the 'sexual rights' of the young or gays or bisexuals or exhibitionists or fetishists ignore any parallel set of duties. What if our 'liberated' fourteen-year-old should become pregnant? Will she or her boyfriend be responsible for the care of the child? Of course not. The state, via the DSS, will perform that task. Similarly, the rights of 'cottagers' should not be limited by any sensibility towards those who might want to use the gents' toilet for another purpose. So extreme is the absence of any sense of responsibility in the AIDS field, that there has been a serious debate as to whether an HIV-positive individual has a duty to tell a partner of his HIV status. The repugnant depths of this self-seeking attitude were captured in the July 1996 issue of the HIV/AIDS magazine *Positive Times* in an article by Jeremy Cantry about the 'endless possibilities for a quick shag' at the annual PRIDE march for lesbians and gays. 'So what does pride mean anyway?' Cantry begins. 'A celebration of community? A sense of fellowship? A sense of anger? Shouting in the streets? Flaunting it? For those of us with HIV, perhaps a time to recognise the solidarity of our community? Nah, for a London-based gay man it's fresh meat from the provinces, innit? And for provincial gay men the chance to shag one or more of those gorgeous, sophisticated metropolitan queers . . . Pride, with all those possibilities, all that energy, all that euphoria and drug-induced high, amplifies all the usual problems about casual sex for us positive people.' The problem being, do you tell your pick-up of your HIV status? Cantry explains that he 'went through a phase of revealing my status to potential shags if I thought it likely that I'd want to see them again afterwards'. He says he is now more open but concludes, 'It's OK not to mention your status. It doesn't make any difference, because, after all, you're not going to do anything unsafe, are you? Don't you fucking hate that? Of course you might do something unsafe. Unsafe for him, for you or for both of you. And anyway, what's unsafe for you if you're positive? Jury still out on that!' Could there be a more chilling celebration of the creed of the self?

In its glorification of personal gratification, its failure to recognise any moral boundaries, its infantile demands for more Government action, its creation of an army of amoral public servants, and its assertion of 'dutiless rights' (to use the phrase of the political philosopher David Selbourne) the AIDS lobby is certainly a metaphor for our times.

Our infantilised society is now riddled with this cult of personal gratification. We are encouraged not to show restraint or patience in our food, our entertainment, our sports, our cars, our homes. 'Move in NOW for just £10' scream the estate agents' slogans outside the newly built estates on the greenfield sites near my home. 'An INSTANT quote, even INSTANT cover' blares the ungrammatical advertisement for insurance. 'Zero to 60 miles per hour in just 5 seconds,' purrs the car salesman. We demand instant food and drive-through burgers. We want our microwaves, our computers, our word-processors, our TV and CD remote controls to act instantly on our commands. 'Come on! Come on!' we shout impatiently at the PC screen or the laser printer during the few seconds it takes for an extraordinarily complex operation to be completed. Tens of thousands of banking staff are made redundant because we cannot bear to queue and would rather operate anonymously over the telephone. Like children, we sulk or throw a temper fit when asked to wait – hence the growing incidence of those ridiculous nineties phenomena: road rage and trolley rage. Teachers complain that many of their pupils are almost uncontrollable because, at home, their every whim is gratified. They are never taught to 'wait their turn' or accept an order. Even the official wording of the civil marriage ceremony has recently been shortened to speed up the process – as if a few minutes during the wedding should matter when a couple are, supposedly, committing themselves to each other for life.

Immaturity is becoming a national pastime. The traditional process of passing from irresponsible adolescence into responsible adulthood is now under threat. We have a growing flock of permanent teenagers, aged anything from twenty-five to fifty-five, who see any commitment, any talk of duty, as a threat to their personal freedom. Still trapped in their worlds of rock 'n' roll, joints and jeans, they wander from one job to another, from one relationship to another, from one flat to another, seeking nothing more than a 'bit of a laugh'. But we must not criticise. It is their lifestyle choice – even if they have to be regularly cared for by the DSS or the local council's housing department.

Infantilism is further reflected in the terror of making anything too difficult for our nineties generation. Everything should be understandable, 'relevant', appealing. So in our history curriculum, we have to teach lessons about 1966 rather than 1066. Our Church sermons have to allude to the last episode of *EastEnders* rather than the Letter of Paul to the Ephesians. Our universities are crammed with undergraduates on courses in 'media studies' or 'cultural studies' rather than chemistry or classics. Many TV programmes, especially those for young people, move hysterically from one item to another in fear of boring the viewer. Budding artists will no longer think that they need to learn the difficult technical crafts of drawing and painting, when they can, like some of their colleagues, become instant celebrities by hanging a piano upside-down or filling a house with concrete and pretending they have some message about nineties society. Cricket, that quintessentially long-winded English sport, has been sent into decline by the desire for instant gratification. The only county matches that now attract any crowds are the one-day events.

For the libertarian Conservative, none of this matters. The immediate demands of the individual must predominate in a free-market society. If the consumer wants out-of-town shopping centres, if the student prefers media studies to engineering, if the gay man wants to cruise in the woods, then so be it. If there is a demand for IVF treatment from lesbians or websites on the Internet for sado-masochists, then the market should meet it. The Church, the MCC,

Parliament, the BBC, the institution of marriage, the NHS or the Monarchy, like the rest of the economy, must adapt to the needs of the consumers in the nineties. They are the servants of the public, not its educators.

The pragmatic politicians of the current Government would deny that they have adopted such an aggressively consumerist stance. Is not Michael Howard's tough penal policy evidence of a strong commitment to strengthening the civic order? Have not the education reforms demonstrated a laudable desire to overcome the feeble relativism of the last thirty years? Has Peter Lilley not been courageous in ignoring the demands of the welfare rights lobby? Perhaps, but there has also been much movement in the opposite direction. The liberalisation of the divorce laws is one example. The expansion of legal aid is another; the health service reforms, where money is supposed to 'follow the patient' another. So is the absurd 1989 Children Act, with its host of regulations to enforce the 'rights' of children, as if children can have 'rights' when they have no responsibilities. The 'Right to Buy' for council tenants at hugely discounted rates, the encouragement given to easy credit and mortgages, the priority given to borrowing rather than saving – a contradiction of the Thatcherite doctrine of thrift – are part of this all-pervasive consumerism. The thrust of the Citizen's Charter also fits this mould. Almost every public service now has a charter, setting out the 'rights' of customers: how to complain, how to apply for compensation, how to demand satisfaction. We have the Parents' Charter for Schools, the Passengers' Charter for the Rail Network, the Benefits Charter for welfare claimants, the Patients' Charter for the NHS. What is missing from all these charters is any expectation of duties from the holder of these consumer 'rights'. The parent has no duty to ensure that homework is done. The patient need not worry about compensation if he misses an appointment or wastes the doctor's time with a trivial call-out. Indeed, the 'Patients' Charter' only reinforces the childish attitude that the NHS has a bottomless pit of money which should meet every single demand made upon it at no charge, from sex-change operations to free medicines for the slightest sniffle.

The European Union is just as keen on the 'rights' agenda. Indeed, the Union's entire social policy, set out in its Social Chapter, aims to provide, in the words of the European Commission, 'a framework for the guarantee of fundamental social rights for workers, including legal measures, financial support, specific action programmes and co-operation in the social field through the setting up of networks and partnerships for the exchange of information and experience'. These 'fundamental' rights set out by the Union include: 'the right to improved living and working conditions', 'the right to vocational training', 'the right to maternity leave', 'the right to paternity leave', 'the right to minimum rest periods', 'the right to time off for ante-natal examinations', 'the right to information' about the workplace, and 'the right to protection from unwanted conduct of a sexual nature or other conduct based on sex affecting the dignity of women and men at work'. The EU has proposed a 'guarantee of minimum living standards for the elderly' and expanded 'social protection' for all, to ensure that no one has to exist below 'the European decency threshold', an arbitrarily fixed sum of about £12,000 a year. In promoting these rights, the EU has developed a fetish for portentous annual public relations campaigns: 1992, for instance, was designated 'The European Year of Safety, Hygiene and Health Protection at Work'; 1993 was the 'Year of the Elderly and of Solidarity between Generations'. An extravagant bureaucratic web, made up of the European Court of Justice, the Court of Human Rights, the Commission, and the European Parliament supports those who feel their 'rights' have been denied.

The expansionary European social and economic programmes define individual 'rights' so vaguely and widely that almost any want or demand for state intervention can be dressed up as a 'human right'. Failure by a Government to provide jobs, increase pensions, raise wage levels, lengthen holidays, expand education, or build more homes can be seen, not as a political problem but an infringement of human rights. This concept is far removed from the pre-twentieth-century idea of civil and natural rights, which enshrined the individual's freedom from, rather than dependence on, the actions of the state. John Locke, the late seventeenth-century philosopher, who believed in 'the inalienable right to life, liberty and property', would have been astonished to discover that, three centuries later, so many 'rights' amount to no more than demands on the public purse.

For all Tony Blair's rhetoric about responsibility – in his March 1995 *Allied Dunbar/Spectator* lecture he said that our rights must 'reflect the duties that we owe' – we can expect this social and economic 'rights' agenda to be extended if Labour takes power. The party is committed to strengthening race- and sex-discrimination laws, and one of its Shadow Ministers has already introduced a Bill into Parliament to outlaw all forms of discrimination on the grounds of 'sexual orientation'. Labour will sign up to the European Social Chapter, thereby extending workplace rights'. Labour's environmental policies include a 'Charter of Environmental Rights', featuring a 'right to clean air', a 'right to clean drinking water' and a 'right to compensation' for environmental damage. A new 'Environment Division' of the High Court is proposed to 'encourage responsible individuals and groups to take out public interest cases'. There will be a 'Freedom of Information' Act, giving the public new rights of access to Government records. For ramblers, there will be a 'right to roam', for mothers a 'right to childcare', for health-food enthusiasts a 'right to information' on labels and packages.

Most of these measures can only encourage the spread of infantilism through our society, where the Government is seen as the provider and protector for everyone, where foolishness or unhappiness can only be ended through more regulations and more subsidies.

What needs to change

It will not be easy to change this public mood. Throughout this century, the concept of 'progress' has been based on the belief that the state should take on ever wider responsibilities to meet the 'social and economic rights' of the people. The reforms of the Edwardian Liberal Government, inspired by Lloyd George and Churchill, the extensions of national assistance and housing in the twenties and thirties, the great expansion of state activity under Attlee's 1945 Government (partly a legacy of the wartime control of the economy), and the corporatism of the Heath and Wilson Governments have all contributed to this movement. Even a supposedly radical Conservative Government has not seriously attempted to reverse it. Both taxation and public spending have never been higher.

But we cannot continue like this. With a growing number of elderly at one end of the population scale, and more young people staying in education until their early twenties, the demands on the state are becoming unsustainable. We must therefore try to change the public expectations of Government action. The re-establishment of a universally accepted moral code must be central, enabling individuals to look beyond their own immediate self-gratification. The first steps towards such a goal were set out in the last chapter.

The media also has a vital role. Too many programmes, like the *Rantzen Report* or *Watchdog* and, on occasions, the main news bulletins, act as cheerleaders for the querulous, rights-led infantilism, demanding corporate action to deal with every grumble and mishap. Even the highly respected *Today* on Radio 4 is sometimes treated as a sounding-board for the prodigal urges of pressure groups. It would make a pleasant change if a few campaign spokesmen were treated as roughly as any Minister, and if TV researchers showed the same cynicism towards the professional complainants and consumer or welfare 'rights' experts as they do towards companies and the Government. Sweeping statements about 'more resources' and 'greater Government support' – which can even come from supposedly impartial reporters – should no longer go unchallenged. This would not be as hard as it seems. Just as station heads now monitor their output for offensive or racist material, so they could be urged to do the same for irresponsible and uncosted items.

Far-reaching changes are needed in the way our political system operates to halt the ratchet effect of spending demands. It is grotesque that, even after the controversy of the Nolan report, MPs are still allowed to act as paid representatives and consultants for companies, lobbying and pressure groups, as long as they declare their interests. This practice must be made illegal. The defence of the existing arrangement is that MPs need to 'keep in touch with the real world'. They must do, yes, but paying professional politicians lobbying fees does nothing to achieve that.

MPs should be encouraged to have real jobs, not political consultancies. One of the greatest failings of our present system is that far too few MPs have any experience of the world outside politics. Hardly any of them have worked in commerce, business, or industry. Many are no more than souped-up councillors, researchers, trade unionists and lobbyists. This modern political caste only strengthens the culture of spending demands, for the professional politician has devoted his career to winning the support of vested interests rather than saying 'no' to them. Two reforms could be introduced. First, no one under the age of forty should be allowed to run for Parliament. A twenty-year gap between the student union hustings and the

Parliamentary campaign trail might discourage even the most ardent political hack. Second, if MPs were banned from holding consultancies and sponsorship, and their present £40,000 salaries were halved, then they might be forced to seek proper jobs.

Ah, but how could they do their constituency and Parliamentary work in such circumstances? Easily, for most of an MP's workload consists of dealing with the unceasing expectations of an infantilised society: taking up every single one of the most trivial or unjustified complaints from constituents, meeting one pressure group after another, speaking in the House in support of more regulation and more legislation for this or that problem. It would be of the greatest long-term benefit to the public if MPs were not able to do half this work. In fact, Parliament should be closed down for much of the year. Its sittings only incite the hysterical cry of our modern age that 'something must be done' on everything from exploding aerosols to a mild flu epidemic. There is a dangerous symbiotic relationship between the media and our politicians, whereby any problem that is reported in the press or the news is quickly 'raised in Parliament' – usually so that a certain MP can gain some publicity – and is then translated into a demand for Government action. Can it be a coincidence that our nation appears to function more happily in August when Parliament is not sitting? We should extend this period into other seasons.

The access of pressure groups, trade unions and lobbyists to the political process should be considerably tightened. They should no longer be treated as impartial experts when presenting their views to Select Committees, or providing briefings on legislation. They should be prevented from paying the salaries of MPs' researchers or providing 'office facilities'.

The number of Ministers and Parliamentary Secretaries in Government – currently over 100 – should, like the sittings of the Commons, be heavily reduced. Though many work eighteen-hour days, much of their time is filled with self-generating activity, such as holding press conferences, launching 'exciting new initiatives' or setting out some three-point action plan to deal with some media-discovered problem. And they also have to respond to the barrage of demands from the pulpiteers of infantilism. 'We asked the relevant Minister to appear on this programme, but he refused to do so,' the presenter of some 'consumer affairs' programme will arrogantly announce.

Would it not be much better if there were no 'relevant Minister' in the first place?

Some of this also applies to local government. As in Parliament, too many municipal chambers are dominated by professional politicians. And because they spend all their time on council business, they now expect a full-time public servant's salary. If councillors' allowances were severely restricted, they would also be compelled to earn a living.

Local government in Britain takes up a quarter of all public spending. Like other elements of the public sector, it mirrors the outlook of the infantilised society, with its bellowed complaints about 'underfunding', its eagerness to regulate, its belief in catering for all the whims of its citizens. Where once municipal institutions might have been a bulwark against the 'rights' culture, they are now amongst its loudest advocates. This change has been partly caused by the Conservatives' centralising measures over the last eighteen years, which have divested local authorities of much of their power. Council tax-capping, the Uniform Business Rate, compulsory competitive tendering, and standard spending assessments (SSAs) have been instrumental in this development. Around 85 per cent of local authority funding is now controlled by Whitehall. A degree of central control was inevitable after the antics of hard-Left councils like Liverpool and Lambeth, whose indulgence in political ideology led to catastrophic mismanagement and appalling services. But the consequence is that local councils, now stripped of their responsibilities over finance, have become as infantilised as parts of the public. Like municipal Olivers, they can just keep asking for 'more' without having to worry about the bill.

To end this mass irresponsibility, local authorities should have their independence restored. Capping should be abolished, and business rates returned to local control. But to increase accountability and prevent the abuse of power, I believe three conditions must be imposed. Elections should be held every year, with either a third or a quarter of councillors being elected on two- or four-yearly cycles. More controversially, each business or employer should have an additional vote. This would ensure that the voice of those who actually create jobs in the local area is not ignored. It might also encourage business-owners to become involved in local politics. Such a move could be seen as undemocratic but, in reality, what is democratic about using taxes from businesses to bribe your party's natural supporters? The business vote might reintroduce an element of fiscal prudence sadly lacking from too many of our municipal chambers.

Local government has been at the forefront of the creation of the New Public Servants. That salariat could start to be reduced with the reforms outlined above, as local councils would be forced to concentrate on providing services rather than campaigning. The axe must also fall on the New Public Servants beyond our town halls. The most obvious way to achieve this is to increase pressure on funding and introduce more ring-fencing of budgets so that they respond to real need rather than the passing fashions of the media. Who is a local health trust more likely to let go, a doctor or a Turkish women's anti-smoking health adviser? In particular, a sense of balance and judgement must be applied to the vast £270 million AIDS budget. It is absurd that, after more than a decade of safe-sex messages, the state employs a growing number of condom distributors, 'cottaging and cruising workers' and sex trainers. Too much of the AIDS industry has become an employment racket for gay rights activists and their ideological soulmates.

Another blow to the 'rights' agenda would be the repeal of the Citizen's Charter and its bureaucratic offspring. Like so many initiatives in our public life, the Charter has achieved little except the creation of work for civil servants and a growing sense of grievance from the public. We do not need these charters. Nor do we need their tiresome cousins, the vacuous 'Mission Statements' which have become increasingly popular in the public sector, setting out 'core values' and 'key objectives' and carrying some exciting new logo. Too often they are no more than statements of the blindingly obvious – 'our aim is to protect the public from crime' announces the silver-haired Chief Constable of the local county police after advice from a group of twenty-five-year-old marketing consultants – or a complete irrelevance to the way an organisation operates. When I was on Islington Council, we buzzed with 'statements of values', 'customer charters', 'complaints procedures', and 'service agreements', but Mrs Jones could still not get her toilet repaired by the housing department and the lifts remained broken in her block.

The modern sacrosanctity of consumer 'rights' should be challenged. The Children Act, with its absurd elevation of the supposed 'rights' of children, has proved a disaster, with teenagers now encouraged to sue their parents, and one father held in police detention for trying to discipline a badly-behaved son. The Act has also confused the role of welfare professionals in looking after children, for rights are not always the same as needs. For both attention-seeking adolescents and our amoral, anti-family New Public Servants, the Act has proved a boon. It should be abolished and replaced with new legislation which emphasises, not 'rights' of children, but duties of care towards them.

The idea of a 'right' to have children, no matter what the costs, the medical obstacles or the living arrangements of those involved, should also disappear. Infertility treatment should only be available to couples who have been legally married for at least three years. The belief that the NHS should provide artificial insemination for lesbian couples or single women who 'feel the biological clock ticking away' is one of the more grotesque consequences of the cult of self-gratification. On a wider level in the NHS, we must face the reality that some form of priority or 'rationing' must be attached to different medical treatments. We should no longer pretend that every treatment, no matter how minor or what the condition of the patient, should be immediately available at no cost. This approach only breeds resentment because individuals frequently have their expectations raised, then find them dashed by lengthy waiting lists. Nor do I think it outrageous that some of the elderly are now asked to make a contribution towards the cost of their place in a residential home. There has been much spluttering about the injustice of residents being forced to sell their (often empty) properties that they intended to pass on to their children. But why should the state have to meet the entire bill for asset-wealthy individuals simply to allow the retention of a substantial inheritance for children who have avoided the responsibility for their parents' care? Because of the destruction of family commitments in our dutiless age, we now want the state to be the main carer for the elderly, yet we still expect the privileges of property arrangements that belong to a family-oriented society. It is time such double standards were exposed.

The primacy of consumerism can be confronted in other ways. We need build no more 'out-of-town' retail centres. They might meet the immediate convenience of the car-bound shopper, but they can tear the hearts out of local towns. Next time you hear one of the supermarket giants announce how many jobs they will create in a new development, just think of all the jobs they will destroy among local businesses. Nor should we surrender to the demand for yet more housing developments on green-belt land – certainly not the two million envisaged by the Department of the Environment. This demand is largely the result, not of population increase (the UK population has increased by little more than 1 per cent in the last decade and the birth rate remains static) but of marriage and relationship breakdown. If it were no longer seen as the duty of Government to ensure there is 'affordable housing' throughout the land, some might be less relaxed about reneging on their family commitments.

Future chapters will look in more detail at possible changes in policy towards the family and the welfare system. What I have outlined here is the case for breaking free from the ratchet effect of the rights agenda which continues to infantilise the populace. We have a right to pursue happiness, but not to have it provided by the state.

CHAPTER THREE

The Culture of Grievance

'This is exactly the kind of precedent we need to fuel our new campaign. It will put tobacco companies on guard and help those trying to pursue claims in this country.' – Pamela Furness, Chief Executive of Action on Smoking and Health, celebrating the verdict of a Florida Court to award damages against British American Tobacco for causing 'health injuries' to two smokers.

'As Lesbians we sometimes drink because we experience problems from the way our sexuality is perceived by others, especially where children are involved.' – Advice leaflet for the publicly funded London body, Lesbian and Gay Alcohol Counselling.

'Social security legislation and the benefits system do not recognise the existence of a multi-racial/cultural society. The prevailing lack of access is an illustration of the racism of the benefits system, which is further aggravated by the power to misuse direction.' – Campaign statement from the Committee for Non-Racist Benefits.

'Instead of seeing the law as a restriction on the rights of clients, social workers should know how they can use legislation to challenge oppression.' – Article in *Community Care*, July 1996, by Beverley Burke, a lecturer in social work, and Jane Dalrymple, social work student.

'The primary purpose of youth work is to challenge and where possible redress all forms of inequality.' – Service statement on youth services from Bath and North East Somerset Council.

'She got what she deserved – I should get the money, not her. I hadn't done any work in the English lesson but she had no right to stop me leaving the classroom.' – Schoolboy James Christie, demonstrating his lack of remorse over the incident in 1989 which left Coventry schoolteacher Hazel Spence-Young permanently disabled.

'The levels of heat in many nightclubs are a health risk, raising people's body temperatures above World Health Organisation maximums for the workplace. At least 500,000 people a week are at risk, according to the Ergonomics Society. It calls for more research to be undertaken so that the Home Office can issue guidance to licensing authorities to take steps to control heat stress in dancers.' – Report in the *Daily Telegraph*, April 1996.

That last item illustrates the mood of the infantilised society. We want the freedom to do as we please, but we never want to live with the consequences. Like children, we have to be nursed and guided through all our activities, from the workplace to the nightclub. We must be cocooned from all life's vicissitudes by state regulation and funding. In an irresponsible age, if we eat too much, drink too much or take drugs, the fault lies with the Government for failing to provide sufficient 'advice' and 'counselling'. If we perform badly at our jobs, we can say we have not received adequate training or we have been suffering from 'stress'. If we remain on welfare, it is because race, class or sex prejudice stops us finding employment. In the nineties, some of us want neither pressure to work nor pressure at work.

If any misfortune should befall us, we should not treat it as an accident or the result of our own errors. We have to find someone to blame – usually the Government or one of its agencies. Every problem can become a claim for compensation, every difficulty a chance to sue. As Lord Templeman, a retired Law Lord, said last year on the BBC TV *Public Eye* programme: 'My first concern is that what I would call bad luck has gone out of the window. People now look for someone to blame, anybody but themselves, whereas many accidents are purely bad luck.'

The litigious society is also the victim-led society. By abandoning the concept of personal responsibility, we have created a modern culture where people feel permanently aggrieved by their circumstances. Individuals can turn their victim-status into the defining characteristic of their identity. Instead of encouraging people to break free from the experiences of trauma, abuse or deprivation, we urge them to wallow in their victimhood, to parade their suffering across the airwaves, to use their emotions as a vehicle for campaigning. The victim is accorded a special place in our society, sought out by counsellors, lawyers, talk-show hosts, and pressure groups. If the victim can prove multiple suffering so much the better. 'Multiple discrimination has drastic effects on the lives of black lesbians and gay men,' says an advice booklet from the publicly funded Campaign for Lesbian and Gay Employment Rights. 'For example, a black lesbian might move from one job because of heterosexism, to another where racism might prevent her from being promoted, to be sexually harassed in the next job.'

We have 'victim television' through shows like *Oprah Winfrey* and *Ricki Lake*, where participants recount the most grisly experiences. We now have 'victim art', where the victim-status of the artist or the subject matter is thought to add weight to the work, never mind its quality. So a jumble of clothes in the centre of the floor of the Serpentine Gallery is said to carry an exciting message about the homeless. Last year, the Arts Council and the Department of Health paid £17,000 to sponsor an exhibition of 'AIDS art' in the Walsall Museum and Art Gallery. This featured test-tubes filled with the HIV-positive blood of the artist, and a set of red ribbons stained grey with the ashes of a woman who died of the disease. Where once public figures retained a dignified silence over the distress of their childhoods or private lives, now they treat them as marketing tools. We have Tony Blair talking at Labour's conference of his father's stroke and John Major boasting of the poverty of his Brixton upbringing. We have victim-led campaigns dominating the formulation of public policy, as occurred in the demands for a ban on handguns after the Dunblane massacre. The Snowdrop campaign amounted to a form of emotional blackmail. Anyone who queried the efficacy of a total ban on guns was treated as a sadist. Anything less than whole-hearted support for the prohibitionists was regarded as an insult to the memory of Hamilton's tragic victims.

We have seen the same policy-by-emotion over drugs, most clearly through the hysteria that followed the self-inflicted death of ecstasy-consuming teenager Leah Betts. Was there ever a more pointless and incomprehensible poster campaign than the one which bore the slogan 'Sorted' beside Ms Betts's beaming face? Our society has the most puerile double standards about drugs. As I argued in previous chapters, we pander to a self-gratifying youth culture, encouraging adolescents to 'express themselves' and enjoy their freedom. We revere their empty music. We admire their grotesque fashions. We praise their raw energy. Yet, when one of them dies through indulgence in a common recreational habit, we suddenly switch into emotional over-drive. We elevate Ms Betts into the position of victim/heroine, transforming her from a party-goer into a crusader for moral change. In such a context, any campaign against drugs is doomed to failure. If we refuse to be judgemental about youth lifestyles – respecting 'diversity' in the words of the latest so-called 'moral' code – then how can we expect our exhortations to be heeded on this single issue? If we treat drug-users as 'victims', then how can we take a tough stance against drugs? The *Parent's Guide to Drugs and Solvents*, published last year by the Health Education Authority, encapsulates the problem of trying to impose judgements in a moral vacuum. Parents are told that the guide will help them 'talk to your children about drugs in a more informed way'. But parents are also warned: 'Don't lecture – remember how it felt to be lectured at. Don't preach – being "holier than thou" does not help a child.' As a society we have to make up our minds about drug-taking. Either we treat it as a criminal habit and hand out serious punishments to drug-users or we reduce drugs to the status of alcohol and tobacco, bringing back responsibility to the users for their habits instead of pretending that they are all innocent victims preyed on by evil dealers. The present duplicitous stance only encourages infantilism while doing nothing to reduce the incidence of drug-use (more on this in Chapter 7).

The infantilism and victimhood of our age are also reflected, very expensively, in our legal system. The law courts and tribunals have become the engines of a new grievance industry. The virtues of stoicism and courage are disappearing under a flood of compensation claims, legal aid green forms, and tribunal applications. Police now sue their employers because of the stress of their emergency duties. Pupils sue their schools because of their poor grades. Smokers sue tobacco companies because of their nicotine addiction. In one ludicrous case in 1995, a married woman who had had a sixteen-year affair with a property developer sued him to cover her debts. She said that her lover 'encouraged her to live the high life'. But, as with drug-taking or smoking, no one forced her to follow such a lifestyle. With choice comes responsibility.

The compensation culture reaches few more absurd depths than the case of Cyril Smith, a cancer patient from Portsmouth, who in 1996 said he would sue doctors at his local hospital because he had lived much longer than they had predicted. In 1992, he was told that he had only three months to live. Commenting on his demand for compensation for loss of earnings and mental anguish, Smith said: 'You can't put a price on the emotional toll of this nightmare,' though that is precisely what he seemed to be doing. And what about the emotional toll on his family if the original prognosis had been fulfilled? As one doctor said: 'It's astonishing. People will sue for anything these days, absolutely anything. All one can ever do is give an estimate – a few weeks or a few years. Even that can be wrong.'

The law used to uphold the values and traditions of our society. Now it is being used by some as a battering ram against them. Take the case of Jason Cooper, a twenty-three-year-old from the East Midlands who, in February 1996, announced that he would be suing social workers at Derbyshire County Council for 'neglect' when he was in care as a disturbed teenager. This 'neglect' consisted of sending him on a series of lavish trips around the world, including visits to Denmark, Spain, the Caribbean (for three months), and Disneyworld and Seaworld in Florida. He was also taken on an African safari, a skiing holiday in Norway and tours of Italy, Germany, France, Holland and Sweden. That is the sort of adolescent life that even the son of a Surrey stockbroker could not expect. It has been estimated that Derbyshire Social Services spent more than £50,000 on Cooper. But to no avail. He complained that no one had taught him the basic skills he needed for life. And what were these skills? 'How to apply for all the state benefits, like signing on the dole and applying for housing benefit.' Because he received 'no help in finding accommodation and had no knowledge of the welfare system', he said he was soon hooked on drugs and became a criminal to fund his habit. As a result, he saw himself as one of society's victims: 'I am entitled to be compensated for the life I lead through no fault of my own.' To be fair to him, he did show some insight into the inverted values of the social services system: 'I would not be in the mess today if someone had been a bit tougher with me then. I was getting things I didn't deserve.'

Is it surprising that there is confusion about our values when our courts can award £13,500 to a convicted IRA bomber in compensation for ankle injuries she suffered when she tripped on a pavement in her home town of Newry in Northern Ireland? Or when a woman is awarded £110,000 for being held in police custody for four hours? Or when a car thief is granted legal aid to sue his local authority after his finger was trapped in a cell door in a secure unit? Or when prisoners are awarded £5,000 each in compensation for the stress they suffered during the Strangeways riots?

Those two traditional agencies for protecting society, the police and the armed services, have been badly hit by the compensation culture. Both have had their authority undermined by a string of legal actions and complaints about discrimination. Damages awarded against the police are now thought to total about £60 million a year, including legal bills and staff costs. In May last year, juries awarded £630,000 against the Metropolitan Police in three cases alone, one of which was mentioned above. In one of the other two cases, a man was awarded a staggering £302,000 after he was hit over the head with a truncheon and required five stitches. To put that award in its context, if a person lost all four limbs in a criminal assault, they would only receive £250,000 compensation. As the Chairman of the Metropolitan branch of the Police Federation has said: 'For lawyers, suing the police is a growth industry. We have to remember this is all public money, taxpayers' money.' Groups like the Gay and Lesbian London Police Monitoring Group, which receives £26,000 from the National Lottery and £42,000 from London boroughs, keep up the pressure on the police. Yet too many police officers themselves have jumped on the compensation bandwagon. As much as £11 million has been spent over the last five years on dealing with sex-discrimination cases, money that could probably have been saved if the police were more rigorous and efficient about handling internal complaints. Even worse has been the action by 150 South Yorkshire police officers in claiming compensation for the trauma of dealing with the Hillsborough disaster – even though the families of the victims have been refused any payments. Early in 1996, it was agreed to pay out £1.2 million to fourteen officers who had been trying to rescue people at the Leppings Lane end of the ground. The logic of this move defies belief. Surely these officers were only doing their public duty. Emergency staff, as their job titles imply, are paid to handle traumatic incidents. Where will the Hillsborough ruling take us? Will ambulance staff be compensated for rushing to the scene of a motorway pile-up? Will doctors and nurses be awarded damages for the stress of performing life-saving operations day after day? Will soldiers feel encouraged to take legal action against the Ministry of

Defence for being sent into a battle zone? In fact, we have already seen the first signs of such an absurd development, through the action launched against the US Air Force by the families of British soldiers killed by American 'friendly fire' during the Gulf War. The implication behind these (thankfully unsuccessful) cases was that even war should be made safe.

Again, like the police, the armed forces are increasingly beset by claims for damages. Almost £55 million has been paid in compensation to pregnant women discharged from the services, after a ruling from the European court that the British policy breached European employment laws, even though the women had signed contracts in the knowledge that pregnancy would result in dismissal. One woman, a former Royal Navy nurse, was awarded £350,000 while thirty women have been paid more than £100,000 each. Claims from women of harassment, of 'unfair' postings after a return from maternity leave, and of differing levels of redundancy payments are now reaching the courts and the tribunals in increasing numbers, damaging the *esprit de corps* of the services.

The legal aid system has become another prop in the culture of litigation. When it was established in 1948, it was meant to provide access to justice for the less affluent. Now it only helps the very rich and very poor. Average earners, though they have to fund the system through their taxes, gain nothing from it. Costs continue to spiral out of control as an unholy alliance of lawyers and litigants use public funds for their own personal gain. Spending has doubled in the last five years to £1.4 billion, though access to funds has been increasingly restricted. The waste in the legal aid system has become a scandal, for lawyers actually have an incentive to drag out cases in order to increase their costs. Also notorious have been some of the recent cases funded by the Legal Aid Board. Dominic Trusted, for example, a wealthy Old Etonian, was granted legal aid last year to sue the law firm Clifford Chance in a dispute over his great-uncle's £50 million will. Though his claim for £1 million was dismissed by Justice Jonathan Parker as 'without substance or merit', the public still had to pay Mr Trusted's legal bill of £250,000. In April 1996, Andreas Pavel, a German inventor living in Italy, was given legal aid to sue the Japanese firm Sony in the High Court over his (unsuccessful) claim that their personal stereo infringed his patent rights. This case cost the taxpayer £500,000. The Government admitted that £8.3 million was paid to lawyers representing Kevin and Ian Maxwell during their long trial for fraud, while the businessman Roger Levitt and three other associates were legally aided to the tune of £3.7 million in defending charges of alleged fraud in 1994. Less expensive – but more bizarre – was the award of aid to ex-RAF officer Simon Foster in his attempt to force his health authority to grant him a sex-change operation. Every attempt at reform of this system has so far failed, largely because it remains in the hands of lawyers who benefit from its continued expansion.

Almost as discredited as legal aid is the industrial tribunal service. When the service was established in 1964, its aim was to provide a simple remedy for those who had suffered workplace injustice. But, as the blame-passing, victim-led mentality has gripped the nation, so the tribunal system has become riddled with frivolous and vindictive cases. As former Chairman of the Personnel Committee of Islington Council, I saw how a threat to 'take the Council to a tribunal' had become the knee-jerk reaction of too many dismissed or disciplined employees. On some occasions I had to attend tribunals as a witness, often on utterly hopeless actions. On one afternoon, while I was speaking at a hearing about the sacking of an alcoholic, along the corridor, a different session was listening to the complaint of a transvestite Hackney Social Services employee who was aggrieved that he had been barred from wearing a skirt at work. Both complainants lost their cases. But they did not lose any money. For tribunals are free. Costs are never awarded against the applicant, no matter how much an employer has to spend in fighting a case. The potential money and time wasted on even the least meritorious case can act as an incentive for the employer to settle before a hearing.

Reflecting the expansion of the grievance culture, the number of tribunal cases has grown rapidly in recent years. In 1981 there were 45,000 such cases, compared to 88,000 last year. The service now costs £25 million a year to run. Most of the cases – more than 60 per cent – involve claims for unfair dismissal. But sex and race claims are becoming more frequent. According to the tribunal service, the number of sex-discrimination cases increased by 42 per cent between 1993 and 1994. This trend has been exacerbated by removal of the upper limit on awards for sex discrimination, following (as usual) a

European Court ruling. Three years ago the ceiling was £11,300. Now payouts of ten times this sum are not unknown.

Perhaps the most grotesque example of the new trend was the case of Alan Bryans, a lecturer at Northumberland College who, in July 1995, was awarded almost £30,000 after being called 'an Irish prat' by one of his work colleagues. As a result of such comments, Mr Bryans was off sick for six months with a stress disorder and had to undergo counselling. The total cost to the taxpayer of this case has been estimated to be around £100,000. As Willie Mills, the Principal of Northumberland College, ruefully commented after the tribunal had decided Mr Bryans should receive damages for racial abuse and victimisation: 'I can't recall the number of times I've been called a Scots bastard. I haven't gone seeking compensation yet.'

Mr Bryans was supported, inevitably, by the Commission for Racial Equality, a vital element of the grievance industry. The Commission spends £16 million a year and employs 250 staff – seventeen of whom earn salaries above £30,000 a year. £270,000 is also spent on 'conferences', some of them held, no doubt, to discuss the underfunding of race-relations work. The CRE seems to exaggerate the incidence of racism in Britain, partly by campaigning on pitiful cases like Mr Bryans's. What call is there for a race-relations bureaucracy in a society without deep racial divisions? To keep the grants flowing from the public purse, the CRE therefore needs to portray Britain as a racist country, to devise new forms of discrimination, invent new categories of victimhood, and run new campaigns against prejudice.

A CRE report, entitled the *Second Review of the Race Relations Act*, illustrates the Commission's anxiety to spread its field of operations, providing yet more scope for professional complainants. Among the thirty-one recommendations in the report are: a new wider definition of indirect discrimination; the extension of the Race Relations Act to childminding; a statutory ethnic monitoring requirement on all employers; a new power for the CRE to demand 'affirmative action' from employers to promote equality; a new discrimination division within the industrial tribunal service; legal aid to be extended to race cases at tribunals; and more action to combat racial discrimination 'on the European front', including the expansion of the European Convention on Human Rights. Such a regime would involve a massive growth of bureaucracy, and, no doubt, litigation.

The grievance-mongering of the CRE is carried out by other

quangos and pressure groups. The Equal Opportunities Commission, which spends £7 million a year and employs 177 staff, has a vested interest in increasing the number of sex-discrimination claims. The absurdity of the E O C's position is that the majority of their complaints about employment now come from men, proof surely that their goal of equality in the workplace for women has been reached. The European Union's Social Commissioners make work for themselves with their rafts of directives and regulations about 'workplace rights'. The Health and Safety Executive is just as bad, with its TV adverts about the terrible agonies inflicted on employees by going to work. You can be sure that one aim of such campaigns was to increase the number of complaints that the HSE receives, keeping their officers busy for the rest of the year.

LAGER, the Lesbian and Gay Employment Rights campaign, has a team of caseworkers seeking out lesbians and gay men who are 'having trouble at work primarily because of discrimination'. One of their publications, *All in a Day's Work: A report on anti-lesbianism in employment and unemployment in London*, gives an insight into the victim-obsessed mindset: 'The adoption of the Race Relations Act and the Sex Discrimination Act, whilst having outlawed sackings on the grounds of race and gender, have merely led to employers giving other reasons for dismissal such as bad time-keeping or absenteeism.' So no one should be disciplined for malingering, is that what they mean?

The trade unions are also adept at filling the airwaves with questionable statistics and apocalyptic warnings about suffering in the workplace. Keen to promulgate the concept of 'workplace victims', they help members to take legal action against their employers. In 1994, a social worker, supported by the local government union UNISON, won a test case against Northumberland County Council when the High Court decided that he should be paid £200,000 compensation for the work-related stress which had forced his retirement. The way was now open for a flood of stress-related claims, warned UNISON in gleeful tones.

In this modern culture of complaint the idea of stress is spreading like a plague. A survey last year by NATFE, the trade union for college lecturers – not normally an occupation associated with traumatic duties – claimed that 'more than 90 per cent of lecturers feel stress at least some of the time'. One stricken lecturer was said to be 'affected by the shakes and diarrhoea' while another, perhaps even more disturbingly for her students, 'developed an eye twitch' because of her 'relentless 23-hour teaching load'. As the principal of North Tyneside College, Lawrence Toyte, wryly commented during the Alan Bryans case (Bryans also had a job in this college): 'Stress? These days the word appears in just about every other document that crosses my desk.'

During the commemorations of the D-Day landings in June 1994, the BBC hired teams of 'stress counsellors' to help staff cope with the trauma of filming the events in Normandy, a facility unfortunately denied by the shortsightedness of Eisenhower to those who participated in the original landings. Other public bodies and firms have appointed their own counsellors, instituted 'stress management' programmes and set up 'stress awareness workshops'. My neighbouring county of Bedfordshire, for instance, says that absence through 'excessive levels' of stress is costing £3 million a year and has instituted a £30,000 programme to provide a 'round-the-clock telephone advice service' and 'face-to-face counselling'. You don't even have to be an adult to be suffering stress. According to the Advisory Centre for Education, 'five-year-olds are now showing signs of stress'. One primary school in Camden, North London, has recognised the problem and 'called in professional psychotherapists'. What a symbol of our age – publicly funded therapy for stressed-out infants.

A doctor recently said to me that we have 'institutionalised helplessness in this country'. Almost every form of feeble or unacceptable behaviour can now be excused on the grounds that the perpetrator is suffering from a medical condition. This condition can absolve the employee and transform the threat of disciplinary action into a demand for 'support' or 'counselling'. Even the plain idle have been defended by certain psychotherapists on the grounds that they are the victims of a problem over which they have no control.

We have never lived in a more healthy society. Life expectancy for men, which was only 45.5 years in 1901, has now reached 74. Death rates for the under-65s, one of the key indicators of the health of the nation, have fallen substantially in the last half-century. In 1951, the death rates within this age group were about six for every thousand men and almost four for every thousand women. Now they have fallen to just under three and two per thousand respectively. Yet while society becomes healthier, so the grumbles about health grow louder. We now have magazines like *Men's Health* analysing every tweak, ache and strain. The hypochondriac is a role model for many modern Britons. The numbers receiving incapacity (formerly invalidity) benefit have increased by nearly half a million in the last five years. Any attempt by the Government to restrict this generosity is met with a chorus of wails about injustice to the sick. We are scourged by indefinable new illnesses like 'Tired All The Time' syndrome, Seasonal Adjustment Disorder (SAD), and Attention Deficit Disorder (ADD), and the medically unproven Total Allergy Syndrome which allows its sufferers to abnegate all responsibility for their own existences.

Myalgic encephalomyelitis (ME) is another ailment which, like stress and ADD, has become the source of the most bitter controversy. Its symptoms – headaches, tiredness, depression, numbness – are as vague and varied as its causes are unclear. It has neither a clear diagnosis nor any agreed cure. There are thought to be about 150,000 sufferers in the country and most are undoubtedly in real physical distress. But, no matter what the permanently outraged ME Association and Action Group for ME say, others are using ME as a vehicle to avoid work, particularly in the more indulgent public sector. Indeed, a Labour MP once said to me, 'Why is that the only victims of ME in my constituency are teachers and social workers?' Last year, a computer programmer with Her Majesty's Stationery Office won a case at an industrial tribunal after she was sacked for appearing twice on a TV dating show while on sick leave for three months. She claimed to be suffering from ME, which made her too 'weak and sleepy' to turn up to work. Yet this did not stop her appearing on Anglia TV's *Love Call Live*, where she told viewers that she wanted to meet a 'hunky Chippendale' – a little energetic, you might have thought, for an ME victim. Her manager was furious and ordered her not to appear again on the show. Three weeks later, still on sick leave, she was defiantly back on TV with news of dates with four admirers. 'She was full of beans,' complained her boss to the tribunal. No matter. The panel ruled that she was unfairly dismissed, because the appearances took place out of working hours. However, it was decided that she was 40 per cent to blame for her sacking and ordered that she receive no compensation, since she had already been awarded £9,000 by the Civil Service Appeal Board at an earlier hearing. Not that the claimant cared: 'I am very happy because it is a victory for

my fellow sufferers of ME. I've already had my money out of it and
the tribunal hasn't cost me a penny.'

In *Diary of a Lost Benefit – My ME and I* in the *Guardian* in March
1996, one ME victim set out the range of support she required:

'My lack of earning capacity puts pressure on the family. We are not affluent
and I am increasingly dependent on my benefits. They help pay the high fuel
and phone bills caused by my being housebound, the taxi-fares, labour-saving
equipment, and takeaway meals on bad days. A private practitioner helps
me manage the ME. Dietary supplements boost my flagging immune system.
I drink bottled water. Once keen gardeners, now I am unfit and my husband
too busy: I pay an occasional gardener. Private sporting activities and play
schemes keep my children happy in school holidays, while enabling me to
pace myself. Holidays are an essential break from the four walls of home
and a health change from polluted city air. (I am also asthmatic.)'

The all-enveloping care of the state is in evidence again.

When I was the Chairman of Personnel at Islington, chairing
disciplinary panels, I became well acquainted with the grievance-led
approach. Employees charged with the most serious offences would
explain how they were the victims of discrimination or unsympathetic
management or some mysterious ailment. One care worker, accused
of maltreating and racially abusing black residents in a council home,
said that, as an HIV-positive gay man, he was the victim of homophobia. A park attendant, with a shocking record of sickness and absenteeism, said that her health problems were the result of 'coming out' as
a lesbian. One of my colleagues at her disciplinary hearing was
unconvinced, asking her: 'You're a lesbian. So that explains an absence
of two weeks with athlete's foot?' A black housing officer, caught
illegally sub-letting properties to Yugoslavian refugees, claimed the
investigation against her was motivated by racism. A teacher, who
remained at home on full pay for more than four years because of
procedural wrangles over her position, claimed to be the victim of
sex discrimination when she was finally made redundant.

Another frequent excuse used by defendants to explain their actions
– or inaction in some cases – was 'lack of training'. One employee,
caught washing his car outside the council office when he should
have been on the reception desk, complained that he had never been
trained in the correct procedures. A social services officer, charged
with 'inappropriate sexual behaviour' with residents of the home

where he worked, said he had received inadequate training from management. Such nonsense elevates training into a panacea which can make the idle diligent, the foolish wise and the dishonest trustworthy.

This is the problem with the equal opportunities, victim-oriented culture that prevails in much of corporate Britain. It takes no account of character. It gives no weight to individual responsibility or ability. It presumes that all are capable of reaching the same level of achievement. If someone is not doing his job properly, it is not his own fault but rather the result of his circumstances. As G.B. Shaw wrote in *Mrs Warren's Profession*: 'People are always blaming their circumstances for what they are. I don't believe in circumstances. The people who get on in this world are the people who get out and look for the circumstances they want, and if they can't find them, make them.'

In another London borough where I was employed as a researcher in the early nineties, I witnessed the most ludicrous grievance-fest in my own office. One audio-typist refused to do any word-processing because the term was not specifically mentioned in her job description. Her immediate line manager had taken out a grievance against her own boss, complaining of racism, while this boss had also submitted a formal grievance against the Head of the Unit, charging him with sexism. The whole affair was an utter farce, and while the wheels of the bureaucratic complaints procedure turned, barely a stroke of useful work was done. The irony is that the very qualities in which 'good' employers (like this authority) take pride – trade union involvement, concern for staff welfare, generous conditions of service, anti-discrimination policies – only foster this climate of complaint while those who are in need of real protection, like textile workers in East End sweatshops or contract cleaners in the leisure industry, lose out. Driven by their ideological obsessions, the professional grievance-mongers are ignoring the real workplace victims. The meat packer who loses her £2-an-hour job with only one week's notice has suffered a good deal more than the college lecturer who's been called 'an Irish prat' a few times.

Given the leniency of too many public employers, it is hardly surprising that they have higher levels of sickness absence than the private sector. In social services, for instance, 8.3 per cent of staff were off sick during a given week in 1995, compared to 4.5 per cent in the economy as a whole. In Nottinghamshire Social Services

Department, absenteeism cost £8 million in 1996 with 10 per cent of the workforce off sick every day. When I was at Islington Council, sick leave was costing the council more than £11 million a year. It is the same with racial discrimination. The largest single category of complaints to the Commission for Racial Equality in 1995 involved local government (311). This is not because local authorities are the most racist employers, but the very opposite. They are so preoccupied with anti-racism that they encourage their employees to see discrimination everywhere. There is an infallible principle at work here: the more an organisation trumpets its equal opportunities policies, the more vociferous will be the complaints of inequality. One of the more inane cases that the CRE has recently supported was a complaint in 1994 from a Ms Yasmin Kutub, a black feminist, who claimed that she had not been appointed to the job of housing support worker at a women's refuge for abuse survivors, Washington Women in Need, because of racial discrimination. The complaint was plainly absurd. It would be hard to find a more ideologically correct institution than WWIN, with its race and gender awareness courses and its equal opportunity policy statements. Yet WWIN's very concern with oppression left it vulnerable to a race obsessive.

Our New Public Servants are adept at spreading this grievance mentality. This is particularly true of the social-work profession which noisily peddles the myth that Britain is a society riven by 'oppression' and 'discrimination'. *Anti-Racist Social Work: A Challenge for White Practitioners and Educators* is a book by Lena Dominelli which reflects this ethos. Ms Dominelli is quite explicit about the political aims of social work: 'Social work is not an apolitical activity which can ignore power relations and the unequal distribution of resources in society.' She also argues that 'Professionalism will have to be redefined in terms of white practitioners taking sides against practices endorsing racial oppression,' and warns that 'in a climate of public spending cuts, the state becomes a force intensifying social workers' responsibilities as agents of social control.'

Ms Dominelli's opinions may sound extreme, but they actually fit in with the outlook of other social services practitioners. Such attitudes are not surprising, given the training that social workers undertake. More concerned with reforming society than serving the public, more interested in 'raising consciousness' than learning professional skills, the courses leave trainees dangerously ill-equipped for their difficult jobs. The University of Durham, for instance, boasts that its programme for the diploma in social work addresses 'issues of oppression and anti-oppressive practice from both individual and structural perspectives, making these issues integral to all aspects of teaching and learning'. The Leeds Diploma 'recognises the powerful links between personal and political issues and asserts the need to challenge inequalities and oppressions wherever they may arise'. At the University of Humberside, the programme 'aims to prepare students to become critically reflective about their work and to practice effective social work in a changing social world, challenging discrimination with respect to all oppressed groups'. Such comments are repeated throughout the course notes for university diplomas in social work. Yet the British Association of Social Workers, in its *Report into Ethnically Sensitive Social Work*, complains, unbelievably, that 'the majority of workers expressed their disappointment at the lack of coverage of race and racism on qualifying courses.'

Social services may be at the forefront of the grievance industry but many others have followed their example, from gay men's health workers to equality officers in local government. At Islington Council, we had a Lesbian and Gay Committee, a Race Equality Unit, a Race Equality Committee, a Women's Committee, a Women's Committee Support Unit, and Race policy advisers dotted throughout the organisation. Despite eighteen years of Conservative rule, such structures have become common throughout local government. The activities organised by councils to celebrate International Women's Day every year on 8 March show the municipal victim-culture at its worst. In 1996, Bristol City Council spent £10,000 on local events, including a 'Wicked Women's Festival – a gathering to celebrate our power in our constant struggle against patriarchal oppression', induction courses for 'Asian women only in weight-training', and a multi-cultural gathering led by the Single Parents' Action Network to 'celebrate women's inspiration and strength in surviving discrimination, poverty and disadvantage'. Birmingham City Council had a budget of £24,000 for Women's Day, and its programme featured 'Egyptian dancing', training seminars, 'lesbian story-telling' and 'celebrations of women in Black, Arab, Irish and Bangladeshi cultures'. In Luton, a group called Drugline hosted a 'Health and Beauty Day for Women Drug Users' ('reflexology to promote health and soothe stress available free to women drug users'). Yet some of the victim specialists were still not happy. Sarah Hewes, a lesbian radical, bizarrely asked after the 1996 festival if 'Women's Day has any room for lesbians any more?'. What Ms Hewes wanted is an 'International Dyke Day, which has nothing to do with gay men or straight women.' She probably will not have to wait too long.

The BBC has also succumbed to the grievance industry. Last year it spent £4 million on its Equal Opportunities Department, which performed such vital tasks as running courses for women on *Changing Your Experience* ('A two-day workshop to help women develop confidence and personal power') and participating in a 'European weekend workshop on journalism, training and development in multi-cultural societies', an event which took place in June 1995 at the appropriately named Adolf Grimme Institute in Germany. One of the more offensive features of this bureaucratic extravagance is that the main aim of the equal opportunities programme has already been achieved. The BBC set a target of 8 per cent black employment in the workforce by the year 2000. That target was reached five years early. But, like the New Public Servants elsewhere in Britain, the BBC's equality bureaucrats cannot admit success. To do so would be to make themselves redundant. So instead they think up new exercises to combat alleged gender and race imbalances, and devise ever more inappropriate training courses.

And the victim specialists have an enormously powerful weapon with which to protect themselves: emotional blackmail. Any challenge to their squandering ways can be dismissed with accusations of homophobia or racism or sexism. In the warped values of the grievance culture, to attack the equality spendthrifts is to attack the whole concept of equality.

The irony of this position is that it actually worsens the very problems that the New Salariat was meant to solve. Colour, gender and sexuality now become defining characteristics rather than points to be ignored. There is no greater race obsessive than the anti-racist, who sees individuals only in terms of their racial origin. Similarly, the gay rights activist divides the world into gay and straight, while the radical feminist indulges in the most crude stereotypes based on gender. As a result, we achieve the very opposite of equality. Instead of treating everyone equally, we give preferential treatment to those from 'oppressed groups' in the name of combating prejudice. The most crude example of this was probably the Labour Party's decision in 1993 to adopt women-only shortlists for Parliamentary selection, a policy which an industrial tribunal later deemed to have contravened the 1975 Sex Discrimination Act. The Appleby Report on the running of Lambeth Council and the White inquiry into Islington discovered similar cases of unfair discrimination in favour of blacks and gays. Even Whitehall has been found guilty of reverse race discrimination in its recruitment methods, giving black candidates interviews when they had failed preliminary tests.

The explosion in the popularity of counselling can be seen as another part of the culture of complaint. No accident today can occur without the rush of counsellors to the scene. No school examination can be held without a counsellor on hand to mop a brow or wipe away a tear. No university campus or doctor's surgery is complete without a team of counsellors. And, as the media informs us, they are always 'trained' or 'professionally qualified'. Why the adjectives? We do not talk about 'trained' doctors conducting surgery or 'qualified' pilots flying 747s. The emphasis on their professional status only seems to underline the questionable nature of the benefits of their work.

In the Britain of 1995, Churchill would be urged to offer the British people not 'blood, toil, tears and sweat' but more resources for post-Blitz trauma counselling. The 'finest hour' would be a session at the stress-management workshop. Yes, we could fight – but only for a claim of hurt feelings at an industrial tribunal.

It has been estimated that in Britain today there are almost 15,000 full-time counsellors (the British Association of Counselling has 13,000 members), while a total of 110,000 professionals, like probation officers or marriage guidance workers, are engaged in some form of counselling as part of their work, dealing with up to 750,000 clients.

The subject of drinking amongst the over-fifty-five age group demonstrates the victim-fixated mentality of some of our professional counsellors. In 1995, the Health Education Authority and Age Concern voiced anxiety at the 'under-reporting and under-recognition' of drinking amongst the elderly. They launched a survey of this group. To the horror of researchers, some older people 'talked openly about how much they enjoyed drinking alcohol'. What a disgrace. There was only one answer: offer them counselling. But, unsurprisingly, the HEA and Age Concern encountered some reluctance. 'There is a view among some professionals, including GPs, that (older people) don't have anything else in their lives so a little alcohol won't hurt. In the nicest possible way, I think doctors collude with this way of thinking, explained Kate Mortimer of Age Concern to *Community Care* magazine. Many of the drinkers themselves are just as uninterested. 'The majority of people we see are non-changers. They are happy with their drinking and they don't see it as a problem,' said Mike Ward, manager of drug and alcohol services at Surrey Social Services Department. But such a relaxed attitude cannot stop the zealots. They can try to force 'this difficult client group' to change, either through 'motivational interviewing' or by 'sending a skilled counsellor into the home once to twice a week.' You would think, given all the bleats about underfunding, that Surrey Social Services would have something better to do with their time and money.

Equally predictable is the concern with discrimination, thinking that every 'oppressed' group needs special services, whether it be the elderly or Asians or black women. Drinking is a problem, and heavy drinkers are society's victims. It is racism or homophobia that drives them to the bottle, so the reasoning goes. Alcohol Counselling and Prevention Services in London, a municipally funded body, runs a distinct service for lesbians and gay men. EastEnders have their own 'East London Lesbian and Gay Counselling Service', while the Haringey Irish Community Care Centre has an *Alcohol Services Networker*. ACAD (Advice and Help on Alcohol and Drugs), based in Bristol, provides a 'counselling service for African, Caribbean, Asian and Black drinkers within the Bristol area'.

A glance at the prospectus for the Foundation Training Programme in Counselling at the City University in London highlights this excessive egalitarian spirit. The programme, we are informed, 'addresses social power issues in the context of institutionalised oppressions which affect individual and community development. It is committed to the "acceptance of difference" and challenging discrimination on the grounds of gender, race, disability, sexuality, nationality, religious belief, employment status, social class, size, HIV status, age and marital status.' The prospectus also contains potted biographies of the trainers for this course, like Lucy Aston who explains that, 'as a white, middle-class woman living in the nineties I am aware of the external and internal oppressions that society holds for each individual.' Bernadette Shiels says that 'as an Irish woman, I have struggled with the temptation to conceal my accent and dilute my culture in response to the existing turbulent climate between England and Ireland. I censor my own free speech and I feel it is only safe to discuss Irish matters amongst fellow Irish people.'

The current Conservative Government has given a major boost to the counselling industry with its 1996 Divorce Law Reform, which will statutorily expand the number of marriage-guidance counsellors, mediators and advisers. The ostensible aim behind the Government's emphasis on mediation was to strengthen marriage by forcing couples to discuss their problems before embarking on the divorce process. Yet, like the race-relations bureaucracy and the social-services progression, the new mediators will actually have an interest in the continuing collapse of the institution of marriage. The more couples that break up, the more work for them – and the more funds they can demand from the Government.

In one respect, it might seem odd that the grievance industry, with all its quivering indignation about equality and prejudice, should have enjoyed such a boom under the Conservatives. Yet, as the last chapter showed, it is the Thatcherite rhetoric of individual rights that encourages us to sue, to blame others, to ignore our wider responsibilities, to feel aggrieved when our ambitions are blocked. It is no coincidence that some of the entrepreneurs of the Thatcherite eighties, like Ernest Saunders and Roger Levitt, have been among the biggest users of legal aid. Another example of this mentality is the disgraceful modern practice of senior Ministers clinging on to office through every catastrophe and scandal, blaming the press, the Opposition, civil servants, everyone but themselves. So pervasive have such attitudes become that the long-held principle of Ministerial responsibility has been all but destroyed. It is certainly a principle that meant little to William Waldegrave and Sir Nicholas Lyell during their undignified wriggling over the Scott Report on Arms to Iraq. The Cabinet even invented a new adverbial dispensation, the idea that it was acceptable to mislead Parliament, as long as it is not done 'deliberately'. 'The buck stops anywhere but here' – to misquote Harry Truman – is a new maxim for the nineties.

But we can expect little better from an incoming Blair Government. Buck-passing is a way of life to many socialists. I saw this frequently in Islington Council. When the Education Department one year incurred an overspend of £8 million, its two directors blamed the Finance Department, their own departmental accountants, their Chief

Finance Officer, their personnel records, underfunding by the Government, and the old Inner London Education Authority. Equally absurd was the claim of 'scapegoating' made by one of my colleagues during a disciplinary hearing against the headteacher of a dismally failing comprehensive, which had just received a scathing report from HM Inspectorate of Schools. You cannot 'scapegoat' someone who is actually paid to take responsibility. Yet we see this term regularly misused by Labourites. Thus when Derek Lewis was sacked as Director General of the Prison Service, Labour said he had been 'scapegoated' for the Whitemoor and Parkhurst fiascos.

Labour would further strengthen the grievance industry by extending the incentives to litigation. Attempts to limit the legal aid budget have been criticised by the party as 'denying access to justice'. A Labour Government will establish a new 'community legal service' with 'regional legal committees'. Legal aid will be provided for litigants at an industrial tribunal. Tougher discrimination legislation will be accompanied by a more powerful Commission for Racial Equality and a new Minister for Women in the Cabinet who 'will have the power to scrutinise all major legislation to examine its impact on women.' The network of women's officers across Government Departments will be expanded, their work co-ordinated by a central unit in the Cabinet Office. There will be more in-depth ethnic monitoring of schools and employment, with all the usual accompanying 'targets', 'positive action' programmes, and training and 'awareness-raising' exercises. Greater European integration under a Europhile Labour Government will further widen the scope for litigation. Some leading socialists are calling for yet more grievance-led regulations to be imposed from Europe, such as a 'new European race-relations directive', and the publication of a *European Anti-Racist Handbook* setting out foreigners' rights and means of redress. Labour-dominated local government, with its wasteful equality bureaucracies, has already pointed the way.

What needs to change

But this is not the direction we should be moving in. The culture of grievance is already too strong in this country. The most effective way to begin weakening it is by cutting off its funding. Here are four immediate steps that can be taken.

First, legal aid for all civil actions should be abolished. It should be reserved only for defendants facing criminal charges in the crown court. At present, the legal aid system is working as a corrupt racket for lawyers. The National Audit Office has refused to endorse legal aid accounts for the last four years because of 'significant and material uncertainty as to their propriety and regularity'. And there can be few greater outrages in nineties Britain than the subsidies granted by the state to those seeking divorce or damages against the police. Like so many other structures of our infantilised society, the legal aid budget assists, not those in real need, but the pseudo-victims, who know how to play the system.

In July 1996, the Lord Chancellor announced a series of reforms to improve the management of legal aid. The scheme is to be cash-limited for the first time. Those who lose their cases risk having to pay their opponents' costs. All litigants must make a minimum contribution. In reaching its decisions, the Legal Aid Board can take account of an individual's resources, the chances of winning and the importance of the case. None of this goes far enough. The system is still in the hands of those who thrive on its expansion. The Gordian Knot must be cut and the civil aid abolished. If that prevents a would-be divorcee from going to court, or a millionaire accused of fraud from receiving £200-per-hour legal advice, or a welfare claimant, backed by some lobby group, from suing the Government, then so much the better. Perhaps we might stop perceiving litigation as the solution to every problem.

Second, in order to stop frivolous cases at the industrial tribunals, litigants should have to pay a contribution towards the administrative costs of the service, in all cases where there is no physical injury. The idea that someone, without any risk to themselves, can sue their employer for 'hurt feelings' is childish. (I do not think it wise to compel applicants to pay their employers' costs, as some have suggested. That would only encourage the hiring of expensive lawyers by defendants.) Moreover, the limit on all awards, which was abolished in 1993, should be reinstated: £15,000 should be the maximum.

Third, the £16-million-a-year Commission for Racial Equality should be abolished. It no longer serves any useful purpose beyond the employment of ideologues and activists. We already have powerful laws in this country to punish those guilty of racial harassment, incitement to racial hatred, or clear racial discrimination. We do not need a purposeless bureaucracy to back them up. If racism is still as endemic in this country as the CRE claims, thirty years after the first Race Relations Board was established, why should we continue to fund its work, which, by its own admission, has been ineffectual? Once again, it is the pseudo-victims who benefit from the Commission's services, not the terrified Asian woman with excrement and lighted matches shoved through her letterbox most evenings. We should concentrate on practical action against real racists – such as gathering evidence against Neo-Nazis and evicting thugs from public housing – rather than indulging the 'oppression' theorists.

Fourth, the £7-million-a-year Equal Opportunities Commission should also be closed down. The fact that more men are using its employment service than women shows that it has now outlived its purpose. Its continuation will only mean more trivial actions. The other problem with the EOC is its failure to recognise the realities of our society, such as the fact that women are far more vulnerable in the event of a car breakdown. The EOC recently used its bureaucratic might to prevent the Britannia Rescue Firm from promising to give priority to stranded women drivers. As usual with the equality zealots, theory has been elevated above reality.

The disappearance of the CRE and EOC should begin a concerted run-down of the equality industry. The panoply of quotas, targets and preferential treatment should be outlawed by a tightening of employment discrimination laws. It should no longer be possible for an organisation like the Arts Council to run an advertisement such as this for two traineeships in the publishing industry: boasting that the Council has 'an equal opportunities policy and warmly welcomes applications from ALL sections of the community', the notice explained that 'the traineeships are offered only to those of Black and Asian ethnic origins.' Similarly, the BBC should no longer be able to offer, as it does now, 'bursaries for trainees of African, Asian and Afro-Caribbean origin'. Nor should health authorities and local councils be able to recruit gay men's counsellors, or female drug-addiction workers. The pressure on employers, especially in the public sector, to indulge in equality monitoring should be ended. We now even have the farcical situation where some organisations ask about 'sexuality' on job application forms ('How would you describe your sexual orientation: lesbian, gay, bisexual or hetero-sexual', says the monitoring form from the 'Off The Record' Youth

Counselling Service in Croydon). What is the point of seeking this information? To ensure that the workforce represents the sexually-oriented balance of the population? But we can never know what that balance is. So it is just another futile exercise in the equalities charade.

The training for some of the New Public Servants, especially social workers, should drop its obsession with discrimination. The number of social-work courses which boast of having an 'anti-discriminatory approach' at their centre is disturbing. It would be much better if such training concentrated on the development of skills rather than sub-Marxist and Freudian theorising. Another unwanted quango, the Central Council for Education and Training in Social Work (CCETSW) which has played a key role in ensuring the dominance of the victim-led outlook, should be wound up. Universities and colleges could be responsible for their own courses and become directly accountable to the Department of Health.

As mentioned in the last chapter, the ring-fencing of budgets for certain health and other public services, where funds are restricted for use on stipulated functions, would be a major blow to the New Public Servants, who are an integral part of the grievance culture. It might also lead to a reduction in the number of taxpayer-funded counsellors and therapists, who would have to show that they were both meeting real needs and providing tangible results, not just empathising with the irresponsible and the feckless. We should stop treating all alcoholics and drug-addicts – some of the biggest users of counselling services – as society's victims. Such services only encourage irresponsibility by promoting the doctrine that individuals have no control over their habits. Even in the nineties, there is still such a thing as willpower. The growing demand for more counselling services for a bewildering range of 'oppressed' groups (the London Irish Women's Centre refers to the needs of those who are 'doubly or triply discriminated against such as travellers and lesbians') should be resisted, especially by the grant-givers of the National Lottery.

Just as the media should be more rigorous with the spending demands of pressure groups, so they should also be more sceptical of the self-serving claims campaigners make about suffering and oppression in Britain. The dirges on 'stress' from Action for ME or the Health and Safety Executive should not be treated as sacrosanct, nor should the claims of workplace angst from trade unions.

Reducing the £25 million campaign budget of the Health Education Authority would be another way of puncturing the swelling balloon of infantilism. At present, the fact that most of the HEA's publicity is so predictably impotent only fuels demands for more spending. If we continue to eat too much and the Government fails to reach its arbitrarily fixed weight-reduction targets, the HEA calls for more expensive campaigns. This is exactly the same as the CRE with racism: the worse they perform, the more vital are deemed their services. We should no longer listen to such siren voices. We have to take back responsibility for our lives.

CHAPTER FOUR

The Loss of Nationhood

'The series of six 30-minute programmes for transmission in July and August will break new ground for television. It will tackle major British issues from a black perspective but also, by reporting from the Caribbean, USA and Europe, give prominence to foreign stories which are high on the black agenda.' – BBC Press Release, October 1995, announcing the launch of a new African-Caribbean news programme.

'The era of the nation state is drawing to a close.' – David Martin, Labour MEP and Vice-President of the European Parliament, in *European Labour Forum*, Winter 1990.

'I'm really confused about what British is. What does it mean? I really haven't a clue . . . I think there is a danger of fascism if people in authority start going on about what they call "British values".' – Views of Ruth Dalton, seventeen-year-old A-level student, February 1996.

'Clearly there are implications for adults involved in childcare and parenting in a society that promotes a "white" norm. If we want to bring up our children to understand equality then adults have to challenge and unlearn their own conditioning, prejudices and biases.' – From an article on *Toys, Games and Race* in *School's Out* magazine, Spring 1994, by Nandini Mane of the Working Group Against Racism in Children's Resources.

The teenage daughter of a friend of mine recently asked her classmates if they felt proud to be British. Not a single one said yes. Sadly, such attitudes are all too common today. Patriotism is seen by many as the last refuge of the eccentric or the fascistic.

It should not be surprising that this is happening in our infantilised society. The decline of personal responsibility has undermined the sense of wider obligations to the nation state as well as to other people. Generations that have been brought up to love only themselves cannot easily love their country. The long-held belief in sacrifice for the greater patriotic good must seem absurd to the adherents of the new cultural ethos. Self-gratification precludes the idea of laying down one's life for one's country.

This development is not new, however. Doubts about pride in Britain have occurred throughout this century. The First World War, with its carnage on the fields of the Somme and Ypres, forced many to question the virtues of the patriotic call to arms. Within eight years of its close, the country had a Prime Minister, Ramsay MacDonald, who had openly opposed Britain's involvement. The pointless deaths on the Continent also created the pacifist climate of the twenties and thirties, symbolised by the famous resolution passed by the Oxford Union debating society in February 1933, that 'This House refuses to fight for King and country.' Appeasement was allowed to flourish in this atmosphere. The anxiety of most to avoid war was demonstrated by the outpouring of relief when Chamberlain returned to Heston after signing the Munich agreement in 1938.

As the historian Andrew Roberts has pointed out, the idea that the whole British nation rallied behind Churchill throughout the Second World War contains an element of myth-making, partly woven by Churchill's own romantic rhetoric. Strikes continued, particularly in the vital mining and shipbuilding industries. There was a widespread black market. The celebrated use of the London Underground as air-raid shelters began as an act of civil disobedience against the authorities. Crime reached record levels in 1941. Looting and burglary were common during the blackouts. Morale in parts of the army was low. Churchill himself felt that 'our soldiers are not as good fighters as their fathers were.'

It would be wrong, nevertheless, to exaggerate such problems. For there was a national wartime spirit. Almost anyone who lived through the war speaks of it. If Britain had not been working together for a common purpose, it would have been impossible for the Government to impose rationing, or evacuation, or conscription without serious disruption, to have Anderson shelters in most homes, to organise the Home Guard and the ARP, to turn out Spitfires and Hurricanes from the aircraft factories with such remarkable speed, to have survived the Blitz with barely a voice being raised in favour of an armistice. Propaganda can only succeed if it has 'the ring of truth'. The tales of Britain's wartime grit, of 'standing alone' against Nazi Germany, continue to have such resonance since 1945 because they are based on reality. Churchill was not wrong when he told the cheering crowds in Whitehall on VE Day that 'this is your victory'.

It is difficult to imagine such a sense of purpose being fostered today in a national emergency. When counselling is required for every circumstance, and when feebleness, indiscipline and irresponsibility are treated as medical conditions, how could some cope with the real threat of invasion or annihilation? How would our modern army of professional complainers, litigants and 'rights' campaigners deal with ration books and bombed-out homes? Would the infantilised be able to raise their vision beyond their next demand on the public purse? Would the multi-culturalists and anti-racists, with their loathing for Britain's heritage, show any commitment to the national cause? Could the established Church provide a clear lead?

The sense of nationhood that existed in 1945 has been dangerously eclipsed. One of the major forces that built it then, victory over a mighty adversary, has obviously disappeared. But fifty years of peace, allied to this mood of infantilism, cannot fully explain how pride in our country has become a derided concept.

The loss of empire has played a part. A nation which had, at the beginning of this century, governed a quarter of the earth's land mass and spread its language, culture and political systems throughout the world, could not give all this up without damage to its confidence. Empire was part of the British psyche, until the second half of this century. Our colonies provided employment for our administrators and missionaries, our soldiers and sailors. They gave us their raw materials and a captive market for our manufactured goods. Our literature (Forster's *A Passage to India*, Orwell's *Burmese Days*, Somerset Maugham's Malayan stories), architecture (Lutyens's grand classical plans for New Delhi), music (Elgar's *Pomp and Circumstance*), and sport (the Ashes series against Australia in cricket, the Commonwealth Games in athletics) were heavily influenced by Empire. Reputations of great public figures like Robert Baden-Powell, Dr Livingstone and Lord Kitchener were built through the Empire. Politics in late Victorian or Edwardian Britain was dominated by Imperial issues, whether it be Ireland, protectionism or the South African War.

The descent from the world's greatest imperial power to a middle-ranking European nation has been astonishingly swift, occupying less than fifty years. Few nations in the history of mankind have given up so much so quickly and with so little reluctance. That orderly transfer of power to the former colonies should, in itself, be a source of pride. So should the establishment of the Commonwealth, a near-unique body that shows the affection in which Britain is still held by those countries which were once, supposedly, weighed down with the imperial yoke. One of Nelson Mandela's first acts as President of the new democratic South Africa was to return his nation to the Commonwealth.

This institution serves as a rebuke to all those who see the British Empire purely in terms of economic greed and military conquest. Those were undoubtedly motivating forces, but the altruistic desire to spread the values of Christian civilisation was also important. Why else would thousands of able young men choose a life of isolation in the Sudanese or Indian civil service? In our age of relativism, when the mud hut is to be treated no differently to Norwich Cathedral and a tribal mask is seen as just as fine a work of art as Turner's *Fighting Téméraire*, we are encouraged to despise the arrogance of the imperialists. Yet many of those who served in the Empire believed, not in the brutal subjugation of alien races but in their civilising mission to establish order, justice and good government. The aggrandising exploits and racial theories of Cecil Rhodes should not be taken as representative of the attitudes of all colonialists. As that noblest of imperialists, George Curzon, wrote during his travels through Asia:

'Out here in the East one cannot fail to be very much struck by the stamp of men which represent the British Government. I record it to our credit and praise that – so far as my experience goes – our home Government is served by as able and enlightened a body of men as ever carried or sustained a conquering flag in foreign lands. The industry, capacity and the service of these men are beyond praise.'

It is a delicious irony that, forty years after the 'winds of change' blew through Africa, colonialism has been reawakened by the most fervent anti-imperialists. 'Why isn't the West doing something?' is the cry from Third World campaigners that accompanies every report of civil war, mass killings or economic breakdown. Those who once cheered the departure of the Western powers from Africa now demand their return. Under the guise of 'peace-keeping' or 'providing humanitarian aid', Britain, France and the USA are urged to take over the administration of independent African states. Like the colonial governors, we are deemed responsible for maintaining the civic order. When genocide occurs in Rwanda, this is somehow our fault for 'standing idly by' and 'failing to intervene'. The same liberal activists, always so quick to blame poverty in Britain on our Government, never ascribe poverty in African nations to the incompetence or corruption of their local Governments. We should not heed their bleatings.

Associated with the loss of Empire has been our comparative economic decline. In the country which experienced the first Industrial Revolution, it is now almost impossible to buy a car built by a British company. The great names of British manufacturing, Handley Page, Armstrong Siddeley, Austin Morris, have disappeared. The engineers who once equipped the world like the shipbuilders on the Clyde and the Mersey have departed for the history books. No longer the workshop of the world, we are now dependent on investors from the Far East to reduce our unemployment figures. 'Made in Britain' is almost a heritage sign rather than a market label.

To many economists and free-market Conservatives, the decline of British industry is an irrelevance. There is no difference between making money from selling hamburgers or building aeroplanes. As the late Nicholas Ridley wrote in *My Style of Government* in 1991: 'I do not think it is a disaster if we become an economy primarily based on the service sector. It isn't vital, as socialists seem to think, that we have a large manufacturing sector.' Besides, such critics argue, British industry has been in decline throughout this century, because of poor management, irresponsible unions and low-quality, uncompetitive goods. Even in the Edwardian age, the supposed zenith of Britain's economic and imperial grandeur, there was a chorus of anxiety about our failure to match industrial competition from Germany and the USA. We have long proved unable to exploit our genius for invention. The world's first commercial jet airliner, for example, was the British De Havilland Comet. But it was soon superseded by the Boeing 707 because of metal fatigue in the former's structure, thereby destroying Britain's chance to dominate a new era in aviation. Concorde, the first supersonic jetliner, was a similar commercial failure. And let us not be romantic about a British car industry of the seventies which produced both the militant Derek 'Red Robbo' Robinson and the Austin Allegro. Is it not better, we are asked, for us to concentrate on the sectors of the economy where we excel, like financial and property services, broadcasting, telecommunications, pharmaceuticals, bio-chemistry and civil engineering, rather than harking back to some non-existent golden age of British manufacturing? The world is now a global marketplace. The national ownership of individual companies is no longer important, we are told. What matters is where they invest and create jobs. If the Germans want to build their cars here, the Dutch their televisions, the Taiwanese their computers, the Japanese their washing machines, and the Americans their vacuum cleaners – all products made more efficiently than we have ever managed – then that can only benefit our economy.

This all may be true in the narrow terms of the balance sheet. But it ignores the importance of our industrial strength in developing a sense of national identity. For nationhood requires its symbols. Like our flags, myths, history, and institutions, industrial success has been woven into the tapestry of our British culture. Brunel's suspension bridge at Clifton is as much an image of Britain's greatness as the statute of Nelson in Trafalgar Square. The radiator grille of a Rolls-Royce is almost as powerful a representation of Britain as the Union flag. The Mini is an embodiment of the English character: eccentric, dogged, humorous, unpretentious and reliable. A chain of estate agencies or IT consultancies could never inspire the same patriotism as the slipway of one of our erstwhile shipbuilding giants or a company turning out the finest Sheffield cutlery.

The argument is both economic and emotional. If a large, advanced nation like ours had no manufacturing base, large parts of the service sector which provide to industrial companies – property, marketing, IT, banking – would become redundant. It is also natural to take greater pride, or have greater job satisfaction, in something visible and tangible, particularly when it is made by a British-based company.

The free-marketeers, thinking in purely economic terms, might sneer at such nostalgia. The British motor car and ocean liner belong to the same economic dustbin as the Great Western Railway, the steam engine, and the gas lamp. The nation's heritage means little to them beyond the profits from the museum or theme park's admission charges. Nationhood is an irrelevance. It has no price; it cannot be bought and sold. Patriotism, like morality and spirituality, are outdated emotions for the market economists.

Such thinking allows French companies to buy some of our water and electricity utilities, and BMW to take over our only volume indigenous car-maker. It is impossible to think of French or German Governments acting so blithely over the loss of control of core parts of their economies. The alleged sale of British weapons to Saddam Hussein (which had to be paid for by the British taxpayer under the export guarantee scheme) is probably the most extreme example of this abandonment of any sense of the wider national interest beyond immediate financial gain.

The same outlook has caused untold damage to our national sporting strength. To our modern breed of sporting administrators, what matters is the profit from TV deals and sponsorship, not the national interest. While our players fail to reach the highest standards in almost every sport against other countries, our domestic clubs are basking in unprecedented wealth. In football, we have failed to win a major championship since 1966, yet our Premier League is among the richest in the world. In cricket, our record is appalling. We have never won the World Cup and have not beaten the West Indies in a series since 1969. Yet the county clubs continue to look after their own, refusing to institute a competitive divisional championship or remove any of their pathetic, money-grabbing limited-over trophies. In tennis, Wimbledon is highly successful, one of the four Grand Slam tournaments, producing huge revenues for clubs but Britain has failed to produce a winner since 1936. In athletics, we have won just two Olympic golds in the last three tournaments, despite all the money that has flowed into this recently professionalised sport. The bickering over TV profits in rugby union shows a warped sense of priorities, especially when our four national sides are so far behind the skills of the three great rugby powers of the southern hemisphere.

What is particularly offensive about our international weakness at sport is the predictable bleat about 'lack of resources' from those in charge, when they are now so awash with money. Complaints of 'Government underfunding' are the first refuge of the terminally irresponsible, from social workers to sports administrators. If 'under-investment' were really the cause of Britain's problems at the last Olympics, then why are some of the poorest countries on earth, like Kenya and Morocco, so much more successful than we are? Why have the Caribbean islands, hardly renowned for their affluence, beaten us at cricket for nearly three decades?

Our sporting failures, like the decline of industry, mean nothing to the balance-sheet cynics of the free market. The Ashes are, after all, no more than a miniature Victorian urn. They carry no prize money. Nor does victory in an Olympic event. Alan Shearer will earn more in a season with Newcastle United than a career with England. But sport, more than any other aspect of our lives except war, is capable of building a spirit of national unity. The mood of elation and despair during the 1996 European Football Championship could have been achieved by no other modern event. Indeed, perhaps the only outlet for unashamed patriotism is now through sport. I remember, as an eighteen-year-old Northern Irish schoolboy, walking through Edgbaston in 1981 after England's astonishing Ian Botham-inspired victory in the fourth Test over Australia, greeting total strangers by the hand and literally dancing in the streets with drunken Brummies. And doing the same in London in 1990 after England's roller-coaster defeat of the Cameroons in the World Cup quarter-finals.

The multi-culturalists and New Public Servants have been as suspicious of such outpourings of national joy as the free-marketeers have been cynical. For they see every demonstration of British patriotism as nothing more than the assertion of our racial superiority. Riddled with their feelings of guilt over colonialism and discrimination, they lapse into a form of inverted racism, loathing every feature of their own culture. I was amused, during the build-up to the aforementioned game against the Cameroons in 1990, by the number of 'progressives' in North London who paraded their support for the African side simply because they were up against England.

But there is little amusing about their efforts to destroy our sense of nationhood. In the name of combating 'Euro-centric attitudes' and 'cultural imperialism', that is what they want to achieve. Nothing in the last thirty years has more insidiously undermined confidence in our national heritage than multi-culturalism. The anti-racist obsessive can only see Britain in terms of the 'oppressed' ethnic minorities and the 'oppressor' white majority. It is the task, therefore, of all our public institutions to reduce this 'oppression' by eliminating any manifestation of pride in our country. The virulent anti-racists believe that it is not the duty of minorities to be assimilated into our society, but for our society to abandon its own culture in order to accommodate minorities. Thus, as one Asian woman doctor from the Royal London Hospital in Whitechapel complained to me, it is doctors who are sent on courses to learn Bengali and Gujarati while the patients are never encouraged to learn English. Quite rightly, the imperialists of the nineteenth-century Raj have been criticised for not attempting to appreciate Indian culture. Yet if the mildest attempt is made to uphold English culture in language or symbolism, it can be greeted with accusations of racism. When the North Luton Conservative Association proposed in October 1995 that schools should have to display the Union Flag, a portrait of the Queen and the Ten Commandments, students at the local sixth form college asked if 'racial hatred were involved in the policy'. What a tragic commentary on the values of our age that our national flag and an image of our Head of State should be seen as racist. After the 1996 European Championship match between England and Germany, one writer on black issues, Jean Simpson, said that: 'Amid the national frenzy of flag-waving, even die-hard black soccer fans said they felt alienated, if not threatened. Many blacks still feel that patriotism equals racism.' Reporting that many blacks in Britain had supported Germany (hardly a nation renowned for its racial tolerance) because they regarded 'England as the enemy', she warned that 'there is still a lot to be done before the days arrive of Afro-Saxon football.'

The anti-racist brigade hate the idea of an integrated, harmonious Britain. They feed on the racial divisions. The fascists of the BNP and the National Front are, paradoxically, their greatest allies in their portrayal of Britain as a society where, according to one educational pamphlet, 'racism is embedded in the everyday practices, customs and procedures of our society.' They are so hung up on their views that they refuse to recognise the genuine progress that has been made towards creating more tolerance and openness. Instead of concentrating myopically on 'oppression', they should acknowledge the real success stories of black people in Britain.

We now have six black and Asian MPs, including two Labour front-benchers and one Conservative. Less than ten years ago there were none. A recent winner of the Booker Prize, Ben Okri, is black. The General Secretary of Britain's second biggest union, Bill Morris, is black. A black woman, Heather Rabbatts, Chief Executive of Lambeth, is one of the youngest and most highly-regarded local authority heads in the country. Lenny Henry is one of Britain's most popular comedians. Trevor McDonald was chosen to front the revamped *News at Ten* because opinion polls showed he was ITN's most popular newsreader – hardly evidence of endemic racism from the British public. Moira Stuart is one of the BBC's longest-serving newsreaders. Businessman Swraj Paul was recently made a peer. Linford Christie and Paul Ince, both black, have captained England's athletics and football teams respectively. Blacks and Asians, like Bruce Oldfield and Shami Ahmed, have been at the forefront of the expansion of British businesses. In film, fashion and music, some of our brightest international stars have been black. Many of Britain's public services, especially the NHS and London Transport, have been dependent on the skills and dedication of employees from ethnic minorities.

None of this is good enough for the ideologues. Clinging, almost gleefully, to the belief that racism is worsening in Britain, they demand more Government action, more ethnic monitoring, more 'awareness training', more blacks in every position, more censorship of 'racist' material, more funding for race bodies, more 'culturally sensitive' services, more 'anti-racist' teaching in schools and universities, more 'positive action' programmes, more legal rights for the 'oppressed', more race regulations. Like ex-public school Marxists ashamed of their backgrounds, the anti-racist pulpiteers feel ashamed of their own country, its history and its culture. Ignoring all the achievements of our nation, they turn Britain's past into little more than a tale of slavery and exploitation. Peter Fryer, a journalist writing of the late Sir Keith Joseph's observation, when Education Secretary, that 'pride in one's country' should be fostered in British schools, said: 'Let the pupils be told how English racism arose and what its role has been in the validation of colonialism.'

'A people without history is not redeemed from time, for history is a pattern of timeless moments. So, while the light fails on a winter's afternoon, in a secluded chapel, History is now and England,' wrote T.S. Eliot in the *Four Quartets*. Through the campaigns of the multi-culturalists over the last thirty years, we are fast becoming a people without a history. As with the teaching of Christianity, we are so terrified of upsetting minorities that we can no longer promote the study of our own rich past. Richard Hoggart, in his autobiographical *A Local Habitation*, in a passage about his education in pre-war Leeds, wrote: 'Our history when external, was imperial history – Wolfe dying on the plains of Abraham, above all the paradigm of the gallant English soldier and gentleman (an officer, of course) . . . Our internal history was more concerned with the Wars of the Roses than the plights of the peasantry.'

We do not want a return to such a limited understanding of history. But the pendulum has swung so far in the opposite direction that many of our school pupils now have no knowledge of our past whatsoever. The narrative approach of teaching dates, kings and events may have been narrowly focused, but at least it imbued most of our young people with the story of our islands. Now the past is truly 'a foreign country' to our nineties generation. The project-based, sociological approach deprives students of any sense of continuity or context. They might be able to empathise with a British sailor at Trafalgar, but they know nothing of the battle's significance. They might grieve at the suffering of a nine-year-old child labourer in a Lancashire cotton mill but do not know why the Industrial Revolution occurred. As a result, the historical ignorance amongst our young people is frightening. A survey in 1995, held shortly before VE Day, of 1,600 pupils showed that a quarter of children aged 11 to 14 could not name Hitler as the Nazi dictator; half did not know that the Battle of Britain was fought in the air; 60 per cent did not know what the Holocaust was. In a study commissioned in 1993 by the *Reader's Digest*, just 2 per cent of seventeen-year-olds knew the dates of William the Conqueror's invasion, the end of the Second World War, the Spanish Armada and the Coronation of the Queen. Last year, a Gallup survey of sixteen- to twenty-four-year-olds showed that just 27 per cent of them knew that Queen Victoria was our longest-reigning monarch, 20 per cent could name Christopher Wren as the architect of St Paul's Cathedral and only 10 per cent knew that King John signed Magna Carta. What these findings clearly demonstrate is the absence of any concept of British heroes from the modern teaching of history. This is another symptom of the relativism of our age where the lives of Sir Francis Drake or William Gladstone are deemed no more worthy of attention than that of a fifteenth-century farm worker. Such attitudes also reflect the Marxist belief that our history is entirely shaped by social and economic determinism rather than the actions of individuals. Hence the degeneration of some so-called history teaching into sociological theorising, without any attempts to instil knowledge about the past. GCSE candidates with the London Examining Board can now study 'leisure and tourism', 'cinema, radio and television since 1940', and 'race relations in a multi-cultural society since 1945'. In 1996 the Midlands Examining Board removed all five of its British history papers, which had enabled pupils to specialise in the Victorian period and Tudors and Stuarts. The Board's History Project paper now covers the impact of 'white Americans' on 'Plains Indians'.

A glance through current history textbooks highlights this problem. You will not find any national heroes in *History Fast Track 1750 to 1900* which features neither Waterloo nor Trafalgar but is very concerned about female coalminers. *Britain in the Twentieth Century*, published by Longmans and 'designed for 14- to 16-year-olds', gives just two brief mentions to Winston Churchill, neither of them as our wartime leader. It then devotes three pages to racial discrimination, which includes these pejorative and ahistorical statements:

'There was growing evidence by 1980 that black children were underachieving in most schools, and that lessons, books and teaching materials reflected white, English attitudes... During the 1980s many local education authorities adopted anti-racist policies to improve the school performance of ethnic minorities. Through the appointment and training of teachers and the production of new teaching materials, schools tried to overcome racist attitudes. However, the progress made in schools was not matched in all other public services. Police forces especially seemed to harbour racist attitudes and behaviour.'

That sounds more like a briefing from the Lambeth Council Labour Group, circa 1985, than a schools history textbook.

The same emphasis on empathy rather than knowledge pervades the *Teachers' Resource Book on Themes in Twentieth Century World History*, published by John Murray, which encourages pupils to imagine themselves in the lives of ordinary people. For the British character ('Bert Higgins') in 1916, they are told: 'You are an extreme socialist, believing in the ideas of Karl Marx. You are aggressive towards the rich. Prepare some good Marxist slogans using words like capitalist, proletarian, exploitation etc. Your teachers will help you.' Does the child who plays 'Bert Higgins' of 1916 know anything about the Somme, or Jutland, or the fall of Asquith, or the Easter Rising in Dublin? No, but he knows how to fight the class war.

The multi-culturalists who now dominate our local education authorities have been at the forefront of these moves to jettison our past. Yet they are guilty of the most flagrant double standards. For while they dismiss any attempt to promote the understanding of the 'white, racist' heritage of Britain, they have no qualms about celebrating the past of other cultures. The heroes of Britain are lost in a fog of sociology, but black heroes are to be cherished. 'All children need the opportunity to identify with black heroes and heroines so it is important that they have books in which the leading characters in both realistic and imaginative stories are black', says the Early Years Trainers Anti-Racist Network. Hackney Council's *Black History Month* included book displays on 'Positive Images of Black Heroes and Heroines' and exhibitions on 'black achievements'. Imagine the howls of outrage from Hackney's anti-racists if some local group organised an exhibition on positive images of British heroes, featuring, say, Churchill (imperialist), Wellington (racist), Shakespeare (anti-semite), and Cromwell (anti-Irish).

The contempt in state education for all things British extends beyond history. It encompasses religion, the English language, geography, science, even mathematics. In 1995 the head of a Lambeth Council appointment panel justified the shortlisting of a Nigerian chef for a post as a Maths teacher with the words: 'It is real-life maths with Ibo cookery. I thought it was an innovative way into maths.' A white maths teacher, who was already teaching at the education centre in which this post was advertised, was turned down for the post because she had supposedly 'failed to grasp the equal opportunities issues involved in working in the inner City.' Two educationalists have written of 'racism permeating the teaching of science, for Western racism is part of the structure of Western capitalism and all its institutions, including science.'

The multi-culturalists see discrimination everywhere. Local authorities employ 'race inspectors' and 'ethnic minority advisers' to check school activities and lessons for the slightest hint of prejudice. The Government's own guidelines on the National Curriculum state that schools must 'make every effort to ensure that the Standard Assessment Tests they produce avoid ethnic or cultural bias.' And 'Children should also be made to understand that the use of chopsticks, fingers and cutlery are merely different ways of eating and no one way is better or more "proper" than another,' says the Commission for

Racial Equality's booklet, *From Cradle to School*. Development tests for young children can be dangerous, warns the BBC's Education Unit, because 'many of them have been standardised on white, middle-class children.' Toys and games have to be vetted with rigour. 'Britain is a racist society,' writes Babette Brown in *Nursery World* magazine, 'and racist images are often transmitted through toys and learning materials.' Dolls, alphabet books, games, food, and dressing-up clothes: all must reflect 'cultural diversity' and 'challenge stereotypes'. 'Teach children to write their names in different languages. Have posters around displaying a variety of scripts and encourage children to get familiar with the sounds and shapes of a variety of alphabets,' urges Nadini Mane of the Working Group Against Racism in Children's Resources. The tragedy of this multi-racial farce is that we are no longer teaching British children the basics of their own language, never mind those of other cultures. In *British Racism, Miseducation and the African Child*, Dimela Yekway epitomises the views of the anti-racists. Through its 'Euro-centric bias' our education system 'becomes a psychological strait-jacket which alienates the African child from himself. Education becomes a process of imparting white, middle-class values. The system is hell bent on perpetuating the old colonial relationship.'

It is not just white children who lose out through this obsession with multi-cultural, multi-lingual teaching. Because of the terror of 'imposing' so-called 'white' values, ethnic minority children, particularly those from Caribbean backgrounds, are being deprived of the skills of literacy and numeracy with which to compete in our society. Far from overcoming racism, the ideologues are actually trapping black children in their disadvantaged backgrounds. Just as the race-fixated priorities of too many social workers have failed to deliver quality social services, so the warped values of too many educationists have prevented the delivery of quality education. As one Asian activist, Arshad Darr, said after the riots in Bradford in June 1995: 'Going on about racism is a mistake. Our children go to school speaking only their own language and are then put into schools where 90 per cent are Asian. Children have to be taught that it is all right to compete for a good education.' Those words should be ringing in the ears of every anti-racist who believes that teaching English is a form of 'cultural oppression'.

In practice, the outstanding performance of many Asian children in British schools proves the nonsense of the claims from the multi-cultural gurus. If British schools were as tainted with racism as they say, why is it that Indians achieve better examination results than any other ethnic group, including the white population? A recent study in the London Borough of Brent, which has the country's largest ethnic population, showed that one in three Asian boys achieved five or more GCSE passes at grade C or above, compared to one in four white boys and one in six West Indians. The figures for Asian and white girls were one in two, and one in four for West Indian girls. The reason for the Asian success is not hard to find. Their stable family backgrounds provide strong motivation, discipline and role models for children. Almost half of African-Caribbean children are brought up in lone-parent households, in contrast to less than one in ten of Indian children.

The destructive ethos of multi-culturalism now exists throughout our public institutions, furthered by the efforts of our New Public Servants. A Home Office report in 1995 warned that the training of probation officers gave 'disproportionate attention to anti-discrimination issues, which are important but should not be an obsession.' Youth and community work, like social services, is scarred by such attitudes. One publication from the Association of Community Workers, entitled *Community Work and Racism*, absurdly claims that 'your primary role as a white worker is to challenge white groups and white institutions.' It further argues that training programmes are needed 'for white people to develop a new white identity which is not the identity of the oppressor.' Even that mildest of British professions, planning, has succumbed. Last year, the Royal Town Planning Institute suggested that planning controls might be applied less strictly to ethnic minorities because they are racially disadvantaged. The Bar Council, the body which represents barristers, has introduced a new 'equality code'. This sets out procedures for 'monitoring the ethnic origins of applicants' and urges employers to consider 'positive action' to deal with the 'under-representation' of particular groups. Chambers are also warned against relying on good A-levels or high-class degrees when recruiting, as this could be 'indirectly discriminatory to ethnic minorities'. As a result of a tribunal case brought by the Commission for Racial Equality against British Rail in 1991 (settled before hearing), BR agreed to change their selection procedures for train drivers because they could be construed as discriminatory. One of the CRE's charges was that the Number Search Test for potential drivers 'even if it was shown to be relevant to job performance, would clearly put minority candidates at an unfair disadvantage because of the need for familiarity with the order of the English alphabet.' This is the descent into the madhouse. Should BR really employ train drivers who are unfamiliar with the English language? What about learning new safety procedures, reading training manuals, or understanding vital communications?

Local government has become almost as notorious as the CRE for its multi-cultural mania. Tower Hamlets last year spent £15,000 celebrating the 25th anniversary of Bangladesh, which broke away from Pakistan in 1971. If the local Bengali community wanted to mark this occasion, fine, but why should it be a municipal matter? In the same borough, Labour councillors justified a grant to a Bengali advice centre which had been hit by management problems by claiming that 'ethnic minority groups need not have such a high degree of internal organisation as others.' In October 1995, in the week that Birmingham announced the closure of three libraries, two swimming pools, and three old people's homes, the city council also decided to make a grant of £10,000 towards a firework display to celebrate Diwali. Supposedly cash-starved Kirklees Council spent £69,000 in 1995/96 on 'international liaison' to 'increase public awareness of global interdependence' and to support local groups with 'links to India, Pakistan and the Caribbean'.

Universities have similarly been urged to adopt a multi-cultural approach. Alan Ingle, secretary of the University of East London, has explained that his board has instituted a new 'equal opportunities action plan' to deal with complaints of 'Eurocentrism'. That rallying cry of the student union movement, 'No Platform for Racists or Fascists', has been so widely interpreted that anyone who disagrees with the multi-culturalists' agenda is ostracised, thus destroying the concepts of academic freedom and open debate, two of the bulwarks of our tertiary system. When I was involved in student union politics in the mid-eighties, this 'No Racist' campaign had become so virulent that even certain polytechnic Jewish societies were banned. The sinister logic goes like this. Zionism equals racism; Jewish societies support Zionism; these societies are therefore racist. One of the most repellent events of my student life was a debate on this ban at the NUS Conference in Blackpool in 1985, when so-called 'progressive' delegates hissed speakers from the Union of Jewish Students before they had opened their mouths. In the name of anti-racism, they had lapsed into the most puerile anti-semitism.

This is the paradox at the heart of multi-culturalism: those who see the world in purely racial terms promoting racial division. By constantly emphasising the differences between races, they militate against integration. By promoting an extreme form of 'cultural diversity', they undermine racial harmony and national unity. By condemning British cultural traditions as racist but refusing to criticise any features of other cultures, they end up with the nightmare of the Salman Rushdie affair where 'liberals' condoned – and even marched in favour of – the public burning of a book by a British Asian writer. Both the National Front and the political multi-culturalists think that identity is based on racial origins. Like the gay activists fixated with sexual orientation, the anti-racists can perceive people only in terms of skin colour. Thus the BBC feels it has to produce programmes from a 'black perspective' and bewails its own alleged 'élitism' in failing to reach ethnic minorities, who 'think of the BBC as remote, traditional and mainly white', according to a 1995 strategy review. What, precisely, are these 'white' programmes? *Top Gear*? The *Six O'Clock News*? *Gardeners' World*? We should not be surprised that Bernie Grant, a supposed champion of black rights, has adopted the same policy on voluntary repatriation as the National Front. Both of them feel, from different perspectives, that blacks have no place in this country.

One of the tragedies of modern Britain is that we have allowed the two racist political extremes to define the terms of our British nationhood. The far Left spreads guilt about our past. The far Right preach racial hatred. As a result, too many of us have fallen into confusion instead of pride about our Britishness. The Union Jack and the national anthem are not sources of unity but division. My wife, who is an American but has lived here for fourteen years, has often expressed astonishment at this feature of British life. Cynics might sneer at the devotion shown in the United States to the Star-Spangled Banner but I sometimes wish we could capture a fraction of their citizens' instinctive patriotism. In an interesting article in the *Guardian* in September 1996, the black journalist Gary Yonge described a visit to the US National Association for the Advancement of Colored People:

'There seemed to be only three higher authorities to which the speakers called upon – God, the Constitution and the American flag . . . Throughout my time in the States I have met no African-American who does not place some faith in these common reference points. Britain, in contrast, has no written constitution, is far less religious and you would not get a Union Jack within five miles of a political meeting full of black people.'

The same is true of our nearest continental neighbour, France, which does not appear to evince our nervousness about national sentiment. The communists are just as passionate singers of the Marseillaise as any Gaullists. Even the smallest Hôtel de Ville proudly flies the tricolour. To most Frenchmen, the idea of worrying about 'Euro-centrism' or 'white, Franco-bias' would seem absurd.

Neither the French nor the American face the difficulty we have, that our nationhood is so closely bound up with the person of our sovereign. As patriots, we are expected to show allegiance, first and foremost, to the Crown. Our national anthem is about our monarch rather than our country. In our criminal courts, the Crown is the symbol of justice by the state (*Regina versus* . . .). Our political system is based on the concept of 'the Crown in Parliament'. Our great national events, like the FA Cup Final, are led by the Royal Family. The Queen is head of the armed services and the Anglican Church. The Royal Mail, the honours system, the charters of universities and cities, the Prison Service (eg. HMP Wandsworth), charities (RNIB), and the arts (Royal Opera House) reflect the dominance of royalty in our public life. The problem is that this structure can only be effective if the authority of the monarchy is universally accepted. As Will Hutton says in *The State We're In*: 'The Royal Family has to rely on its unimpeachable behaviour for its continuing legitimacy – and this is beyond the capacity of any human family to generate.' Particularly in our age of media intrusion when every move by our Royal Family is captured by the telephoto lenses of the tabloid press. Edward VII might never have reached the throne if the press of his age had been equally willing to spread the news of his sybaritic exploits across their front pages.

The House of Windsor has, however, recently behaved like a dysfunctional family, with both the Princess of Wales and the Duchess of York displaying all the worst traits of our age of self-gratification. Even the most committed monarchists must have had their faith in the institution badly dented by the grisly pantomime cast of Major Ron, James Hewitt, Johnny Bryan, Steve Wyatt, and Budgie the Helicopter. The mystique that is so essential to the monarchy has been exploded by the ill-advised parade of public confessionals from younger members of the Royal Family. Walter Bagehot, in *The English Constitution*, wrote that 'we must not let in daylight upon magic.' With Dimbleby, *Panorama*, and *Hello*, we have had a blowtorch.

Largely as a consequence of these antics, republicanism is now a serious political force in Britain. But because the monarchy is still the symbol of our nationhood, it is difficult to be both a British republican and a patriot. How can you sing our national anthem if you do not believe that the Queen should be reigning over us? The monarchy has been in crisis before, of course, such as at the time of Edward VIII's abdication, and during Queen Victoria's long withdrawal from public life in the 1860s after the death of Prince Albert. Yet the dangers to the monarchy are much greater now, for we no longer live in an age of deference. Authority is taken for granted much less easily. The democratic instincts of our time make the hereditary principle much harder to defend when the beneficiary of that principle is widely disliked.

Another source of our confusion over our Britishness stems from the rise of nationalism within our own borders. Any call for a unifying sense of Britishness can appear weakened by the demands of separatists from Scotland and Wales. Opinion polls in Scotland in recent years have shown almost a quarter of the population supporting Alex Salmond's pro-independence SNP. Some of the fervent Scottish nationalists – in the true spirit of fractious nineties anti-racism – see themselves as a different racial group who, like blacks and Asians, have been oppressed by the English colonialists. It was noticeable during the VE-day celebrations in the summer of 1995 how few events were held in Scotland. We are already beginning to see the first, tell-tale cases of 'anti-Welsh and anti-Scottish discrimination' at industrial tribunals. The Scottish actor, Tom Conti, has written of his repugnance at the anti-English siege mentality that now exists in some circles. One of the dangers of this mood is that it creates a reverse reaction among some of the English, who start to resent the subsidies that they have to pay to Scotland – Government spending per head of population is 20 per cent higher north of the border, though unemployment is now lower – and become indifferent to the unity of the kingdom. The demand for self-government can be infectious, with Cornwall and the Isle of Wight now boasting their own separatist movements.

Yet I believe this problem has been blown out of proportion. The vast majority of Scots and Welsh do not want independence from Great Britain. Even many of those who might vote for the SNP are not necessarily seeking separation. When Roseanna Cunningham won the Perth and Kinross by-election for the SNP, much of her vote came from disillusioned Tories who could not stomach voting Labour. They are hardly likely to be in the vanguard of an independence movement. Indeed, much of the present Celtic nationalism stems purely from an anti-Conservative, rather than anti-British, mood in Scotland. If a Labour Government is formed after the next election, containing a phalanx of Scots at its head (Tony Blair, Gordon Brown, Robin Cook, George Robertson, Chris Smith, Ann Taylor, Donald Dewar) then some of this feeling will evaporate. The demand for a Scottish Parliament may be similarly diluted, especially when the implications of its tax-raising powers become known. In Wales, the call for independence is even weaker. Similarly, Labour's plans for Welsh devolution are less far-reaching than those for Scotland. And it should be remembered that when both regions last had the chance to vote for devolution, in 1979, they failed to do so in the necessary numbers, 40 per cent of the total electorate.

We should also see Scotland and Wales in the context of history. Wales was conquered by Edward I in the fourteenth century and was formally united with England under Henry VIII. The Scottish and English thrones have been together for almost four centuries while the United Kingdom of Great Britain has existed since the 1707 Act of Union, far longer than the United States, Italy, or Germany. Wales and Scotland have heavily influenced the development of Britain as one of the great powers, from the ideas of Adam Smith to the mercurial premiership of Lloyd George, from the shipyards of the Clyde to the collieries of the Rhondda valley, from the Welsh Fusiliers to the Gordon Highlanders. The interwoven relationship continues in our age. Our economies are unified. So is our political system. Since Harold Wilson, every one of the five leaders of the Labour Party has been Welsh or Scottish or has sat for a Welsh seat. In our present Tory Cabinet, the Deputy Prime Minister, the Foreign

Secretary, the Home Secretary and the Lord Chancellor are either Welsh or Scottish. Could modern British culture be studied without reference to R.D.Laing and Dylan Thomas, Alex Ferguson and Ryan Giggs, Anthony Hopkins and Sean Connery, Shirley Bassey and Billy Connolly? Such a heritage cannot be overturned by a few separatist slogans.

A more serious threat to Great Britain's existence as a sovereign state comes from the European Union. Rhetoric about 'partnership', 'solidarity', and 'subsidiarity' cannot hide the fact that the EU is driving towards the creation of a unified federal Europe. That is the goal of its institutions and its bureaucracy. Integration – or 'ever closer union' – has become the *raison d'être* of the EU. The nation state is an obstruction along that path. It is better that our politicians face up to this reality instead of pretending that the European project can be shifted in a different direction. Such an attempt would be no more successful than trying to persuade Gerry Adams to sing *Rule Britannia*. As one publication from the European Commission in 1992 put it menacingly:

'The European Community has to proceed towards a federal-type European Union, now that there are several actual or potential applicants waiting to join. Member State governments of all political shades know that absolute national sovereignty is no longer a realistic option. They understand that formerly sovereign nations can only continue their economic and social progress and continue to have an influence on world affairs, if they pool their resources and accept that their fate is now intertwined.'

This is not what the British people supported in 1975. We voted to retain our membership of a Common Market, not to join a vast integrated social and political 'Union' which would destroy our national sovereignty. The descent from a Common Market to a European Community to a European Union was carried out in the most insidious fashion without any democratic mandate. And the concept, so beloved of EU bureaucrats, of 'pooling sovereignty' is a nonsense. National sovereignty is not something that can be sliced and shared. It can only be passed from one body to another.

The integrationist instincts of the EU can be seen throughout its operations. The demand for 'harmonisation' of working practices is one example. The introduction of a common foreign and security policy is another. So is the creation of a European-wide passport, now to be followed by an EU identity card. The regulatory interventions of the Commission in the fields of consumer and environmental policies have become notorious. Cheeses, double-decker buses, condoms, beaches, office furniture, and footballs have all been subject to the unwanted scrutiny of Brussels.

That pitiful talking shop, the European Parliament, is constantly seeking to expand its remit, in the name of increasing democratic accountability within the union. But you cannot enhance the role of the Euro Parliament without diminishing the sovereignty of national Parliaments. It has certainly proved itself hopelessly unfit for any greater powers. Like some irrelevant students' union, it fills its time with posturing and gesture politics. Bureaucratic necrosis is reflected in its shambling twenty-eight-strong committee structure, dealing with such exciting issues as 'Culture, Youth, Education and the Media', 'Regional Policy' and 'Women's Rights'. Most of its members are second-rate political hacks, whose sole qualification for office is their ability to subsidise their waffling with public funds. Their bloated £80,000-a-year allowances for 'secretarial assistance' are a scandal, as are the widespread abuses of travel subsidies. As one MEP's researcher has candidly admitted:

'Everyone's on the same gravy train. The MEPs get £155 a day just for signing in here, and all their travel is paid for. A lot of them sign in and get the first plane home again. They also get £2,340 a month for office management, but the office, fax and telephone are all free. That money is basically just for paper.'

More money is wasted through the ridiculous arrangement whereby the Parliament spreads itself between two centres, Brussels and Strasbourg, with a secretariat in Luxembourg. The cost of moving staff between these centres comes to more than £100 million a year, while the rent on the two centres is £800 million. The idea that this body should be the democratic engine of an integrated Europe is laughable.

Nowhere is the damage to national sovereignty more clearly demonstrated than in the judicial activism of the EU. Laws passed by the British Parliament are rendered increasingly meaningless because of the jurisdiction of the European Courts of Justice and of Human Rights. Parental smacking, for instance, may be outlawed in this country, not through legislation passed by the House of Commons, but as the result of a test case taken by a twelve-year-old boy to the Court of Human Rights. The ban on homosexuality in the armed forces could be judicially removed in a similar fashion. Liberals might applaud such developments, but the destruction of our own laws can also work against them, as happened over the inability of our Government to ban veal exports. Perhaps the most offensive decision of the European court has been to allow Spanish fishermen who register in this country to have access to our fishing quota. The fisheries policy has become an emblem of our loss of sovereignty. Even European treaties can be superseded by the European lawyers. At Maastricht, Britain specifically opted out of the Social Chapter. Now the European Court of Justice has imposed a maximum forty-eight-hour working week. Against the spirit of the Maastricht opt-out, the EU is using the backdoor method of widening the scope of 'Health and Safety' legislation to force Britain to comply with a raft of social regulations.

Our existence as an independent state will finally be destroyed by European economic and monetary union under a single currency, due to take place in 1999. Neither of our two main political parties has ruled out Britain joining, and the Liberal Democrats are positively enthusiastic. The abolition of the pound and the creation of a European central bank would reduce our nation to the status of a county council, with the Chancellor no more than a municipal treasurer, waiting on the decisions of unelected European treasury officials. We would lose all control of our economic destiny. Political union is bound to follow. Those, like Tony Blair, who claim that there is 'no constitutional barrier' to a single currency, are simply wrong. There is no case in history of a currency union between independent states not acting as a precursor for their political unification (the *Zollverein* was an important step towards the creation of a unitary Germany in the nineteenth century). That is why the Euro-federalists are so keen on the idea. As Jacques Delors, the father of modern European federalism, has said:

'Economic and monetary union will not be possible without corresponding democratic and political integration. How can we envisage the existence of a powerful independent central bank, controlling a currency used by 340 million people, without corresponding political and democratic developments, without having a European political entity?'

The single currency is founded on political dogma, not economic reality. Not only would it remove national sovereignty, but it would also increase unemployment, worsen poverty and reduce competitiveness in many parts of the Continent. Without horrific upheaval and social dislocation, you cannot drive together fifteen divergent economies, each with differing tax systems, levels of public expenditure, trading patterns, and standards of living. The House of Commons Social Security Select Committee was right to warn in November 1996 that a single currency could result in British taxpayers having to subsidise the generous state pensions of other EU members, a development which would raise our public debt from £5,000 per head to £30,000, since few EU states have the same level of private pensions as us. Even if we did have to bail out other countries' national pension schemes, the levels of borrowing required to fund them would impose crippling interest rates throughout Europe. In this country we have already witnessed the disastrous consequences of the European Exchange Rate Mechanism, which we would have to rejoin if we were to apply for membership of EMU. The overvaluation of the pound drove us into recession and put more than one million out of work. The day our economic recovery began in 1992 was the day we left the ERM.

The ERM fiasco exposed the economic nightmare that would greet us under full monetary union. This is what the Euro-enthusiasts never address. Instead of dealing in hard facts, they resort to internationalist platitudes and juvenile abuse. Those who oppose their grandiose visions are 'Little Englanders' or 'petty nationalists'. The 'march of time' is on their side, they believe. When the pensions problem was raised in Parliament, they airily claimed that it amounted to nothing more than the 'clutching of straws' by the Euro-sceptics. But their flatulent language is hopelessly at odds with the shambles that is the EU: a structure that spends more than half of its £65 billion funds on its inefficient Common Agricultural Policy, that is, according to its own auditors, losing up to £2 billion a year through fraud and lax management, and whose civil service and Parliament have become by-words for bureaucratic waste and incompetence. What has the EU really achieved: economic prosperity? low unemployment? industrial innovation? higher living standards? rising productivity? social cohesion? Hardly. We have less unemployment in Britain (7.5 per cent of the workforce at the time of writing) than in France and Germany, precisely because we have refused to accept all anti-competitive edicts of Brussels. That is why the federalists are so enraged with us. Our relative success stands as a contradiction of their theories.

European integration is the triumph of theory over rationality. Like other theories of our age – such as the belief in child-centred learning – it flies in the face of common sense. 'You must have faith,' the founder of the Common Market, Jean Monet, told the Labour Leader Hugh Gaitskell, when attempting to persuade him to adopt a more Europhilic policy. 'I believe in reason,' Gaitskell rightly replied.

It was Gaitskell who, in the Labour Party Conference of 1962, spoke of the destruction of 'a thousand years of history' if Britain were to join the Common Market. His words are even more pertinent today as we are dragged into 'an ever-closer union'.

What needs to change

If we are to retain our sovereignty and independence, we have no alternative but to begin negotiating our withdrawal from the European Union. The status quo is not an option since the EU is determined to press ahead with integration. If we were to remain a member of the European club, we would have to accept this. Europhiles, with their gift for overblown rhetoric, pretend that life for Britain outside the EU would be a disaster. We would lose our access to trading markets, we are warned. The bounty from European social funds would disappear. Investment from the Far East would go elsewhere. Our citizens would be deprived of their social 'rights'. We would slip into the twilight existence of some decayed imperial power instead of enjoying a bright economic future shared with our Continental partners. As usual, it is not explained how any of this would happen. The EU could not impose trading sanctions against us since that would be contrary to the GATT agreement. EU membership is hardly an overwhelming factor in the attraction of foreign investment. Geographical position, language, and low unit labour costs are more important. Far from missing the benefits of EU social funding, we would have a financial benefit from withdrawal, since we currently make a net contribution to the EU of more than £3 billion. What is more, we could decide where to spend this money rather than have such decisions dictated by Brussels. Nor would our public agencies have any further need for 'European Units' and 'European Officers' whose sole task is to penetrate the EU's bureaucratic web of regional and social funding.

It is not as if European countries outside the EU have fared badly. Contrary to the predictions of local Europhiles, Norway has flourished economically since its people rejected membership in their recent referendum. Like Norway, Britain has never been an integral part of continental Europe. The story of our island over the last two centuries has been as closely bound up with the development of the Empire as with Europe. Until our entry into the Common Market, our closest ties lay with the Anglo-American alliance and the Common-wealth. Both these relationships have been developed through a shared language and business culture, and legal and Parliamentary traditions. It is nonsense to pretend, as one Euro-enthusiastic Liberal Democrat did with me, that I have more in common with a German than an Australian. For a start, the German and I could not even speak to each other. And even if he had a rudimentary smattering of my language, I could hardly ask him about news from *Neighbours'* Ramsay Street or the latest score in the Ashes test. It may be impossible to rebuild our links with the Commonwealth which were so tragically thrown away twenty years ago, but that is no excuse for allowing the continued subversion of our independence. The argument that the globalisation of economies makes the EU more necessary should be stood on its head. Globalisation actually makes the corporatism of the EU a dangerous irrelevance. If we are to compete on an international stage, surely it is much better to have economic independence rather than being locked into the bureaucratic quagmire of Europe? I do not see the Tiger economies of the Far East rushing to form a vast trading bloc. They do not believe that prosperity lies in the surrender of control over their own economic destinies.

The very process of withdrawal would open a debate about our sense of nationhood. The Euro-federalists would be forced, for the first time, to be open about their aims instead of pretending we can have both national sovereignty and political union. They would have to confront the patriotism about which they are so unbearably pompous. It will not be enough to sneer at national pride as mere 'jingoism'.

Extricating ourselves from the quagmire of Europe will not be enough. We must reinvigorate patriotism in other ways. Perhaps the most simple change would be to reform the national curriculum for history in schools so that it actually teaches pupils about the story of our country. We must no longer be in thrall to the nostrums of political correctness. Children should have to learn about the events of the past which have shaped our present. A purely social history cannot provide this sort of understanding. How much, for example, does the life of a twelfth-century peasant differ from that of a fifteenth-century one? The fashionable emphasis on developing 'skills' with which to interpret historical sources should also be abandoned. Historical knowledge must come first. Without such a background, study of sources takes place in a vacuum. Anyway, as Chris Woodhead, the excellent Chief Inspector of Schools, asked me once: 'What exactly are "problem-solving skills"?' Some GCSE questions in historical interpretation could be answered by a ten-year-old through the application of mere common sense rather than any historical knowledge.

In teaching British history, we must not be afraid of the multicultural pulpiteers. As Roy Strong has pointed out, previous generations of migrants to Britain, like the Dutch in the sixteenth century or the Huguenots in the late seventeenth century, have adapted to British culture and taken the British past as their own. The guilt-ridden obsessions of the anti-racists should not prevent our post-fifties generations of arrivals from the Commonwealth from learning about the history of their new home. If the children of ethnic minorities are kept in a cultural cocoon, how can they be expected to assimilate into our society? The same applies to celebrating heroes and myths from our heritage. There is nothing more racist than the assumption – usually made by patronising white liberals – that, because of skin colour, a heroic figure can only inspire allegiance from his or her racial group. Is not Nelson Mandela an inspiration to both black and white? Was not Churchill's romantic language of 1940 a rallying cry against tyranny across the globe?

Nor should we be afraid of demonstrating our national allegiance by flying the Union Jack in schools and on public buildings. In a near decade's involvement in local government in London, I cannot recall ever seeing any representation of our national flag at any school or education centre. Sadly, for too many people, especially in the inner city, the Union Flag has been hi-jacked by the thugs of the extreme

Right like the BNP and Column 88. But the answer is not to surrender it to these racists but to reappropriate it for the mass of the British people. In Ireland, the tricolour is not seen as the symbol of the IRA, no matter how many times it has been draped across the coffins of some murdered terrorists. Our New Public Servants in local government have, predictably, played their part in the down-grading of the Union Jack. In 1995, Labour-run Warwick District Council tried to ban the village of Whitnash from putting up a flagpole to fly the Union Jack on VJ Day. A Labour member of the planning committee explained the thinking behind the decision: 'There was a concern that a noise nuisance could be created in windy weather.' A more patriotic outlook is required from some of our bureaucrats.

The stumbling block of the monarchy can be overcome in two ways. Either, the Royal Family can reduce its unpopularity through a period of quiet, solid public service. Or the Crown can be gradually phased out and replaced by a presidency. I would not personally favour abolition, not because I am an ardent monarchist but because, if we are to revive our sense of nationhood, the last thing we need is a major division in the public over the removal of our most long-lasting institution. It is certainly possible to revive the fortunes of the Royal Family, especially now that those twins of vulgar self-absorption have left the scene. Queen Victoria did it in her time in little more than twenty years, the republican mood of 1873 giving way to the nationwide celebrations for her Diamond Jubilee in 1897. In our own age, the Princess Royal has shown what can be achieved by doing one's duty. The Queen's Golden Jubilee in 2002 could be a catalyst for a renewed monarchical popularity.

Most of the current debate over reforms to the Queen's consti-tutional position is so much froth. Our monarchy is in crisis because of the antics of its junior members, not because of the Queen's prerogative powers or her role as Supreme Governor of the Church of England or Head of the Commonwealth. Most British people neither know nor care about such niceties. And the anger against the House of Windsor's wealth largely arises from Diana's wardrobe and Fergie's globe-trotting. Recent reforms such as the introduction of Royal income tax, the reduction in the Civil List and the opening up of Buckingham Palace to the public can help to lower this resentment.

It is essential that the media, especially the tabloid press, starts to reduce its lurid coverage of the Royal Family. How can any reverence be attached to the institution when the stories of the Royals' former lovers are so expansively and noisily paraded in public? The Prince of Wales has been part of this problem, of course, with his undignified televisual confession of adultery. But now the Diana roadshow has collapsed, the Press Complaints Commission should be tougher with editors over intrusions into private lives.

Three other steps could be taken to revive our nationhood. First, our National Anthem is unsatisfactory, since it relates only to the person of the sovereign rather than our country. We should have a new anthem to which republicans as well as monarchists can feel allegiance. Elgar's *Land of Hope and Glory* would be my choice. For me, no other piece of music approaches its patriotic inspirational quality. The annual joyous flag-waving at the Last Night of the Proms shows how much it is loved by the public. Some critics would argue that it is too closely associated with the Tory party. That is only because we have allowed it to be. The point about the fascist Right appropriating the Union Jack also applies here. Elgar's great work should not be the property of one political party. Labour should sing it at the end of their conference instead of that dated dirge, *The Red Flag*. And if the Liberal Democrats used it as well perhaps they might not be so witteringly enthusiastic about Europe.

Second, we must revive our sporting prowess. Nothing is better guaranteed to restore our national pride than a clutch of Olympic medals, a World Cup in football, or the return of the cricket Ashes from Australia. In the immediate term, we must encourage our sports clubs and institutions to put the national interest first. The pinnacle of any player's career should be representing our country, not gaining a large pay packet or winning some domestic trophy. In too many sports, the demands of the domestic game tend to undermine the skills of our most gifted individuals. We have no problem in producing fine players. We just iron out their special talents in the treadmill of a professional career. Lancashire County Cricket Club has already set an example by allowing the England captain, Mike Atherton, to withdraw regularly from their fixtures. Others should follow. In the longer term, we should have centres of excellence for each of our major sports to hone the skills of our top athletes, though much of the cost could be borne by our TV-enriched sports administrators rather than the taxpayer. We must also encourage more competitive sports in schools. As the former England football manager, Bobby Robson, has said, 'There can't be many leading sportsmen who did not begin at school. Destroy the seed and there is no harvest.' The Government's unambitious target of at least two hours of sport a week is not being met at present. British children have an average of just 90 minutes' physical education a week, the lowest in Europe. Schools in France and Germany have twice as much PE as in Britain. Some of the damage has been caused by the egalitarian instincts of too many local authorities, where the very idea of 'winners' and 'losers' is seen as oppressive, and any games played must be 'non-gender-specific' – in case the boys do better than the girls. So we end up with the most feeble sessions of aerobics or rounders. Almost as damaging has been the market-oriented sale of playing fields by schools and local authorities to developers in order to raise more cash. In my former borough of Islington, the seventy-two schools possessed not a single field or athletics track. We need to restore such facilities. Funds from the National Lottery and the Sports Aid Foundation would help, but, again, sports clubs themselves could do much more. If Newcastle United has £15 million to spend on one player they are certainly financially equipped to help local schools.

Third, we need a national British day of celebration, as the Americans have 4 July, the French Bastille Day and the Irish St Patrick's Day. At present we have nothing except some bonfires on 5 November to mark a bungled assassination plot that took place almost four hundred years ago. The burning of effigies of Guy Fawkes has no patriotic meaning. There have been some recent calls to revive the feast day of St George but this can only be an exclusively English, rather than British, event. The solution is to abolish one of the May bank holidays and make 15 September, Battle of Britain day, our national holiday. The great success of VE day in 1995 and the growing support for the revival of the two minutes' silence on 11 November shows the memory of wartime courage still strikes a chord with most of the public. This date has all the necessary ingredients. It commemorates one of the most significant moments in our history, when we stood near the 'abyss of a new dark age'. It is full of romantic overtones: the brave pilots, the 'finest hour' language of Churchill, the sense of struggle against tyranny. It embraces not just England but the whole of the United Kingdom, and, indeed, the Commonwealth. It invokes exactly the spirit that we need to recapture: sacrifice, duty and heroism. It revives the image of those British characteristics that we seem to be losing, like detachment, steadiness and dignity. Even its very name exudes patriotism. An annual tribute to 'Our Finest Hour' would be the surest way to inculcate future generations with a sense of the greatness of our past.

CHAPTER FIVE

The Loss of Authority

'I don't want to be told what to do, ever.' – Unemployed ex-public schoolgirl, interviewed on *Listen to the Future*, BBC2, July 1996.

'Mum lets me stay out until three a.m. and she lets me go where I want with who I choose.' – Sara, fifteen-year-old girl, interviewed in the *Sunday Telegraph*, June 1995.

'Throughout their contact with pupils, teachers should demonstrate an understanding of anti-sexist issues. We wish students to have a heightened awareness of sexism when working with children and expect them to be able to take practical measures against it.' – Policy document for Teacher Training College in Sunderland, 1995.

'Strikes are a positive act which students can learn much from. They can learn that, as future workers themselves, they should not be treated as slaves. They can learn that pride, dignity and justice as a worker demands that we collectively oppose the exploitation of our class by yours. They can start to say no to a system which cares little for the general well-being. Maybe then they will not shut up, be forced to die for their country, or kow-tow to some boss.' – Views of Nick Grant, Teacher in 'Media Studies' at Villiers High School, Ealing, in a letter to a local councillor, May 1995.

'The real problem may not be scientific ignorance so much as a pervasive indifference to critical thinking, which springs from a hostile attitude to truth. After moral relativism comes intellectual relativism.' – Views of Dr Piers Benn of the Leeds University Philosophy Department on the growing popularity of astrology, *Independent on Sunday*, January 1996.

Institutions and figures of authority – police, parents, the Church, the courts – are essential to the maintenance of our civic order. But the forces that have built our infantilised society are undermining them.

Marxist egalitarianism encourages us to challenge those in authority, seeing them as no more than the instruments of corrupt capitalism. By extension, for anti-racists, such figures represent the values of a 'white', 'imperialist' hierarchy, while radical feminists see them at the centre of a male patriarchy. For both Freudians and liberals, they can 'repress' freedom by the enforcement of an unwanted moral code. Free-marketeers treat them as an irrelevance at best, and a restraint on market forces at worst. Any institution that opposes the policies of the Tory Right is accused of self-interest.

The collapse of a universally-accepted moral code has been accompanied by the decline in respect for those people and institutions who were formerly seen as agents of the public good. The climate of non-judgementalism deprives them of their moral force. The creed of relativism promotes the belief that the opinions of all are equally valid. In the child-centred school the views of the teacher – or 'facilitator' – have no more authority than those of the children. For an inner-city jury, the witness statement of a police officer is no more reliable than that of a convicted criminal. In our value-free world, the TV astrologer has just as much claim on truth as the Cambridge professor of science. The views of some empty-headed, baseball-capped teenager are treated with the same reverence as those of a World War II RAF veteran. The very term 'our elders and betters' has long been consigned to the same linguistic dustbin as 'illegitimacy', 'perversion' and 'delinquency'.

Those in positions of power are subject to constant questioning and abuse. The media sneers at every institution, treats every politician as if he were some dishonest imbecile. The Church is used as a vehicle for a fifth-rate sitcom like *The Vicar of Dibley*, where Dawn French's character has as much spirituality as a teabag. Programmes like *Watchdog* and *The Rantzen Report* encourage the belief that employers and organisations are motivated entirely by greed. The 'Rights' agenda, of which this consumerism is part, is now geared towards attacking the decisions of those in authority. Rights of appeal, grants of legal aid, demands for compensation and damages against the police are all part of this culture. Few appear to accept institutional judgements any more. Instead of admonishing a child expelled from school, parents now run to their local authority in order to get the decision overturned. 'I'll take this to the European Court of Human Rights if I have to,' is one of the battle-cries of our disrespectful age. MPs, local councillors, health visitors, probation officers, social workers and welfare advisers exacerbate this problem with their own challenges on behalf of constituents and clients. The more decisions of the housing department or the DSS that the local MP succeeds in overturning, the higher his popularity, though not, crucially, his authority. Some of the New Public Servants, like race-relations officers and gay men's health workers, devote their working days to undermining the authority of the present social structure.

This is part of the problem. Many institutions, like local councils, schools and the Church of England, have fatally weakened themselves from within by their appeasement of infantilism and non-judgementalism. The notorious 'Bad Hair Day' advertisement by the Anglican Church, designed to raise attendances, only damaged its credibility while revealing its craven fear of appearing irrelevant. Similarly, the bejeaned teacher, who urges his class to call him 'Mike', lowers his professional status. The local councillor who, like some slovenly teenager, turns up at surgeries and meetings in his leather jacket and 'Man Utd' T-shirt is hardly likely to inspire respect from his ward constituents. Even worse are the MPs – and we could find a few on the Labour benches – who think they can only represent their electors if they dress like the shabbiest of them. Dressing down and false intimacy are inimical to the exercise of trust and responsibility.

The mistake of so many of our cultural leaders is their belief that they must reflect our society rather than shaping it. Every whim of our age has to be accommodated. From the paraphernalia of 'contract culture' to the obsession with 'equality targets', too many of our leading public institutions are now the driven, not the driver. 'Mission statements', 'customer-driven core values', 'performance indicators', 'equal opportunities policies', 'league tables', 'zonal re-organisations', 'devolved budgeting' and corporate imagery are all part of modern institutional life. But the benefits of this jargon-led activity are dubious. The BBC, under its Director-General John Birt, is now a by-word for organisational navel-gazing. 'Birtspeak' has become a slang term for incomprehensible management babble. In 1995 the Corporation spent £9 million on consultants. They have been employed to advise on how to campaign for an increase in the licence fee – the rise needed partly as a consequence of the bloated consultancy bill. Neoteric training courses are another feature of Birtian culture. Senior managers can choose from *Time Management, Leadership Train-*

ing, A Creative Thinking Workshop, Effective Meetings, Handling Conflict, Team Building and *Managing Personal Performance Review*. One week-long residential course for make-up staff, held to raise their 'leadership and management potential', involved personality tests, treasure hunts and games with Lego. At other training sessions, BBC staff have been asked to make paper aeroplanes or compete on exercise bikes. Such management training courses have become all too typical of the quackery that has infected British industry and the public sector. It has been estimated that more than £2 billion a year is spent on management training exercises, but, as the BBC experience demonstrates, much of this money is wasted. The bureaucracy of the Corporation is equally aggravating. Philippa Giles, the producer of BBC dramas such as *Oranges Are Not The Only Fruit*, complained in 1995: 'There is an awful lot of doubling up of jobs. There are cost controllers, production executives and production assessors all doing, I believe, the same job. Having people in parallel jobs just doesn't make sense.'

None of this frenzied corporate activity helps with the BBC's central purpose: the making of television and radio programmes. The same problem exists in the National Health Service. From the army of accountants, contract managers, public affairs advisers and purchasing officers now working in the NHS, it would be possible to forget that the NHS exists to provide medical treatment. As one doctor commented ruefully after it was reported that his local NHS trust had spent £500,000 on refurbishing the offices of its contracts department: 'This is happening while wards increasingly rely upon charity for equipment and clinical services such as physiotherapy are severely rationed for lack of money.' The number of NHS managers has increased by 400 per cent in the past five years. Some trusts are now spending more than 10 per cent of their total budget on management. More funds were swallowed up two years ago when the Department of Health relocated its Management Executive to a new £80 million headquarters in Leeds. The sum of £4.5 million had to be spent on compensating staff for the move but their pain was eased by their new surroundings, which included a swimming pool, interior waterfalls, handwoven carpets, a sports hall, gymnasium, bar and hairdressing salon. Yet, like the BBC, the Department's managers seem incapable of doing anything without outside advice. Between 1991 and 1995, they spent £95.5 million on external consultants.

The knee-jerk resort to consultancies exists throughout Government. Last year it was reported that Whitehall is spending more than £800 million a year on hiring consultants, while an internal Cabinet report said that £130 million a year could be saved if the Government were to make more efficient use of outside experts. That is surely a gross underestimate. What is the point of employing thousands of civil service managers if their work is so regularly performed by consultants? The taxpayer loses out twice.

Consultancies have become one of the rackets of the nineties. I have always found it odd that an experienced businessman should feel compelled to resort to the opinions of some naïve recent graduate, whose toughest decision in life so far has been whether to part his hair on the left or right. In the local authorities in which I have been involved, consultants were heavily used. Yet so often their (extremely expensive) reports amounted to no more than the regurgitation of the views of current directors. Indeed, the growth of consultancy is an indicator of the loss of authority by those running businesses and organisations. It is as if they can no longer accept responsibility for decision making. Only those outside the organisation can be trusted to solve problems.

Another impetus behind this modern devotion to consultancy and bureaucracy has been the Conservatives' market-led approach to the public sector. The privatisation of major industries has been a bonanza for city lawyers, consultants and PR firms. The so-called 'internal market' in the NHS has led to an orgy of organisational change, and this contract culture, with 'purchasers' on one side and 'providers' on another, has been copied throughout the public and voluntary sectors. The accountants have never had it so good. In local government, Tory-inspired compulsory competitive tendering and community care have led to a similar demand for a host of new policy and financial managers. In 1995 a report by the Audit Commission found that, in the previous six years, councils had taken on an extra 50,000 managerial staff. It may appear ironic that a Government pledged to 'roll back the frontiers of the state' should have been a catalyst to an expansion of the white-collar professionalism in much of the public sector. But this development has been a direct result of applying pseudo-business methods to essentially monopolistic organisations. In place of competition, we only have chronic paper-chasing. As Simon Jenkins says in his excellent *Accountable to None*: 'Despite her contempt for it, Thatcher failed to reduce the public sector's appetite and barely contrived to reduce the proportion of the nation's wealth it consumed.'

But Thatcherite contempt has reduced the authority, if not the size, of many of our public bodies and professions. The Tory denigration of doctors, lawyers, BBC chiefs, and teachers – even if it is sometimes justified by their failings and inefficiencies – helped to lower the status of these figures. And it also exacerbated a regrettable siege mentality amongst these professions, some of which began to ape the worst excesses of the trade union movement, harping on about 'rights', 'pay scales' and constantly demanding more funds ('resources') from the Government. Representative bodies like the BMA, the Law Society, and the Bar Council became increasingly outspoken in their attacks on the Government. Nowhere did this change occur more violently than amongst teachers, who by the mid-eighties were vying with the National Union of Mineworkers for the accolade of most militant occupational grouping. The strikes in schools in that decade did untold damage to the reputation of the teaching profession, from which it has still to recover.

The police service has also experienced many of these developments, from greater militancy in its professional body, the Police Federation, to the unwelcome adoption of market-led jargon and structures. A senior Essex police officer complained to me last year about the damage being caused by the importation of alien business methods. 'Yes, we've got to be business-like, but we are not actually a business. We are planning and monitoring ourselves to death. All this emphasis on procedures means we're losing sight of our basic objective: dealing with crime.' Equally irrelevant to the fight against crime, like the BBC's £4 million expenditure on equal opportunities, is the fashionable demand that the composition of the police must mirror our society. Do we really want half of our police officers to be women, when more than 95 per cent of violent criminals are men? Once again, we see the triumph of egalitarian theory over reason. Policing is tough, physically demanding work. Of course, we should recruit able women, but not to the extent of seeking absolute mathematical symmetry. The parade of ex-policewomen seeking damages at industrial tribunals shows how unsuited some of the recent recruits have been to this hard, masculine world. The modish anxiety about 'stress' – dragging in its wake predictable demands for compen-

sation and counselling – is equally misplaced within the police. So is
the focus on 'racism'. There is a vicious circle operating here. Because
the police are seen as racist, few blacks are willing to join. In some
places they could suffer accusations of 'betrayal'. As a result, police
ranks have disproportionately few blacks. The charge of racism is
reinforced, making it all the more difficult to recruit from the black
population. The only solution is to indulge in the usual equal opportunities activities. A 1995 report from HM Police Inspectorate urged
that the police force should become an 'anti-racist, anti-sexist, anti-
homophobic organisation'. The 'hierarchical, predominantly white
male culture of the service' must be challenged, the Inspectors
warned.

Our armed forces, still amongst the best in the world, have also
fallen prey to the equality mania. Last year they instituted an 'equal
opportunities directive', under which selected officers have been
retrained as 'equal opportunities advisers' and new procedures have
been established for dealing with complaints. In the Royal Navy,
regulations against sexual harassment require 'sailors to be made more
aware, more sensitive and more attuned to issues of discrimination',
as if they were maritime social workers. The Army has its own Equal
Opportunities Unit and has drawn up an anti-discriminatory code of
practice on the advice of the Commission for Racial Equality and the
Equal Opportunities Commission. None of this will either produce a
more efficient fighting machine or satisfy the equality zealots. It seems
to me absurd to train men to kill and be killed, and then expect them
to be 'sensitive' about discrimination. Where personnel may be
dependent on each other's courage for their lives, where they may
have to spend twenty-four hours a day in each other's company, we
cannot expect the same culture as might exist in an office. The naval
policy of allowing women to serve on certain craft, in the name of
equality, also strikes me as misguided. Efficiency should come before
anti-sexist theorising. The difficult experiences of many women at
sea – and the justified jealousy of sailors' wives – points to a failure
of the experiment. What is more, it destroys the powerful argument
used against homosexuality in the armed forces, that the danger of
sexual attraction between personnel could undermine morale. As
Captain James Briggs, a former officer who still does contract work
in the navy, wrote last year: 'The continuing scandals involving
WRENS cause me great distress. I feel relieved that I was spared

from commanding and serving with women in the particular confines of a modern warship. I am regularly told that the service has tried hard to make this work but that it simply does not. They tell me that the change destroys the whole concept of "all of one company".'

The modernist fear of being 'biased' or 'élitist' has created a crisis in our jury system, once the bedrock of British justice. Until 1974, you had to be a householder to sit on a jury but liberal minds felt that this requirement did not match the egalitarian mood of the age. As the late Lord Devlin put it: 'Juries are not really representative of the nation as a whole but are predominately male, middle-aged, middle-minded and middle-class.' So all property and age barriers to jury service were removed. Anyone aged between eighteen and seventy became eligible. The paradoxical result has been that, in the mid-nineties, juries are more unrepresentative of the public than ever. Those with jobs and businesses to run – the majority of the adult population below seventy – can usually avoid service, while those without pressing commitments can afford to sit through a long trial. A top fraud investigator, Simon Bevan of Arthur Andersen, has attacked the way businesses encourage their staff to avoid jury service:

'Juries find it hard to get a conviction because the jury is rarely a cross-section of the community. The problem is that whenever someone from any management position – not necessarily very senior – is called for jury service [the courts] invariably get a letter explaining that they are indispensable to the business and seek to be excused.'

The young unemployed should be the last people chosen to sit in judgement through a complex fraud or murder case. At least the 'middle-aged, middle-class, middle-minded' juries of yesterday, so loathed by the reformers, could have been guaranteed to bring some common sense and experience to the courtroom. What experience can a jobless nineteen-year-old offer, except, probably, an empathy with those 'oppressed by the system'? The steady flow of incomprehensible verdicts from our courts – stalkers and fraudsters acquitted, preposterous libel damages awarded – shows how unreliable our juries can be.

The jury in the 1995 trial of drug dealer Ray Lee for the murder of policeman Philip Walters hardly fitted the old ideal of 'twelve good men and true'. Infantilism was writ large at this trial. The murder of a policeman has usually been regarded as the most serious of all crimes, but obviously not by this group, most of whom were in their mid-twenties. Two of them started a very public affair. There were demands for a gym at their hotel and rows over smoking. One court official was reduced to tears by their childish antics. Eventually they had to be discharged without reaching a verdict. As the long-serving Essex police officer (mentioned earlier) said to me about the change in juries: 'People once had a greater sense of responsibility to the society they live in. We recently had a case of a woman juror who fell in love with a robber and went to visit him during the case. Such an event would have been unthinkable years ago.'

The Freudian/Marxist/therapeutic victim-led outlook has caused untold damage to the rule of law and the representations of its authority. When every criminal has an excuse for his actions in his background, or deprivation, or political beliefs, those who try to enforce the law become instruments of oppression rather than justice. Just as there are no longer any absolute standards in moral behaviour, so there are no absolutes in law. Every case 'depends on the circumstances'. A disturbing example of this trait was the acquittal of the four women 'peace campaigners' who filmed themselves vandalising a British Aerospace Hawk jet in protest at the use of such jets against the people of East Timor. On a more gruesome level, the same argument of political motivation for crime has been used by loyalist and republican terrorists in demanding special category status in prison.

Greed, the corrupt child of Thatcherite individualism, has also undermined respect for law and authority. The entrepreneurial spirit carried to a dangerous extreme is one way to explain the plundering of the Mirror Group pension funds by Robert Maxwell, the fraudulent dealings of Nick Leeson at Barings, the frauds of Darius Guppy and the byzantine web of drug-dealing operated by Howard Marks. The rise in burglary and car theft over the last two decades has been partly inspired by the same spirit. One young offender, recently interviewed by BBC TV, explained that it was difficult to be honest when you saw 'people earning more than £300 a week just from crime.' Yet greed-inspired lack of reverence for the law need not involve only serious crime. Tax-dodging, expense-fiddling and moonlighting have become part of our nineties way of life. The Inland Revenue estimates that the black or 'hidden' economy is now worth £46 billion, while a study by Leicester University gave a much higher figure, £65 billion, which would mean a loss in tax revenue of some £15 billion, twice our entire spending on police and prisons.

Our society has developed the most infantile double standards towards the black economy. The middle-class taxpayer might splutter with outrage over benefit fiddles, then be quite happy to pay cash to a builder to get a discount. The cleaner paid in fivers, the video recorder bought from the car boot sale, the van loaded with drink from France for that 'Christmas party', the lawnmower categorised as 'office equipment', the luxury hotel stay treated as a 'business trip', are just as much part of the illicit economy as the creatively-completed housing benefit application form. The Driver and Vehicle Licensing Agency claims that 6.2 per cent of motorists evade their road tax, an increase of 18 per cent on 1989, and now costing the Inland Revenue some £163 million a year. Brewing companies fear that the 'Calais run' accounts for £2 billion-worth of alcohol brought into this country. Illicit trading in tobacco is thought to be costing the taxpayer £1.6 billion. Fraud of income support has reached £1.4 billion a year and that of housing benefit £1 billion, yet it has been estimated by one consultancy firm that 60 per cent of middle-income households are responsible for 70 per cent, or £40 billion, of the total hidden economy. Typical is the view of one middle-class professional, a forty-year-old geography teacher from Hampshire, who earns some extra money through private tutoring: 'I get paid a pittance but at least they give me long holidays when I can top up my income. I don't declare it. I don't owe this government anything.' Except the small matter of his salary. Does this public employee not see the contradiction between tax evasion on one hand and, on the other, complaints about his 'pittance' pay, which could only be increased if tax revenue improved? And while he might rail against the Tory Government for 'underfunding' the teaching profession, he is perversely accepting the Right-wing Tory argument that taxation in itself is wrong, that each individual should be allowed to earn as much as he wants without having to contribute to society.

More than five years' experience at Westminster taught me that, when it comes to fiddling, it would be difficult to beat the performance of some of our Parliamentarians. Those who make the law can show scant regard for its requirements. False car-mileage claims and the employment of a spouse as 'secretary', when no work is involved, are just two of the scams. Fact-finding missions to sunny foreign climes, 26 per cent rises in their salaries, conferences on tropical islands, lucrative 'consultancy' fees, alleged payments for asking questions, and provision of 'research' support have rightly contributed to the weakening of Parliament's authority. MPs cannot preach restraint and responsibility when they behave in such a spectacularly selfish fashion. For all the bleating about 'service' to the public, some of our politicians have benefited from their Parliamentary status to gain wealth they might never have found as private citizens. Would David Mellor have a string of contracts with Middle Eastern companies if he had not entered Parliament? Would Sir Edward Heath enjoy his luxurious Albany and Salisbury homes if he had not been Prime Minister?

Nor have members of the European Parliament won a reputation for their integrity. Many refuse to pay the employer's tax contribution on their researchers' salaries – for which they receive an allowance of £70,000 – thereby netting themselves a profit. As one Brussels assistant has explained: 'The money is paid directly into the MEPs' account and they employ us personally, so they see it as part of their salary and they don't want to give it away. Few are generous and those with their hands in the till are pretty clever about it.'

In a society without a system of ethics, greed has become endemic. The so-called 'progressive' lawyer misusing legal-aid green forms for his own gain, the surgeon arranging for a video company to sell footage of operations, the police officer with undeclared earnings from spare-time work as a security guard, the accountant to the celebrity taking an ever-larger 'percentage', and the football manager with his 'cut' from transfer deals, are all reflecting this mood. Even some of those in the voluntary sector are displaying the same instincts, as a friend of mine discovered when she helped to organise a women's conference in London, and was then surprised to be sent a hefty invoice by an HIV/AIDS group which had provided a speaker, even though no fee had previously been discussed. What's more, this organisation already receives substantial funds from the public purse to do precisely this sort of information and publicity work.

The notorious pay rises of the chairmen and directors of the once-public utilities have, understandably, dented the authority of these organisations. Nothing did more damage to the reputation of

British Gas than the bloated salary of Cedric Brown. PR staff may have claimed with justice that individual increments had no relationship to the company's turnover or the size of gas bills, but such arguments only emphasised contempt for the paying public. The weasel words about 'market rates' and 'competition' hardly applied, since British Gas, at the time, had a monopoly. Despite the furore, Brown's example has been mirrored throughout our economy by company chiefs who have never had to risk anything. What particular enterprise skills are needed to run Eastern Electricity or South West Water? Some of the utility bosses who now set themselves up as 'Captains of Industry' were, in their previous public sector incarnations, no more than upmarket town clerks. But even the town clerks have jumped on the bandwagon. One parish council chief last year managed to wangle himself the grotesque salary of £71,000 a year. From my experience of local government, here is a cast-iron principle that applies to almost any organisational restructuring: salary increases for those implementing change will outweigh the benefits of any savings.

As the last chapter pointed out, the recent loss of the monarchy's authority is largely due to the irresponsible greed of the Duchess of York and the Princess of Wales. The quiet dignity of the Queen and the Queen Mother stands in contrast to the rapaciousness of Fergie and the manic wardrobe-filling of Diana. Both are classic products of our infantilised society. Wilful and self-obsessed, they have supported all the fads of our self-indulgent age, from astrology to anorexia. Despite being two of the richest women in Britain, they absurdly portray themselves as victims. Their problems have never been their responsibility. Blame always has to be attached to someone else: the palace, the Royal advisers, the media, their husbands or their own staff. They have shown no concern for others – witness the embarrassing roll-call of departing assistants and destroyed marriages. Their supposedly 'caring' work for charity has been nothing more than an expensive PR front. If Diana really 'cared', why did she suddenly resign, like a spoilt child, as patron of almost 100 charities when her divorce was settled? As with so many others today, they are trapped in their own self-justifying, pleasure-seeking, tantrum-throwing environments, unable to escape because they have no concept of transcendence.

There is a darker side to our nineties crisis of authority. Lack of respect has, at times, degenerated into violence. Assaults on priests and police officers, teachers and doctors, housing officers and social workers are a growing problem. We now have security cameras on school premises, toughened glass at the counters of DSS offices, and, in one case, an inner-city doctor has resorted to the recruitment of a Russian bodyguard to provide some protection. The British Medical Association has been forced to issue guidelines for GPs on dealing with violent patients, which include the warning: 'In some areas, outward signs of your professional status can attract unwelcome attention. Some of our colleagues prefer to use a comparatively unobtrusive vehicle and wear more casual clothes, carrying any medical equipment in a pocket rather than in the conventional bag.' As the guidelines state in their conclusion: 'The advice in this document may seem to be contrary to our duty to provide care and uphold patient confidentiality. Sadly, the need for it has been caused by social and cultural changes beyond our influence or control.' A recent BMA survey of London GPs backed up the need for such advice: 59 per cent of those in the inner city had received threats of violence, both direct and implied. Even in outer London, 36 per cent of doctors said they had received such threats.

The catalogue of assaults against teachers is indicative of this crisis of authority. In 1995, the National Association of Schoolmasters/ Union of Women Teachers (NAS/UWT), the second largest teaching union, reported that the number of serious attacks against its members had reached a record 51, compared to just 10 such incidents in 1990 and 12 in 1991. The cases highlighted by the NAS/UWT included a woman teacher punched and hit around the head by a secondary schoolgirl, another woman teacher knocked unconscious after being hit with a chair by a Rochdale pupil, a teacher in Darlington shoved down a flight of stairs and a teacher in Northern Ireland sprayed with an aerosol can by a pupil with a record of disruption.

These attacks are part of a wider problem of the breakdown of discipline in our schools. And while we might sympathise with individual teachers who have suffered attacks, the culture of our modern education system must carry its share of responsibility for this breakdown. The concept of 'child-centred' learning and the agenda of 'children's rights' – so eagerly pursued by local authorities and education 'experts' – have divested our teachers of their authority and ability to maintain control. In the infantilised society, the boundaries between childhood and adulthood have been blurred. Wisdom and experience count for little. For the radical educationists, who have been in charge of much of our schooling for the last thirty years, instruction in knowledge and self-control are no more than instruments of cultural oppression. Any attempt to impose ideas about 'right and wrong' – either in promoting good behaviour or in teaching literacy and numeracy – can stifle a child's 'free expression' and 'creativity'. We must never demand too much from children. They should be guided, encouraged, supported, but never punished or admonished. No child should be made to suffer guilt for any action.

As a result of this outlook, too many schools have been turned into centres of ill-organised chaos. The anarchy at the Ridings School in Halifax is just one, albeit extreme, example. Having been educated in two traditionalist schools in Northern Ireland, I have been astonished at the educational shambles of inner-city England. When I worked for Harriet Harman, MP for Peckham, and accompanied her on school visits in the borough of Southwark, I saw the indiscipline and non-achievement that prevailed in many of them. Pupils seemed free to wander around the classroom and, instead of instructing the whole class, the system I grew up with, a teacher would move uneasily from one noisy table to another.

In our 'child-centred' education system, almost every disciplinary measure has been outlawed. Corporal punishment was abolished in 1986. Detention can only be imposed with the permission of parents. The 'house' system, which helped to create order and a feeling of loyalty among pupils, has largely disappeared except in the private sector. The only weapons left to an exasperated headteacher are suspension or expulsion. Five years ago there were just 2,500 expulsions. In the last school year there were 12,500, a rise of some 400 per cent. And the financial cost of this development is phenomenal. By law, each of these expelled pupils still has to be educated, either through personal tuition at home or in a special referral unit. At £5,000 for home tuition or £9,100 for a special referral unit (compared to £1,300 for education in a primary and £2,500 in a secondary) the bill for taxpayers from expulsions has now reached about £90 million.

Yet the sanction of expulsion is becoming more difficult to implement because of the views of 'rights'-fixated education administrators, governors, lawyers and campaigners. Recent successful appeals to the local authority against school expulsion have rightly created a scandal, while one seven-year-old pupil has even been granted legal aid to challenge his exclusion in the courts. In Bradford in February 1995, a pupil who had been expelled after an assault on a teacher and suspicions of drug dealing had the decision overturned by a local authority appeals panel. In West Glamorgan, a local authority tribunal reinstated a girl after permanent exclusion following a series of incidents, including violent attacks and theft. In Sheffield in May 1995, a pupil expelled by the head for threatening a teacher with a knife was reinstated by the governors. In some cases, like that of Nottingham boy Richard Wilding, who is said to have threatened 'to butt' a teacher, only the threat of strike action prevented the pupil returning to school when his expulsion had been overturned.

The most disturbing feature of this saga is the irresponsible attitude of too many parents. In the first half of this century, when both the teacher and the father were in positions of moral authority, the threat of making a report of misbehaviour to a pupil's parents was a serious punishment. But the infantilisation of our society has rendered it almost meaningless in some schools. It is now the admonishing teacher rather than the disobedient pupil who is likely to feel parental wrath. In September 1996, when a five-year-old boy from Essex was expelled from his primary school after he carried out more than thirty attacks on staff and pupils, including punching and kicking dinner ladies, his father's response was to threaten to 'kneecap' the headmistress and wreck her car. The expulsion of thirteen-year-old Sarah Taylor from her school in Halifax, when she was accused of pushing a teacher and being violent towards another pupil, prompted this reaction from her mother: 'I accept that she has been disruptive but she has been driven to it by the teachers. She has been constantly picked on. The teachers haven't given her a chance.' And this from her father: 'Sarah just pushed him [the teacher] away when he grabbed her.' As if pushing a teacher was a matter of no consequence. Matthew Wilson, a ten-year-old from Nottinghamshire, was twice expelled from school in 1995 because of 'continuous and chronically disruptive behaviour punctuated by threats and actual physical violence against pupils and teachers.' His mother fought the move, saying that 'he is not a bully. The teachers are picking on him.' Predictably, parents of some of the nastiest children support the fashionable diagnosis of 'Attention Deficit Disorder', the modern illness which explains away any vicious behaviour. We no longer have the troublemaker, only the medical victim. Has anyone ever been hospitalised because of ADD, other than those who have been at the receiving end of the alleged 'victim's' abuse? Complaints about 'lack of support' for recalcitrant children are equally predictable. When James Christie, a ten-year-old from Coventry, left one of his teachers permanently paralysed after assaulting her, his mother was full of sympathy – but only for her son. 'So he's got a temper on him, but they kept him at the same school. James is just a lovable rogue. He needed help but they didn't give him any.'

With attitudes like this, discipline has collapsed as badly in the home as it has at school. Indeed, the chaos of the classroom often reflects no more than the home environment. Schools do not operate in a cultural vacuum. It is a courageous parent who, today, is willing to swim against the tide of self-gratification and set boundaries for their children's behaviour. Successful parenting is a difficult task, requiring sacrifice, devotion, stamina, but, above all, a framework of values in which children can learn about their relationship to others rather than thinking only of their immediate needs. It might be easy to appease the whining nine-year-old by buying the latest set of trainers. The sulking of the fifteen-year-old might be ended by allowing her to 'stay over' with her new twenty-seven-year-old boyfriend. But such actions can only further the cult of gratification. They will do nothing to instil a sense of responsibility or duty. Lieutenant-Colonel Richard Quirke, commanding officer of the training regiment in Winchester, Hampshire, has been depressed by the lifestyle and attitudes of army recruits in the mid-nineties. Some, he says, are unable to take discipline. 'For the first time in their lives these young people have come up against an organisation that says no, means it and enforces it.'

The modernist belief that authority must be questioned has caused as much damage to the position of parents as it has to other institutions and societal guardians. Those who grew up in the sixties with the idea that 'no child of mine should ever feel guilty' can find it much harder to impose discipline than previous generations, particularly with teenage children. In a 1995 survey of parental attitudes one female local-government worker, with a fifteen-year-old son, confessed: 'He has to have designer everything and I tend to give in.' A father, who works as a driver and has two stepsons, said: 'We try to tell them you don't have to wear designer labels to be a cool person and that is a source of arguments. In the end we usually give in because there is so much pressure on them to have these things.' A seventeen-year-old from Chelsea was delighted that her 'parents are very liberal and don't have many rules ... They are very lenient but I respect them.' Another teenager boasted: 'My parents are not at all strict. As long as I let them know where I am, then they leave me to do what I want.'

Much of this rampant liberalism results from the breakdown of the family – itself a consequence of self-gratification. Without a stable family background, it is much harder to impose discipline on children. And if certain adulterous parents are more interested in their own short-term happiness than the welfare of their children, they can hardly complain when those children are unwilling to show them obedience. Indeed, the guilt that some adults feel over the end of their married relationships has exacerbated the practice of surrendering to the demands of their children. Instead of providing their offspring with routine and stability, they give them treats or brief moments of 'quality time' in order to compensate for their absences. One of the most bitter complaints I have heard from single mothers arises from the way their ex-partners escape the daily pressures of bringing up children and then expect to be thanked for lavishing them with gifts at birthdays and Christmas. Such superficial generosity only obstructs the attempts at regular discipline from the permanent parent.

Moreover, the stepfather or new 'boyfriend' can never be invested with the innate authority possessed by the natural father. It is no coincidence that many of the runaways who cite 'difficulties with parents' as the reason for their homelessness come from broken families. A seven-year-old boy who loves his real father will find it difficult to accept discipline from his replacement. Just as problematic can be the child growing up without any paternal influence whatsoever. Since divorce and single parenthood became more common during the last twenty years, there has been a powerful liberal propaganda campaign to try to convince us that children do not need to grow up in homes with fathers. But, as with so much other liberal theorising (Europe, child-centred education, multi-faithism), it simply does not match reality. Children, particularly young boys, need their natural fathers as role models and disciplinary influences.

This problem is worsening in Britain. Only half of our households consist of the traditional nuclear family. Single parenthood accounts for a fifth of all families. In total, almost two million children under the age of sixteen are living in single-parent households, a higher proportion than in any other European country.

The problem of adolescent discipline in our fractured society is particularly serious because of the 'feminisation' of professions like social work, education and probation. In these three areas, the vast majority of recruits are now women, more than 70 per cent in the case of social work and teaching. While some feminists and liberal academics might welcome this change, anyone with a modicum of common sense must be disturbed. For these three services have an important civilising role in our society. It cannot be right that they should become the exclusive prerogative of women.

Think of a fourteen-year-old boy from a single-parent family, growing up on a sprawling council estate in inner London. He has never met his father, who left home the moment his mother discovered she was pregnant. In his primary school all the teachers are women. Even at the comprehensive he now attends, most of the staff are women. His poor behaviour in the classroom has led to a series of visits from the (female) social worker. He has convictions for burglary which led first to a caution, then to a community service order supervised by a young (female) probation officer. The only men this boy ever meets are drug-dealers and the police. He has no male role models; only mother figures who, by training and outlook, are unwilling to punish him.

According to the Central Council for Education and Training in Social Work (CCETSW), 70.7 per cent of trainees on social work courses are women. The figures are even higher for those who have qualified: 73 per cent of field social workers and 90 per cent of part-time workers in England and Wales. The same imbalance exists in probation. Though 90 per cent of those receiving supervision from the probation service are men, about two thirds of recruits to the service are now women. Ten years ago, just over a third of probation officers were women. Only 32 per cent of new entrants are married. A work force dominated by young, single women is hardly the most appropriate for dealing with male, sometimes violent, offenders. The imbalance is worse in parts of the teaching profession. According to the Department of Education, 71 per cent of teacher-training students are female. In primary schools, the latest figures show that 83 per cent of teachers are women. In the 1960s one in four primary teachers was a man. The Teacher Training Agency fears that, by the year 2010, male teachers will have disappeared completely from our primary classrooms. Even in the more masculine secondaries, where almost half of staff are male, just 4 per cent of teachers are young men. As June Smedley, a retired primary teacher, has put it: 'Boys need role models, particularly as increasing numbers do not live with their fathers. Girls also need to build relationships with adult males. No woman teacher, however able, can identify with the problems of being a boy and growing up into a young man.' Imagine the demands for reverse discrimination from the cultural pulpiteers if 85 per cent of our primary school teachers were men.

The loss of authority towards the young is graphically reflected in our nauseous appeasement of a synthetic youth culture. The inverted values of our infantilised age mean that, instead of guiding young people into the mores and manners of adulthood, adults are urged to embrace the attitudes of youth. Those with the most wisdom and experience are derided while the transient interests of the young are cherished. Figures of authority are expected to listen 'to what kids are saying' – which is often no more than some self-pitying whine. Violent rap singers are lionised because their tuneless outpourings represent 'the language of the street'. Youthful promiscuity is glorified. Nihilistic raves and the puerile antics of Britpop groups are portrayed as the 'cutting edge' of a cultural renaissance for which we should all be grateful. Sneering, loutishness, and foul language – all of them displayed by the wretched band Oasis – are regarded as a form of political statement or vibrant artistic expression. The idea of 'good manners' is seen as hopelessly dated. Deference towards elders is equally archaic. For both the Marxist and the Thatcherite, deference is a throwback to a class-bound era, when each man knew his place in the hierarchical social order. But, in truth, deference is no more than the Christian ideal of showing respect to others. In our inverted society, the only 'respect' (a much favoured word on 'the street') that some young people need show is towards themselves.

Politicians, advertising executives, record companies, TV producers, and Church leaders all crave the attention of the young. In-depth analysis is out. 'Wacky' images are in. Where once banks and building societies tried to emphasise their stolid reliability, now they are keen to show how hip they are, with their promotions showing multi-racial saxophone playing (the Midland), or environmental concern (the Co-Op), or roller-blading (the Halifax). The police are in danger of succumbing to this mood; hence the debate about ditching the traditional helmet, that symbol of law and order which has been part of British policing for 130 years. PC Brian Fenlon of the Police Federation explained why officers in Greater Manchester had welcomed its removal: 'It is only those who have a great deal of service behind them who are against losing the helmet. The young members of the force would rather be wearing baseball caps because that is what the youngsters on the street are wearing.' What next? Baggy jeans and Ray-bans?

We are frequently told about the suffering of today's young people – the limited job opportunities, the student debts, the poor pay, the exam pressures, the threat of AIDS and the prevalence of the drug culture. A consortium of housing pressure groups claimed recently that some 300,000 sixteen- to twenty-five-year-olds were homeless at some stage last year. Chairman of the consortium, former *Independent* editor Andreas Whittam Smith, said society had to 'reverse the discrimination against young people'. Deep scepticism must be attached to this figure. Previous estimates of young homelessness have shown far lower totals. A survey by Shelter in November 1996 found that on a single, given night, just 375 homeless people were sleeping on the streets in twenty-three urban areas – 375 too many, yes, but hardly the national catastrophe painted by Whittam Smith's consortium.

More importantly, pouring new funds into benefits for young people – as the Whittam Smith lobby urged – can only worsen the problem. Many will be encouraged to leave home when not economically independent, thereby putting an even greater burden on local authorities and the DSS. The belief that the state should subsidise the flat-hunting of jobless, unmarried young people is one of the most absurd of our time. When old people are struggling to live on meagre pensions and income support, it is outrageous that some young people, who may have contributed little to society and have all their life-chances ahead of them, should be paid to do nothing. At both ends of the age spectrum, however, we can see cases of family neglect, one of the consequences of our irresponsible new individualism: the impecunious pensioner unsupported by his children or the eighteen-year-old driven out by the abusive stepfather. But the idea that the state should take over the responsibilities of the family is a dangerous one.

The crisis of authority is part of a deeper malaise within our society. We have lost confidence in our morals, our heritage, and our institutions. As the critic George Steiner has written: 'The great majority of us can no longer identify, let alone quote, even the central biblical or classical passages which are not only the underlying script of Western literature but have been the alphabet of our laws and institutions.' The insidious relativism, the egalitarian anxieties about race, class and gender, have deprived our institutional guardians of all their moral force.

The art and literature of our civilisation have been similarly deprived of their authority. Like so much else, the Western canon is seen as either reactionary or irrelevant. As the review editor of *Wired* magazine recently said: 'People's mental landscapes have changed. It is more useful to know your way round an Apple Mac than to know verses from the Bible.' When, precisely, has an Apple Mac ever built a civilisation or given anyone a coherent moral code?

Perhaps even more importantly for our civilisation, the authority of Christianity – and thereby our moral code – has been weakened by both science and superstition. The more extreme rationalist scientists, like Richard Dawkins, who holds the Chair of the Understanding of Science at Oxford University, argue that human existence is nothing more than a physical collection of genes and molecules. There is no creative force in the universe. Our lives have no higher purpose. As Dawkins has bleakly written in *The River Out of Eden*: 'There is at bottom no design, no evil and no good, nothing but blind pitiless indifference.' So belief in any form of transcendent consciousness becomes stupidity. We are materialist creatures, driven only by our own immediate needs. This outlook accords with our late-twentieth-century culture of amoral self-gratification. Greed and selfishness are not just natural; they are now scientific imperatives. The only constraint on our behaviour is the harm we may bring on ourselves, not the damage we may cause to others. So we avoid committing murder, not because it is inherently evil, but because we might end up in prison.

Science has been responsible for many of the greatest material advances of our civilisation. The internal combustion engine, the cathode ray tube, the microchip, the heart transplant, the lightbulb, drug treatment, photography, lycra, the jet engine, the lunar module, and satellite communication all owe their existence to the ingenuity of scientists. Indeed, one of the distinguishing features of our civilisation, compared to primitive societies, is our ever-expanding scientific understanding of the world around us, and ability to exploit that knowledge for our own benefit.

But understanding cannot be equated with divine authority. In a world without God, scientists can be tempted to play the role themselves, creating and controlling human life through genetic engineering, cloning, embryology, and mind-altering drugs. The worry is that these experiments now take place in a moral vacuum. To prevent the misuse of newly-acquired knowledge, we have to trust the personal responsibility of individual scientists, not a wider code of ethics. Almost any line of scientific enquiry can be justified by a reference to some vague concept of 'progress', from full-frontal lobotomies on the mentally ill in the fifties to the growth of human organs on the backs of mice today. 'Virgin births', octuplets for fertile single women, IVF treatment for lesbians, and the destruction of frozen embryos may never have been envisaged by those who first developed successful fertility treatment, but they are the inevitable consequence of allowing science to operate beyond any moral framework.

'When a man does not believe in God, he will believe in anything,' said G. K. Chesterton. The credence given to astrology, which had been out of favour since the Enlightenment of the eighteenth century, is an example of this. Astrology has no scientific, rationalist or astronomical basis, yet its 'star signs' are now treated as factual entities. As the renowned astronomer, Patrick Moore, has argued, constellations have absolutely no significance, rendering the astrological system 'nonsense'. The idea that your birth under a particular sign could affect both your personality and your destiny is foolish in the extreme. Here are some of the people born under the sign of Aries: Marlon Brando, Michael Atherton, William Wordsworth, Norman Tebbit, Harry Houdini, Charlie Chaplin and Neil Kinnock. Have they anything in common except the month of their birth? Yet astrology continues to grow in respectability. Quality broadsheets are now running horoscopes. TV stations have astrological phone-ins. The Abbey National has produced a booklet for customers entitled *Your Astrological Guide to a Secure Future*. Astrology might be dismissed as nothing more than harmless fun, but the problem is that it encourages the damaging modernist creeds of individualism and irresponsibility: individualism because the credulous horoscope reader sees herself (and the vast majority of astrology supporters are women) at the centre of the universe; irresponsibility because astrology claims it is the stars, not our own actions, that control our lives.

Astrology is at the forefront of a growing body of superstitions through which people can abnegate responsibility for their lives: tarot cards, palmistry, crystal-ball gazing, psychometry, reading the runes, and consulting mediums. All these mystical activities exploit the credulous by saying things so vague that they are open to almost any interpretation. One woman, consulting a tarot reader, was told that she would meet 'a wonderful man. He will come from the East, or be travelling from East to West.' Not exactly specific. Is that from East Grinstead to West Byfleet? The popularity of irrationalism is also reflected in the success of TV programmes like *Out of This World*, which never subject claims about the supernatural to the same scrutiny that is applied to science. When Winston Churchill, in his 'Finest Hour' speech of June 1940, spoke of Britain being plunged 'into the abyss of a new dark age' he was probably not thinking of *Secrets of the Paranormal*.

What needs to change

The revival of an agreed moral code, outlined in previous chapters, would do more than anything else to restore authority to the family and our civic guardians. Indeed it is only through such a moral framework that authority can be securely rebuilt. To quote from Cicero's *Republic*: 'For there is a true law: right reason. It is in conformity with nature, is diffused among all men and is immutable and eternal; its orders summon to duty; its prohibitions turn away from offence . . . To replace it with a contrary law is a sacrilege.' The anarchic classroom, disordered home and crime-ridden estates are certainly living under a 'contrary law'. The next chapter will look at the need to revive the family as the cradle of morality, though some of the arguments will be touched on here.

Equipping our police officers, judges, social workers, probation officers, and teachers with a new moral force would strengthen their status more than any new rules or procedures that an interventionist Government could dream up. Indeed, the demand for yet more professional bureaucracy is a symptom of the decline of moral authority. Regulation does not breed respect but the opposite. The public servant constantly forced to resort to the rule-book is only exposing his own lack of authority.

This is why all the equipment of institutional bureaucracy – the creative training courses, the layers of administration, the purposeless hierarchies, the myriad contract agreements, the consultancies – must be challenged. In too many organisations, these bureaucracies have become ends in themselves rather than tools to achieve better perform-ance. Some managers judge their status by the size of their administrat-ive empires. So the Policy Unit Director has to have a Deputy. Both must have their own personal assistants, advisers and researchers. Then, to organise these teams, they need an Administrative Officer, who becomes a Chief Administrative Officer with his own PA, and Deputy. And a press officer is required. But because of his attendance at team meetings, review meetings, strategy meetings, forward-planning meetings, project monitoring meetings, and staff appraisal meetings, he has to have a deputy. So, like the many-headed hydra of Grecian myth, the bureaucracy develops its own internal momentum. In such a climate, lines of communication are obscured and buck-passing becomes rife. Look at last year's shambles over the early release of prisoners from their sentences. No one was to blame because responsibility and accountability had been so diffused.

This is the culture we have to reverse. Too often we have reorganis-ation for its own sake, just to keep the consultants and administrators busy. The baggage of corporate logos, chief officers' perks, and PR departments should be ditched. If managers are paid to run an organisation, then they should perform that task, not hand it over to consultancies. Public institutions should return to their primary purposes, programme-making for the BBC or fighting crime for the police. Supporting vulnerable individuals, not changing society, is the task of social services. Treating patients is the job of the NHS. In this context, the excesses of the internal market must be curtailed. The benefits of the system, discovering the real cost and demand for various treatments, have often been outweighed by the bureau-cratic costs. Longer-term commissioning between health authorities and hospitals, rather than annual contracts, would usually be more efficient.

Part of this cultural change must involve the training of our public-service professionals. I have already argued that the focus on politically-correct issues that runs through instruction for social work, probation and teaching should be ended. The outmoded psycho-babble of Freudianism should have no place in university social-work training. I recently heard one first year social work student talking authoritatively about the 'Oedipal Complex', one of the most fallacious dogmas of the twentieth century. We also need to raise the calibre of students, particularly for those going into teacher training. At present, for too many it is the 'career of the last resort'. A survey in 1996 by UCAS (the Universities and Colleges Admissions Service) showed that trainee teachers have lower grades than any other group of university students. On average they need only a C and two Ds to win a place, compared to two As and a B for medical and veterinary students. Some colleges will take on teacher trainees with just two Es. Equally worrying is the fact that would-be English teachers need only a C grade in the subject at GCSE. How can they possibly teach the rudiments of grammar on such a basis? These standards need radically to be raised. A minimum of three Cs should be required for teacher trainees. To attract a higher calibre of undergraduates the pay for teachers must be raised. At £21,000 primary school teachers received little more than average male earnings (£19,500). Some of the classroom 'workers in struggle' might wear their comparatively low pay as a socialist badge of honour, but this is not the way to attract able professionals. The average pay of secondary teachers is little better, £23,000. I believe these rates should be improved to £25,000 and £27,000 respectively. There should also be continuous increments throughout a teaching career, in order to retain the most experienced staff in the classrooms. At present, a pay ceiling is reached too early. The only way to acquire a salary rise is through moving to a headship or an LEA administrative post. A concomitant of higher pay, however, must be greater productivity through longer hours and shorter holidays. The excuse of poor financial rewards should no longer be available to those trying to avoid commitments to extra-curricular activities. Some of this also applies to social workers, whose average £18,000 a year is too low: £25,000 would be more suitable for this demanding role. The market-led argument that there is currently no shortage of recruits to either profession is irrelevant. It is the quality, not the quantity, of entrants that is disturbing.

Some of the money for this increased pay bill could come from the shrinkage in bureaucracies already proposed. There is no need for local education authorities to retain their sprawling central administrative departments. Money will also be found through a reduction in the number of New Public Servants (anti-poverty campaigners, equalities advisers, race inspectors, women's officers, welfare rights workers) who are so prevalent in the fields of education, social work and health. I looked at one edition (18 September 1996) of the jobs supplement in the *Guardian*'s 'Society' – the Bible of the New Public Servants – chosen at random. In terms of salaries offered, the advertisements for public and voluntary-sector posts from that single issue totalled £6.9 million. Spread over a year, that is the equivalent of £360 million. Here is a flavour of the posts available in that week: *Early Years Quality Development Manager* at Kirklees Council (£27,600); *Gender Equality Manager* at Birmingham City Council (£40,000); *Director* of Dudley Race Equality Council (£24,500); *Research Officer* for the National Housing Federation (£27,600); *Social Regeneration Officer for Poverty Work* at Stonebridge Housing Action Trust (£22,600); *Arts Administration Development Officer* at the Asian Women's Arts Group (£19,300); *Equality Adviser* at the London Fire and Civil Defence Authority (£27,400); *Policy and Development Officer for Black and Ethnic Minorities* at the Haringey Racial Equality Council (£22,000); *Public Rights of Way Officer* at South Tyneside Council (£16,400); *Welfare Benefits Worker* at Hillingdon Hospital (£18,000); *Tackling Drugs Together Co-Ordinator* at Redbridge and Waltham Forest Health Authority (£26,600); and a *Strategic Planning Co-Ordinator* at Oldham Social Services (£26,300).

What we must not do is simply raise taxes to meet the costs of salary increases. Such a tactic has been followed by virtually every Government in the last half of this century. That is why both the size of the public sector and levels of taxation (indirect as well as direct) have never been higher. Raising taxes while continuing to waste their revenues would only worsen the current irresponsibility that many feel towards making an accurate return to the Inland Revenue, a mood that has helped to create our £46 billion black economy. It is telling that in continental Europe, where income tax levels are much more punitive, tax fraud is more widespread than here. In Germany and Belgium, evasion is a national way of life. One of the mistakes of many 'progressives', though not, thankfully, Tony Blair or Gordon Brown, is the idea that high levels of taxation across all social groups are somehow synonymous with a 'caring' society. You do not make people 'care' by expropriating half of their pay packets. You only breed resentment towards both the tax collectors and the recipients of tax funds. Why should the Birmingham garage mechanic be forced to subsidise the bloated salary of the city's 'Gender Equality Manager'? Again, by focusing our public services on serving the public, we can restore their authority and reduce the widespread animosity felt towards taxation.

Higher pay for teachers and social workers might also attract the increased number of male recruits so urgently needed in these two professions. So might the replacement of a 'child'- or 'victim'- centred, emotionally sensitive (feminised) approach with a tougher, more disciplined (masculinised) ethos. Serious damage to the authority of professionals has been caused by the empathetic, feminised approach, evidenced by, for example, the reluctance to highlight mistakes by school pupils for fear of 'hurting' them or to impose any judgements on clients' fecklessness. We should be worrying less about what clients or pupils are 'feeling', and thinking more about what they are doing.

The decline of discipline in schools is a clear example of the 'feminised' approach, where punishment is deemed oppressive. There are few tasks more urgent to the restoration of the teacher's authority than a return to the well-ordered classroom. Part of this can be achieved through an end to 'child-centred' group work, where children are meant to learn by self-discovery and the assistance of their helpful schoolmates. Of course, such crackpot utopianism does not work. So we must go back to the traditional method of whole-class teaching, with pupils sitting in rows of desks. Not only does this make the teacher a more authoritative figure, but it also reduces the strain of trying to run about ten mini-classes at any one time. We also have to restore a system of graded punishments for those who misbehave. At present, there is nothing between a mild ticking-off and full-scale suspension. Teachers should no longer have to seek parents' permission before giving a child detention. Other punishments, such as essay-writing or cleaning away graffiti, could be introduced. Personally, I favour the restoration of corporal punishment in secondary schools. The opportunity for parents to sue or take legal cases to the European Court of Human Rights will be ended by restrictions on legal aid and our withdrawal from the European Union. I agree with the view of John Bourn, headteacher of a comprehensive in Gateshead, who said in September 1996 that the disappearance of the cane had been 'one of the causes of the deterioration of discipline in schools. The cane or belt was a good deterrent for many, an effective punishment for some. It is no surprise that expulsions have risen – there is virtually nothing else heads can do.' One of the virtues of corporal punishment is that it physically emphasises the authority of the teacher over the recalcitrant pupil. The equation made by New Public Servants between child abuse and caning only demonstrates their lack of morality. Indeed, the cane could give some loutish teenagers their first taste of the consequences of wrong-doing. Nor are we talking about the infliction of cruelty on all children. The punishment need be used only sparingly against adolescent boys, who are, after all, the main source of the current trouble in our schools.

Another vital step towards greater school discipline must be the abolition of the system of local authority appeals panels, which has prevented headteachers and governing bodies from exercising their authority. Such panels are riddled with the handwringing proponents of the 'victim culture' and have proved counter-productive to the maintenance of discipline.

It is an ironic reflection of the inverted values of our age that our cultural leaders should be so unconcerned about gender balance where it is vital, in the education and civilising of young people, and, at the same time, should be so anxious about equality in the armed forces, the police and fire brigades, where it is at best irrelevant and at worst detrimental. If women want to join such services, that is fine. But there must be two prerequisites. First, they should never be given special treatment. If the entrants to a certain regiment have to be able to perform fifty press-ups, that should apply equally to women. Nor should complaints about bullying or harassment be treated differently because of the sex of the victim. Second, service commanders should not be compelled to indulge in 'positive action programmes' to rectify a supposed 'gender imbalance'. There will always be only a small number of women who are able or willing to accept the physical conditions of these jobs, especially in the army and navy. A 50:50 split between the sexes is neither attainable nor desirable. Listen to this statement from the London Fire and Civil Defence Authority, justifying a concerted new 'equalities' campaign:

'Fire doesn't discriminate and nor do we. We're totally committed to providing the best possible protection for all London's communities. Part of that job is to understand and reflect the communities we serve – this can be more difficult when the majority of our organisation continues to be white and male. It's an imbalance we're continuing to address with a practical, long-term equality strategy.'

What the Londoners want is the safety of an effective fire service, not the luxury of a sexually proportionate one. Do we really need some nervous firefighter whimpering about stress halfway up a ladder? I also think that naval warships should be exempt from the anti-discriminatory requirement to employ women. After all, we accept segregation in other special circumstances, like hospital wards and prisons. The efficiency of our naval crews must receive priority.

The jury system has been similarly weakened by this relentless pursuit of equality. The belief that juries should mathematically 'represent the community' is absurd. Intellect and experience are more important than ideological correctness. No one under the age of thirty should be allowed to serve. Only self-employed business people who employ less than ten staff should be able to avoid service. A simple test of reasoning powers and literacy should be held before trials to exclude the most idiotic. Moreover the demands on the juries could be reduced by the measures already proposed for restricting litigation, like abolishing legal aid for civil cases.

The authority of Parliament would also be revived by the lower age limit of forty for MPs, and by the de-professionalisation of politics. Indeed, exactly the opposite argument that I used with teachers and social workers applies here. MPs' pay, as I have said earlier, should be cut in order to force them to take other jobs and prevent them being nothing more than messengers of the enfeebled 'rights' agenda. Again, like juries, the House of Commons should be a repository of our nation's wisdom, not a replica of its social composition. The ethic of public service must be restored to our political system, both at a national and local level. Holding public office involves privileges and responsibilities, but should never be seen as a glorified marketing opportunity. The Nolan rules are to be welcomed but could go further in restricting MPs' financial activities, especially political consultancies and payments for advice. It is a sorry indicator of the low standards of Parliament that we have these regulations at all but, until there is a shift in our moral climate, they will be necessary.

The craven surrender to youth, which has become another objectionable feature of our civic culture, must be ended. The views of 'kids today', whether they be about religion, employment, crime or patriotism, should not carry weight simply because of their source. It is quite grotesque that the media should give space and airtime to the misogynistic lyrics of creatures like Snoop Doggy Dog simply because they're 'cool' and black. It says something about our decaying civilisation when supposedly 'liberal' broadsheets run adulatory pieces about gangsta rappers who use words like 'ho' (whores) to describe women. Any criticism of this street talk is, of course, 'racist'. This pathetic willingness to suspend any normal civilised judgements has to be challenged.

We have to restore the idea that adolescents are at the beginning of life's journey and have to be guided by figures of authority. This is what the process of civilisation used to be about – teaching young people to mature into a responsible citizenry. But in our infantilised society, we have lost sight of the concept of maturity because we are so terrified of discipline, restraint or patience. One of the social problems which has exacerbated this trend is our failure to encourage teenagers to be socialised with their elders. This used to happen partly through apprenticeships, the most common route into an occupation. As David Smith, Professor of Criminology at Edinburgh University has argued: 'Before the war, most young people would have entered apprenticeships or some form of employment at thirteen or fourteen. Therefore they were with adults from a young age and the ordinary routines of daily life meant they had to conform. That made an enormous difference. What you have now is a long period in which young people are segregated within their own age group.' Sadly this happens whether they remain in full-time education or full-time unemployment. There are several ways through which this process of socialisation can be revived. One is through an expansion of the programme of Modern Apprenticeships, a recent Government initiative which has not received the attention or the funding it deserves. Surely it is much more effective to give companies an incentive to take on young people in trainee posts rather than paying students to undertake some half-baked, jargon-riddled course that will lead to an unwanted qualification? Another is through the establishment of a nationwide scheme for compulsory community service, which would encourage teenagers to think of their wider responsibilities to society. Already there are many such voluntary schemes for well-motivated youth: the Duke of Edinburgh's Award, Operation Raleigh, the Prince of Wales Trust, Community Service Volunteers, the three cadet forces, and numerous charities. But the people who would benefit most from such schemes, the disaffected inner-city youths, are those least likely to participate in them. An element of compulsion is therefore necessary. I am not proposing a return to National Service, only a duty on those aged between sixteen and nineteen to complete a certain number of hours in community work. The schemes currently in existence could be expanded, while local authorities and non-statutory groups could be given ring-fenced grants to take on young volunteers. Gordon Brown, the Shadow Chancellor, has put forward the excellent idea that a young persons' 'Environmental Task Force' could be funded partly from a windfall tax on the profits of the privatised utilities to carry out tasks such as cleaning up beaches and derelict sites. Similarly, the armed forces, searching for a role since the end of the Cold War, could be told that further cuts will be avoided if they prove willing to set up more cadet organisations and expand the number of places in the Territorial Army. There could be special recruitment drives by the TA in the inner city to attract those who would benefit most from a disciplined environment.

Third, the balance of our welfare system should be further tilted towards the elderly. Benefits, especially rent rebates, for those under twenty-five should be radically cut back. I have seen few more dispiriting figures in my time than the eighteen-year-old living in the bedsit off social security, drinking or doping himself stupid every evening, without ambition or hope. The welfare state was not designed to subsidise such nihilism. Open-ended benefits should be replaced with offers of training, education, apprenticeships or work. Savings from the withdrawal of such benefits should be used to increase the old age pension, which, in 1996, was just £61 a week for a single person. I believe there should be a one-off increase in state pensions, disregarded for the purposes of calculating income support so that the poor do not lose out. (This was the problem with pension increases proposed in Labour's 1992 manifesto. For those on income support, any pension increase would have only meant less benefit from other sources.) Our current generation of pensioners, unlike those in work, have no chance to take out private schemes to enhance their retirement income, and many are living in poverty. In the longer term, as the elderly population continues to expand, personal responsibility for a secure retirement must be encouraged, otherwise the tax burden will become intolerable.

These idea about pensions, benefits and young people's community service will be further explored in the following pages. What I am arguing here is that we have to shift our societal concern from the young to the old. The real 'Lost Generation' of modern Britain is not our youth but our elderly. The over-sixties are patronised, ignored, shoved into homes, put out of sight, looked after by a few dedicated staff, while we work ourselves into a frenzy over the likes of the E-popping Leah Betts. Their manners and morals are derided, yet they passed on a richer national inheritance to us than we will pass on to our children. Respecting their experience and insights, rather than treating them as bingo fodder, would be a start.

I hope I have set out here some ways to restore a sense of discipline, responsibility and authority in modern Britain. And nowhere is this more important than within the family, the subject of the next chapter.

CHAPTER SIX

The Breakdown of the Family

'It can drive you mad, sitting around the house all day with a child. I'd really like a big house in the country with horses and everything else – but wouldn't we all.' – Louise Stanley speaking about her future with her son Sam and her boyfriend Keith, an unemployed man who claims to have eight children by seven different women.

'Traditionally, men have learned self-restraint through working and providing for a family, and self-worth through the love of wife and children. What meaning is there for a young boy in a lifetime without either?' – Norman Dennis, sociologist and author of *Families Without Fatherhood*.

'We simply do not want to be treated different than any straight couple. All we want are the rights we are legally due. We have nothing to hide.' – Jill Percey, who, with her lesbian partner, Lisa Grant, a British Rail employee, sued BR for discrimination when they were refused the same travel benefits as a heterosexual couple.

'Obviously because I'm pregnant, I should be able to get a place from the council pretty quickly because we need a good, clean environment to bring our baby up. We're not claiming benefit yet because I have to sort it all out, but we should be able to claim it.' – Stacey, seventeen, a would-be single mother. The father is her twenty-year-old Gambian boyfriend.

'I do think it is irresponsible to have children without accepting that you will have to be there for them and I think attitudes like that are adding to the problems of young black boys.' – Herman Ouseley, Chairman of the Commission for Racial Equality.

The married nuclear family has been central to the structure of our civilisation. It is the local building block of civic order. It has been the unit through which children are socialised into the adult world. It has taught people about responsibility to others. Through the network of siblings, parents, grandparents, and other relations, it instils an awareness of duties and obligations. It has reinforced the code of morality. It has been a source of security and affection for young and old. It has given emotional and financial support within the home. It has provided a framework for the enjoyment of sexual relations. As the American sociologist, F. Ivan Nye wrote in 1958: 'The human infant has no sense of "right" dress, safe driving speeds, moral sex behaviour, private property or any of the other norms of society, whether custom or law. Conformity, not deviation, must be learned.' The family has proved easily the most successful structure devised for the inculcation of these norms. Indeed, no successful, civilised society has ever been built that was not based on the family of two parents.

The collapse of our moral code over the last three decades has been accompanied by the breakdown of the family. There has, of course, been a symbiotic relationship between these two developments. As morality has fallen into abeyance, so there has been less pressure to sustain the institution of the family. And as the structure of the family has been weakened, so the primary mechanism for civilising young people has disappeared.

The decline of the family is perhaps the most far-reaching social change of our time. Before the seventies, it was taken for granted that the best way to rear children was through a married, heterosexual, committed couple. This ideal was supported by the common law, the taxation system, schools, social services, the Church, the media, and charities. Even in that much-vilified decade, the sixties, unmarried, single mothers were still expected to give up their children for adoption. The landscape of family life has been utterly transformed since then. Now 22 per cent of families are headed by a lone parent, compared to just 8 per cent in 1971. During this time, the proportion of dependent children living in single-parent families has tripled. There are now 1.5 million such families in Britain. Never-married lone mothers account for the largest category of single parents, 540,000 (36 per cent), compared to 480,000 divorced mothers (32 per cent), 270,000 separated mothers (18 per cent), 75,000 widows (5 per cent) and 135,000 lone fathers (9 per cent). Almost a quarter of all unmarried women aged between eighteen and forty-nine are now 'co-habiting' (to use modern parlance), double the number of just fifteen years ago. Though the rate of marriage has fallen by two fifths since 1961, the number of divorces has increased sevenfold over the same period. It is predicted that four out of ten new marriages are now likely to end in divorce.

Britain has the highest rates of both single parenthood and divorce in Europe. With such grim prospects, it is perhaps not surprising that the number of first marriages has fallen dramatically from 390,000 a year in 1971 to just 210,000 a year in 1993, while 36 per cent of all marriages now involve a divorcee. Even more disturbing has been the rise in the number of births outside wedlock, from a rate of just 5 per cent in 1960 – a proportion that had barely changed since the late Victorian era – to 32 per cent in 1994. While liberal apologists for family breakdown claim that two thirds of births outside marriage are registered by both parents at the same address – fatuously pretending that this is some sort of indicator of long-term stability – it is also true that the General Household Survey has shown that seven out of ten never-married lone mothers are living without a stable partner. Other research has demonstrated that 80 per cent of all children born to teenage mothers are without a present father.

These figures tell the story of an institution in crisis. The same forces that have so badly dented the confidence in our values and nationhood are also destroying the family. The climate of moral relativism has played a disastrous role. For the amoralists, a commitment in marriage to a family is just another lifestyle choice. Despite the sacrifice involved in raising children, the devoted married couple are deemed no more worthy of support than the serial adulterer. Everyone is entitled to run their own lives entirely as they see fit. We live in an age where the pain of social stigma is deemed far worse than the consequences of irresponsible behaviour.

In the egalitarian spirit of the times, it is seen as discriminatory to treat marriage more favourably than any other type of relationship. The climate of 'equal rights' for all couples, gay or straight, married or not, has now infected, for example, the provision of pensions, council housing, workplace conditions, adoption policy, fertility treatment, and insurance. The Left-leaning Institute for Public Policy Research last year, in a report entitled *Men and Their Children*, called for unmarried fathers to be given the same rights across the board as married ones. 'I would not be surprised if politicians were not running with this one before long,' said Patricia Hewitt, an IPPR Trustee, before the report's launch. Given the shameful record of our policymakers in upholding marriage, she is probably right. The informal concept of a 'common-law' marriage is now widely accepted, as if it were the same as the real thing. The word 'partner' is replacing 'spouse' on official forms. Companies provide the same perks for such 'partners' as they do for husbands and wives. This was the fatal mistake that BR made in refusing to provide travel benefits to the employee's lesbian 'partner', mentioned in the introductory quotations. Once BR had indicated that marriage had no stronger claims than a casual relationship, there could not be any justification for excluding homosexuals from the scheme.

A gaggle of pressure groups, like the National Council for One Parent Families, Stonewall (the gay and lesbian 'rights' campaign), the Single Parents Action Network, Gingerbread, and the Child Poverty Action Group have strengthened this outlook. A respectable charity like Barnardos sends out information packs for primary schools about adult relationships which have the professed aim of 'encouraging children to challenge prejudice and discrimination', and to 'look critically at media images'. What media images can these be? Rarely does a TV programme give a positive picture of married life. Adultery, rows, lesbianism, domestic violence, and teenage angst are now the staple fare of both soaps and documentaries. Every taboo, even incest, has been noisily broken in our soaps. As I write this book, *EastEnders* is plumbing new depths in its rejection of anything that could be portrayed as traditional home life. The young barmaid of the Queen Vic becomes pregnant, catches her boyfriend in a homosexual embrace with her own brother, and then moves in with the landlord of the Vic, who may, or may not, be the father of her child. Cindy is leaving Ian, whose mother Kathy has also fallen out with her alcoholic second husband. Cindy's lover, David, has children by two other women, one of whom, Carol, is now living with Alan, though he is about to embark on an affair with Frankie. Predictably, in the only stable married couple, the husband is HIV positive. BBC producers might argue that the programme is reflecting urban life in modern Britain. But if the media treats family breakdown as the norm such an explanation can become a self-fulfilling prophecy.

The New Public Servants have played their usual malign role, clamouring for 'positive images' in schools of gay couples and campaigns to 'raise awareness' of the needs of single parents. Housing advisers, welfare rights officers, social workers, 'needs assessment' researchers, and sexual health co-ordinators would be outraged at any suggestion that a legally married couple should merit any different treatment from others. Indeed, in my experience as an inner-city Labour councillor and MP's assistant, the public services actually discriminate against married couples in favour of lone parents. In one case in my ward, an engaged woman was told by a housing adviser that she was far more likely to be given council accommodation if she became pregnant and did not marry her fiancé. In the hundreds of housing applications I dealt with over seven years, very few came from married couples.

This is the tragedy of our tax and welfare system. It is not just indifferent to marriage; it positively works against it. By focusing its resources on the mother-and-child unit rather than on the two-parent married family, it encourages women to treat men as a financial handicap. When access to benefits, lower taxes, housing and childcare are radically improved by unmarried lone-parent status, there is an economic imperative on women to minimise their relationships with men, especially if they are unemployed or in low-income work. This is what the controversial US social commentator Charles Murray has termed the 'perverse incentives' to set up fatherless families. On many housing estates in urban Britain, men have become peripheral to family life, their roles replaced by the DSS and the local authority.

Bureaucratic rejection of marriage has been accelerated in the last fifteen years, despite Tory rhetoric about 'family values'. Tax allowances for married couples have become increasingly worthless, while single parents have been given their own unique cash benefits, and an earnings disregard on the costs of childcare. Child benefit, introduced by the last Labour Government instead of child and family tax allowances, has withered. It now is only about half the value of the tax allowances of forty years ago. Overall, as a result of policies pursued by the Tories, the tax burden on couples with children has worsened significantly compared to single people.

Until the last thirty years, the state recognised that those who take on family commitments should be assisted through the fiscal system. Because the family was the bedrock of the civic order, it had to be supported by the Government. In fact, this was one of the reforms successfully demanded by Victorian philanthropists who were angered that tax policies treated married men no differently from those without family responsibilities. In this century, tax exemptions, allowances, and subsidies have been used to favour the family. The architect of the welfare state, Lord Beveridge, felt that the tax system should be a 'means of maintaining individual freedom and responsibilities and the family as the unit of the state'. The removal of allowances, and the extension of taxation further down the earnings scale, have dramatically worsened the position of families. In 1950, the tax threshold for a married man with two children was 101 per cent of average male earnings. Now the figure is just 30 per cent. To return to the same position as existed in 1950, a one-wage family would have to start paying tax at £170 a week, rather than at £73 a week as occurs now. This trend has accelerated in the last seventeen years of Tory rule. In 1979, a couple on half the average wage with two children under eleven paid only 2.4 per cent of their income in tax. Now the figure is 10 per cent.

Detailed research by the exceptional sociologist Patricia Morgan has exposed how badly our modern tax and benefit system has discriminated against two-parent families. In her pamphlet, *Are Families Affordable?*, she shows that, at all income levels, a single parent with children will always receive more in net pay and benefits than a married man with children on the same earnings. According to Morgan, a 'lone parent with two small children can work for 20 hours at £4 an hour and end up with a net income of £163.99 after rent and tax, while a married father of two small children working for 40 hours at the same hourly rate would take home £130.95.' She also gives the example of a married man with two children who earns £300 a week. After taxes and child benefit, he receives £232 a week. A single person with no children, also earning £300 a week, gets £212, a difference of just £20 a week, far lower than the cost of supporting a wife and children. Miss Morgan continues the argument in her book, *Farewell to the Family*. She points out that, because of state policies, poverty increasingly affects families of those in work. The poor do not consist only of the unemployed and lone parents. In 1991, for instance, '62 per cent of British children in the bottom half of the income distribution were in families headed by a full-time worker.' As she concludes, 'Measured by average after-tax per capita income, families with children have become the lowest income group – below elderly households, single people and couples without children.' This is one of the reasons why so many women are now compelled to go out to work. Far from being inspired by a spirit of feminist liberation, much female employment is driven by economic necessity. And the once-vital role of full-time motherhood now wins little recognition or reward from the state. With so many women forced to go out to work, there is a consequent growing demand for state childcare, publicly-funded nurseries and subsidised childminders. In turn, the expansion of childcare provides a new source of employment for many married women. So we end up in the insane position of paying many women to look after each other's children instead of their own.

Those who are struggling with commitments to their families and their low-paid jobs deserve the most support of the state. Yet they are the ones who, proportionate to their responsibilities, receive the least. Unlike single parents, absent fathers and lesbian couples, the traditional working family does not have a host of pressure groups lobbying for new 'rights'.

Tory measures have damaged the status of the family in other ways. The 1996 reform of the divorce laws gave a statutory basis to the concept of a 'no fault' divorce, another symptom of the non-judgemental society where no blame and no guilt should accrue to any human behaviour, even the breaking of solemn marriage vows. Another unwelcome consequence of the 1996 Act is the envisaged creation of an army of taxpayer-funded counsellors and mediators to resolve the problems arising from the breakdown of married relationships, further swelling the ranks of the New Public Servants. Ironically, these new professionals will have a vested interest in the further collapse of marriage rather than its revival. More divorces mean more work for them. Already, with mind-aching predictability, the counsellors are starting to whine about the underfunding of their work. Here is Sarah Bowler, Chief Executive of Relate, formerly the Marriage Guidance Council, which last year received £3 million of government support: 'It is a disgrace that not enough public money is invested in the welfare of relationships. It ignores the pay-off. Think of the children who would benefit from parents being able to resolve their conflicts.' Yes, but that is not going to be achieved by counselling, especially not by the poorly trained, dogma-driven quasi-Freudians who currently dominate the field. The money would be better spent on providing financial incentives for couples to avoid divorce.

The most serious problem with all divorce-law reform is its promotion of the belief that marriage is an essentially transitory institution.

By making divorce ever easier to complete, the state is signalling the lack of importance it attaches to the marriage contract. 'Liberalisation' of divorce weakens the pressure on couples to stay together when a crisis is reached in their marriage. As Ruth Deech wrote in *Divorce Dissent: Dangers of Divorce Reform*:

'Every increase in the divorce rate results in greater familiarity with divorce as a solution to marital problems, more willingness to use it and to make legislative provision for its aftermath. The pressure on the divorce system leads to a relaxation of practice and procedure in divorce, then to a call for a change in the law, in order to bring it into line with reality, and then to yet another increase in divorce.'

The Children Act of 1989 has been another blow to marriage, since it strengthens the legal 'rights' of unmarried fathers and 'partners' in looking after children. Moreover, barristers are increasingly using the Act to win joint residence orders and rights of 'parental responsibility' for lesbians. Liberal reformers have welcomed this development, arguing that it regulates actual relationships rather than some out-moded ideal. But, as with divorce, state sanction can be equated with encouragement. The introduction, also in 1989, of independent taxation for husbands and wives, was another sign of official indiffer-ence to marriage. For tax purposes, each spouse is now regarded as self-supporting.

Given their self-image as 'the party of the family', it may seem odd that the Conservatives should have presided over such a prolonged assault on the institution of marriage. Yet, for the free-marketeers, why should the family be treated any differently from those other institutions like the NHS, the Monarchy, the Church, the armed services, Whitehall, and local government, that have been compelled to adapt to the new climate? Many Right-wingers dislike child benefit, married couple's tax allowances or mortgage tax relief because they interfere with the market and use taxpayers' money to prop up an institution. It is not the job of Government to be promoting a certain lifestyle. It would be much better, they argue, for the state to treat everyone as individuals and abolish any incentives towards the family. Andrew Neil, the former *Sunday Times* editor, has proposed introduc-ing a radical flat-rate tax system, under which all those earning less than £10,000 would pay no tax, and all those with incomes above this figure would pay a merged tax and national insurance levy of 25 per cent. Benefits would be reduced to the most basic of safety nets. Though it has the attraction of simplicity, this fiscal system would be an even larger disincentive to marriage than the present creaking one. A single man earning £15,000 would be far better off, after tax, than a married man with a wife and three young children. Indeed, for such a man earning just over £10,000 a year, the burden would be almost intolerable. His wife would therefore have to go out to work, whether she wanted to or not, no matter how young the children were. None of this matters to the free-marketeer. The decision to marry and bring up a family is a personal one, no different from buying a house or changing career. Marriage should be a private contract, not a public statement. In an ideology that attaches an economic price to everything, the roles of motherhood, support for a spouse and child-care are literally worthless. It is only by entering the employment market-place that parents can demonstrate their worth.

This market approach is in line with the wider individualism of modern Britain, where people are encouraged to think purely of their own needs and wants. We have responsibilities to neither society nor our own families. If we are bored, dissatisfied or impatient in our marriages, we should be allowed to walk away. Our supposed 'right to happiness' is paramount, never mind the deserted wife or abandoned children. Self-gratification must come before the virtues inherent in family life: patience, duty, restraint, sacrifice. Several leading Tory ministers, like David Mellor, Steven Norris and Cecil Parkinson, have set particularly nauseous examples. Norris, in his memoirs *Changing Trains*, even seems to think there was something commendable about the way he was 'honest' with his wife over his affairs with five mistresses. Alan Clark has paraded his infidelity as if it were a badge of masculine honour.

The American novelist Terry McMillan has said that the trouble with men is that they cannot say no. 'From drugs to alcohol and all kinds of stuff, everything is about instant gratification. They don't understand the meaning of the word "sacrifice". Everything has to happen now.' This may have been true of men since we took our first tentative steps outside the caves. The problem of our society is that we place no restraint on such transient pleasure-seeking, indeed, we sometimes seem to celebrate it, as in the spread of the image of the 'New Lad' through magazines like *Loaded* and *FHM* and programmes like *Game On* and *Men Behaving Badly*. In some masculine circles (the tabloid press, drinking dens at Westminster) Steven Norris's reputation went up as a result of the tabloid revelations about his private life. The culture of individualism, the vastly expanded welfare state and the death of a moral code have freed men from their former duties, turning them from fathers into permanent adolescents. As the sociologist Norman Dennis wrote in *Rising Crime and the Dismembered Family*:

'The separation of impregnation from pregnancy is a fact which allows the man to escape the consequences of procreation in a way and to a degree that is quite impossible for the woman. These things have always been true in all societies. What is new about ours is that the whole project of creating and maintaining the skills and motivations of fatherhood and of imposing on men duties towards their own children that are as difficult as possible to escape, is being abandoned . . . Young men with a short-term view of life and hedonistic values have looked on with quiet delight, scarcely able to believe their luck.'

The cult of selfishness has been given a new spur by modern science. Our society now treats children as a 'right' rather than a duty, and advances in embryology and genetics enable everyone to have that supposed 'right' fulfilled, no matter what their marital status, their sexual orientation, their past history of relationships, or even their age. Infertility treatment, first devised to help childless married couples, is now used as another weapon to destroy the family, the basic unit of our social structure. As Melanie Philips contended in the *Observer* in January 1994:

'We have reduced the procreation of children to a mechanistic production line . . . We see childlessness not as a misfortune but as a denial of a human right. Since rights are now the altar at which we genuflect, we have failed to understand that a culture devoted to gratifying individualism is inimical to the creation of an ethical community.'

When a lesbian couple were refused permission by King's College Hospital in London to engineer the birth of a baby – it was planned to take an egg from one woman, have it fertilized by a male donor, then implant it in the other – an NHS spokesman said that the 'issue of sexuality is not important'. The treatment was refused because it was 'designed for medical infertility'. But why should the sexuality of the couple be unimportant? Such a claim overturns the wisdom of centuries of civilisation, that a child is best nurtured by a mother and father. Pretending that the gender or sexuality of the parents is an irrelevance is yet another modern theory which has no basis in reality. What about the lack of role models for children provided by a homosexual couple? Or the inevitable taunting that will result from fellow school pupils? Or the sense of ostracism by society?

The interests of children are being ignored in a ghastly egalitarian experiment to further the 'rights' of lesbians and gays. Our cultural pulpiteers pretend that nothing is wrong with 'non-straight' parenting. 'There is no suggestion that they will not be able to look after her. People would have to think carefully before deciding that she might be better off in a heterosexual household,' said Donal Giltinan, Scottish Secretary of the British Agencies for Adoption and Fostering, commenting on the case of two Edinburgh men who allegedly paid thousands of dollars to a surrogate mother in the USA to have their baby. How can he be so confident? Several child therapists have told me of the disturbing consequences of being brought up in gay households for individual children's self-esteem and sense of identity. And this is what one twelve-year-old boy, with gay parents, recently told Radio 4: 'I get very depressed. I feel trapped in the middle.' He had even contemplated suicide: 'Sometimes I don't think I should be here at all.' In the same programme, one gay couple, who had a baby through a surrogate mother impregnated with a cocktail of their sperm, grotesquely claimed they had both morality and normality on their side: 'What we did was moral. I didn't consider it to be a wrong thing. We went through the process of any normal couple – except in this case there were three of us.'

The egalitarian theorists inevitably blame such problems on the 'prejudice' of society against gays. Such discrimination can only be overcome by raising 'awareness of the needs' of gay parents and by 'providing positive images' of gay couples, thus creating yet more work for the New Public Servants. The notorious booklet from the Inner London Education Authority *Jenny Lives With Eric and Martin*, the 'Sexuality Project' run for local schools in Birmingham, and the recent teachers' 'resource pack' from Camden and Islington Health Authority *Colours of the Rainbow* have been examples of this urge to 'celebrate a diversity of parenting styles', reinforcing the message that there is no ideal for a family structure. When Tony Blair spoke out strongly last year in support of traditional family values, Ruth Lister, social policy professor at Loughborough University, responded: 'What about those who are lone parents out of choice and homosexual families rearing children? A Labour Government's family policy must be aimed at all families.' As with multi-culturalism, the exceptions are being allowed to set the rules. Just as we can no longer teach Christian values or British history for fear of offending a small number of ethnic minorities, so our New Public Servants will no longer promote the traditional family for fear of offending a tiny number of gay couples. And the numbers are surprisingly small. According to the 1996 General Household Survey, a minuscule percentage of the population, just 0.0014, are living in gay or lesbian households. Such figures reflect two points that we never hear about from 'rights' campaigners. First, the number of gays is far lower than the one in ten figure often cited – even the more conservative one in 30 may be an over-estimate. Second, gay relationships tend to be less stable than heterosexual ones, as any glance at the hedonistic gay scene would confirm. Yet, in the face of such facts, our society is being urged to destroy any support for the traditional family.

Others on the left, apart from gay-rights activists, have joined the attack on traditional marriage. Marxists and radical feminists have seen the family as an instrument of both class and gender exploitation, a symbol of the capitalist patriarchy. Marx himself wrote in *The Communist Manifesto*: 'The bourgeoisie has torn away from the family its sentimental veil, and has reduced the family relation to a mere money relation. The bourgeois sees in his wife a mere instrument of production' (quoted in Gertrude Himmelfarb, *The Demoralisation of Society*), words that would echo today in any local authority 'women's unit' or university centre for women's studies. According to this analysis, women must be freed from the financial, emotional, and sexual dependence on men. Marriage is therefore seen as a form of enslavement. (The US feminist Gloria Steinem once said how difficult it was 'to mate in captivity'.) Enhanced benefits for lone parents, more public housing, an expansion of artificial insemination services, and a statutory right to pre-school childcare would help mothers to escape the oppression of married life. It has been suggested by some critics of traditional marriage that lone parenthood, as a properly supported condition, could acquire a new and possibly even desirable status in society. If it were made more economically attractive, it could challenge the existing social structure. It is a sad commentary on our times that such views have now come so close to realisation. We are now living in an increasingly matriarchal society, where the mother-and-child unit is replacing the traditional family, where men can be seen as nothing more than providers of sperm, where a husband is a financial handicap rather than a source of support.

Some social commentators argue that this does not matter. The family is not breaking down, but merely changing, they say. In a world of great technological advances, globalisation of information, unprecedented individual wealth, and new freedoms for women, we cannot expect the family structure to remain trapped in its Victorian past. Peter Alcock, the Professor of Social Policy at Sheffield Hallam University, holds to this view. In a commentary on the essays of the right-wing American Charles Murray (*Underclass, The Crisis Deepens*), Alcock argues:

'Of course, changes are going on in family structure in Britain; and, Murray is right, levels of illegitimacy are growing . . . But these are part of broader demographic and cultural shifts which reveal changing patterns of parenting but not necessarily the failure of it.'

This is the line adopted by so many theorists and academics in trying to assuage fears about the free-fall decline of the family in our society. Illegitimacy, single parenthood, fatherless families, multiple parenting, and marital instability are nothing to worry about. This is a bit like an accountant trying to explain to the Board of Directors that a turnaround from last year's large profit to this year's heavy loss represents nothing more sinister than a change in the pattern of trading.

The complacency of figures like Peter Alcock is inconsistent with a mountain of evidence about the damaging consequences of the decline of the traditional two-parent family. Teenage delinquency, increasing welfare costs, growing state bureaucracy, mental health problems, poverty, child abuse, adolescent indiscipline, and homelessness can all be blamed in part on our modernist destruction of the family. It has, however, been difficult to conduct a rational debate about these problems. Whenever any social commentators refer to them, the cultural pulpiteers respond with their hysterical mantras about 'the cruelty of attacking single mothers' and the dangers of 'imposing Victorian values'.

Yet it is precisely to lessen the burdens of lone parents that the traditional family should be revived. Bringing up children is an exceptionally demanding task but it is made easier when shared between a mother and a father. I can see nothing 'liberating' for women about giving them the entire responsibility for raising a family while men are free to act as they like. The exponential growth of single parenthood in the last twenty years has been 'liberating' for men, but not women. Trapped at home, often in dire financial straits, unable to work or have a social life, the source of all emotional support and discipline for the children, single mothers can have a brutally restricted and draining existence. To call on men to resume their role as responsible fathers in the home should not be portrayed as an 'attack' on single mothers but an expression of support for them. As one lone parent told the *Exeter Family Study* conducted in November 1994: 'Since my husband left, I have learnt that you are almost always better off with a husband even with problems.'

That *Exeter Family Study*, led by the Joseph Rowntree Foundation and the University of Exeter, exposed the fallacy behind the theory that family breakdown does not matter. Researchers looked at the lives of 'intact' (natural father and mother still together) and 're-ordered families' (involving lone parents, remarried couples, boyfriends, and stepfathers). They found that 'parents in re-ordered families, especially lone parents, were more likely to express concern about their children's current behaviour than those whose families remain intact.' Rates of truancy, psychosomatic disorders, difficulties with school work and a low sense of self-esteem were all higher in children of re-ordered families. Parents in re-ordered families commented on their children's awkwardness in company, and the stresses of access arrangements. In true *bien pensant* fashion, however, the researchers concluded that children from re-ordered families, like those of gay parents, experience these problems because of societal prejudice, not because of the inherent weaknesses of alternative family arrangements. So the answer is the inevitable 'awareness-raising' exercise. 'An important part of the school curriculum would be the acknowledgement of the pluralistic nature of modern life and the exploration of the many forms of the family in which children find themselves.' So our schools should actually be encouraging the acceptance of family breakdown.

The real prejudice that now exists, though, is against the traditional family, as the *Exeter Family Study* unwittingly reveals. 'Intact families were inclined to apologise for their ordinariness.' One family warned: 'You will find us very boring; we like each other and are thankful for what we have got.' This is the Britain of 1996, where happily-married families feel so uncomfortable about their situation that they want to apologise. Stability is now 'boring'. Divorce is cool.

Other research evidence reinforces the *Exeter* findings. One 1995 survey found that children of divorced parents were 'less emotionally stable, left home earlier, and were divorced or separated more frequently'. The number of children under the age of ten now being admitted to hospital for mental illness had increased by 50 per cent in the last three years, according to the Department of Health. Commenting on this finding, a headteacher of an inner-London school in Southwark said: 'Many parents are working harder, families are breaking up, children are being moved to other homes and some face violence and emotional abuse. We must recognise that more children are suffering at an early age.' The One Plus One research charity has found that 'on a variety of measures, the divorced are less healthy than their married counterparts . . . Divorced men are more likely to die from heart disease than married men. Admissions to mental hospitals are four to six times greater among the divorced than the married, and divorced people are four times more likely to commit suicide.'

Divorce is also a financial problem for the Government. According to One Plus One, £3.4 billion of taxpayers' money was spent in 1992 as a direct consequence of divorce, including £2.75 billion in welfare payments, £242 million in legal aid, £80 million for children in care and £165 million in NHS costs. In addition, it has been estimated that companies lose £200 million a year through absenteeism and low productivity as a result of marital splits. Then there is the huge welfare bill of more than £9 billion a year for lone parents.

Homelessness and poverty are also damaging consequences of family breakdown. The increased demand for housing arises not from population growth but from parents separating or teenagers leaving home, often as a result of a difficult new parental relationship. Between 1961 and 1993 the population of Britain rose by only 10 per cent.

Over the same period, there was a 41 per cent increase in the number of households. A recent study of local authority housing showed that more than 40 per cent of allocations made under the 1985 Homeless Persons Act went to lone parents. Lone parents may not be the lowest income group in Britain, as I pointed out earlier, because of the tax and benefit system. But their status traps many of them in comparative impoverishment without a job, since they would lose many of their benefits if they were to receive a full-time wage. In addition they have the problems of paying for childcare. The result has been the creation of a 'dependency culture' in which many lone parents exist entirely on state handouts. According to the National Council for One Parent Families, 72 per cent of one-parent families – 1,086,000 out of 1.5 million – were in receipt of income support in 1994. The General Household Survey classed 71 per cent of never-married single mothers as 'unemployed or inactive'. In 1993, 60 per cent of one-parent families were existing on less than half of average national income, compared to around a quarter of **all** couples with children.

Crime and delinquency are perhaps the most serious results of the instability of modern family life. In an environment without security or masculine role models, is it surprising that so many male adolescents have no concept of maturity or restraint? In the disordered household, where is the source of discipline? If parents act only on their own selfish impulses, how can they expect their children to be obedient and respectful? It is a remarkable lone parent who can continually manage to be both a figure of affection and authority to her children. This problem has been exacerbated, as I said in the last chapter, by the 'feminisation' of certain public services, especially teaching. Young boys from fatherless families can now grow up without seeing any men in positions of authority. The disappearance of jobs and apprenticeships in heavy industry and the growth of female-dominated service industries has further driven ill-educated male youths to the nihilistic fringes of society. Without the guidance of a father or any base in a strong family structure, they can drift into crime and violence. As the Labour MP Clare Short has warned: 'Boys of fifteen or sixteen get into a drop-out culture of the streets: they are sullen and rude. It is a very murky world and it leads to getting money illegitimately. You can see the potential disaster. We are storing up a social crisis.'

The *Cambridge Study into Delinquent Development* (1973) found that for children aged less than ten, the divorce and separation of their parents is associated with future delinquency. Research among boys with criminal records in Newcastle came to the same conclusion. Another study of high-crime areas of Glasgow found that 'traditional, child-rearing patterns of strict, working-class parents appear to offer children protection against delinquency.' As Norman Dennis, author of *Rising Crime and the Dismembered Family* has pointed out, a direct correlation can be made between crime and illegitimacy in the last half of this century. 'Thirty or forty years ago two features of everyday life in England began their extraordinary transformation, the results of which are now beyond denial. One was in the prevalence of criminal conduct. The other was in the attitudes and activities associated with family life.'

Adult men have been just as affected as youths by these changes. Before the modernist revolution in family structure, it was presumed that the responsibilities of fatherhood could reduce delinquent tendencies. The need to care for a wife and children would encourage maturity. Today, we can have no such confidence. The increasing reliance on the mother-and-child unit has helped to render men superfluous in the raising of families. So instead of demonstrating his manhood by his contribution to his family, the delinquent continues to do it through the aggressive methods of male adolescence: thieving, gang warfare, and sexual promiscuity. A research study by the Home Office last year found that Britain now has a new class of 'career criminals', young men who are no longer 'growing out of crime' as they reach adulthood. The study found that, by the age of twenty-five, almost a third of men said they had committed some sort of crime, excluding drug use and motoring offences. Contrary to the bleats of the liberal theorists, the report found higher rates of criminal behaviour among the children of disordered families. The authors feared that 'young men are finding it more difficult and taking longer to make the transition to adulthood. But with the declining number of young people in employment, the capacity for the world of work to provide a rite of passage for young males has diminished.' Our infantilised society has sanctioned the growth of a new generation of permanent adolescents, who have no sense of responsibility to either family or society.

The differing fortunes of the two largest ethnic groups in Britain illustrate this point. More than one in four black families is headed by a lone parent, compared to less than one in ten south Asian families.

The difference is even more graphic when examined in terms of mothers and children. While the vast majority of Asian mothers are married, fewer than three in ten black mothers under thirty have this status. More than 90 per cent of Asian children are raised by married couples. For Caribbean children the figure is just 46 per cent. And the consequences of these differences in family structure are all too clear. Five times more Asians are entering higher education than blacks. One in twelve new undergraduates is of Asian origin, far higher than their proportion of the population. In contrast, Afro-Caribbeans are disproportionately more likely to serve a prison sentence, rent their homes from the public sector, be excluded from school or be unemployed. If the Commissioner of the Metropolitan Police is to be believed, 80 per cent of muggings in inner London are committed by blacks. More than 60 per cent of young black men are without jobs. To our cultural leaders, this is evidence of the frightening racism in our midst. But if that is the case, why do these figures not apply to all non-white ethnic minority groups? If we are such a racist society, why are Indians more likely than whites to own their own homes, be employed in professional occupations, and have higher levels of educational achievement? After all, many south Asian migrants came to this country with far greater disadvantages than Caribbeans, such as a language barrier. The Asian tradition of the family is the answer. Stability, discipline, motivation, and respect for authority are the ingredients of the lives of most Asian children. In contrast, young blacks grow up in disordered families without male role models. Even the Caribbean tradition of the extended family, where relatives, if not the actual father, played a part in child-rearing, has not been translated to this country. The entire burden of raising the family too often falls on the mother alone.

What needs to change

While some of our cultural leaders cling to the notion that the pattern of family life is merely changing, not deteriorating, others have begun to see how disastrous their social revolution has been. Indeed, only a blinkered ideologue could deny that rising crime, indiscipline at school, homelessness, the loss of authority and drug-dealing are wholly unconnected to the breakdown of the traditional family. And the social revolution will gather pace as the breakdown continues. For the children of broken homes are less likely to be able to form stable relationships themselves. They are untutored in the interdependencies of family life. They have no model of stability which they can copy. Rates of divorce, illegitimacy, single parenthood and neglect of the elderly will worsen.

This is the cycle that has to be broken. But because of the climate of relativism, the hands of would-be reformers are tied. If all types of family arrangements (married couples, co-habiting, lesbian, one-parent, step-parents) are equally worthy of support, then it is impossible to favour the traditional unit. That would involve being judgemental about other relationships, the great social crime of our age. 'It is time to recognise that families come in all different shapes and sizes, and what matters is the validity of the family unit, and the closeness of the family unit, rather than how it is constructed,' says Labour's Shadow Health Secretary, Chris Smith, exposing the hollowness of some of New Labour's rhetoric about traditional family values. Afraid of making judgements, the amoral reformers have to fall back on demands for parenting classes in the national curriculum, more sex education, higher rates of child benefit for all parents, more government support services (such as drop-in centres, advice projects, toy libraries, training schemes), more counselling for parents, more parental leave and, above all, more subsidised childcare. The New Public Servants should, it is argued, also have their scope for action expanded, especially in youth work, social services and support for lone parents. In other words, the state should increasingly take over the role of nurturing, caring, and child guidance that was once deemed the responsibility of married parents. Far from shoring up the family, this sort of role for Government authorities can only further its collapse.

Even if it were not positively harmful, none of this activity reaches the fundamental problem: that traditional married family life is now an unattractive prospect. It brings increased financial burdens but is accorded little respect by the Government and its agencies. Despite its responsibilities, it has positive disadvantages in terms of access to housing, welfare benefits or low taxation. It is derided by large sections of the media. And it is a state that becomes ever easier to leave, thanks to relaxed divorce laws, legal aid, and the all-enveloping embrace of the welfare system.

The catastrophic breakdown of the family in Britain over the last thirty years has not been inevitable. If it had been, why has it not occurred to the same extent in the other countries of the European Union? Why is the rate of divorce in Britain so much higher than in Germany or Spain? Why is lone parenthood so much more common here than in Italy or Greece, where just one in twenty families with dependent children are headed by a single parent? The decline of religion in Britain is part of the answer. But deliberate changes in public policy have also been significant. It is time to reverse some of those changes. We must make the fiscal system work in favour of the traditional family instead of discriminating against it. I believe we should gradually phase out child benefit over the next decade and use this money, £6.6 billion a year, to increase married couples' tax thresholds and reintroduce a child tax allowance. At present, child benefit is indiscriminate and expensive, going at the same rate to rich and poor, married and unmarried. The money would be better used to help poor, working families. The changed tax rates for married couples should be large enough to lift out of direct tax those families with an income of less than £10,000 a year (little more than half of average male earnings). There should also be a tax allowance of £500 for each child, up to a maximum of £2,000 a year. As Patricia Morgan has suggested, we should also allow married couples to divide their combined incomes in two so they pay tax at lower rates and can gain from allowances. For example, a one-earner family with an income of £30,000 would pay the same tax as two single earners with £15,000 each.

There are other steps that a Government could take to reinforce its support for marriage. All that it requires is the courage to jettison the creed of non-judgementalism. In public sector housing, married couples with children could be statutorily given the highest priority on waiting lists, above single parents and co-habiting couples. Though young women may not deliberately become pregnant simply to get a council flat, they are certainly led to believe they will have few difficulties over accommodation when they reach motherhood. This situation should be ended. Rates of maternity pay could be made higher for married mothers. Paternity leave is important in encouraging fathers to play a fuller role in the home, but rights to such leave should be statutorily restricted to married fathers, thereby abolishing the bizarre practice that exists in some organisations, like my former council of Islington, where a mother 'can nominate anyone' for two weeks' leave when she has her baby. In school admission policies, priority could be given to the children of married couples, just as religious schools now give priority to church-goers. With regard to the NHS, I have earlier argued that all infertility treatment should be restricted to couples who have been married for three years. Since so many doctors now appear reluctant to make judgements about the provision of such treatment, they would probably welcome this establishment of such simple parameters. The disappearance of publicly-funded artificial insemination for lesbians and virgins – one of the more unsavoury phenomena of our times – would be a welcome consequence. Similarly, public agencies should treat the fostering or adoption of children by homosexual couples as a last resort, when the only alternative is local authority care, rather than the equivalent of life with a married family.

These changes would no doubt be denounced as a means of stigmatising those born outside marriage. But it is exactly this terror of disapproval which has helped to create an amoral wilderness in our society and precipitated the collapse of family life in Britain. Stigmatisation is one of the consequences of having a coherent code of morality. Where there is no disapproval, there are no values. Besides, the long-term problems of a society dominated by fatherless and disordered families far outweigh the immediate anxieties that arise over any lack of support for 'alternative' methods of parenting.

The proposed tax and benefit advantages of married life might slow down the divorce rate. Other steps are necessary. I have previously said that legal aid for divorcing couples should be abolished. It is quite wrong that the state should be subsidising, in such a direct way, the break-up of marriages, especially given the £3.5 billion cost of divorce to the Exchequer. Divorce legislation also needs to be tightened. No couple who have been married less than three years should be allowed to divorce, except in cases of domestic violence. If children under the age of ten are involved, the limit should be raised to five years. It is one of the ironies of the 1996 divorce law reform that, though it mouths the usual modernist platitudes about 'putting children first', it will actually undermine children by encouraging divorce through its 'no fault' procedures. If the welfare of children really is to come first, divorce should be made more difficult. Moreover, there should be no public funding for mediation counsellors, who are employed, under the 1996 Act, to achieve an 'amicable settlement' between separating couples, not to persuade them to stay together. Like legal aid, this amounts to a state subsidy for divorce. The money would be better spent on marriage-guidance counselling. Given that more than 90 per cent of teenage marriages end in divorce, the age limit for marrying should be raised from sixteen to twenty-one. Modern infantilised adolescence is no basis on which to take on the responsibilities of married life. The numbers are not insignificant. In 1993, 6 per cent of all women who married for the first time were under the age of twenty.

One of the reasons why men have found it so easy to evade their responsibilities as fathers is because the welfare state has taken over their role of providing financial support for their families. If they pay nothing in maintenance, their ex-wives and partners simply seek it from the Department of Social Security. It was to end this racket that, in 1993, the Government established the Child Support Agency, one of the most welcome measures of the last eighteen years of Conservative rule. The need for such an institution is a regrettable symptom of our irresponsible age. But few could dispute the soundness of the CSA's founding principle: that fathers should contribute to the care of their children. The first years of its operations have been dogged by controversy. There were demonstrations, debates in Parliament, claims from women's groups that vulnerable single mothers would be harassed by ex-partners, complaints of mismanagement and maladministration. It was argued that the formula for deciding the level of maintenance was too rigid. The CSA was accused of driving fathers to suicide. But most of the agency's problems stemmed from the simple fact that so many men were outraged at being held financially accountable for the first time and were determined to foul up the system. For me, there are few more pathetic sights in the nineties than middle-aged men marching against the CSA, and mouthing slogans about their 'right to a second chance'. What second chance did their children have? In the face of this adolescent hatred, the CSA is achieving remarkable successes. Last year it met its Government target of collecting £300 million in maintenance from absent fathers. It must be allowed to continue its work. One of the fundamental misunderstandings about the CSA has been the belief that it would lead to a sudden improvement in the incomes of single mothers. This was never going to be the case. Its aim has been to ensure that, where possible, fathers rather than taxpayers pay child maintenance.

The row over the CSA shows how far our society has lost sight of the most basic concepts about the duties of parents towards their children. MPs and the press degraded themselves by joining the vicious campaign against the agency and relaying the selfish whines of irresponsible fathers. The Liberal Democrats are still calling for the abolition of the agency, arguing that the courts should take over its role. Such a move would be prohibitively expensive, would line the pockets of family lawyers, and would ensure that only a dribble of cash reached deserted parents. In a civilised world we would not need the CSA, but we are far from that. If its demands provoke a limited form of social engineering, leading to greater caution from adults before they create or leave families, then so much the better.

State encouragement towards the revival of the traditional family can only be successful within the wider moral context outlined in previous chapters. By example and message, the Church, public servants, the media, schools and the monarchy all have a duty to uphold marriage. Instead of worrying about 'same-sex marriages' and the sanctity of homosexual relationships, the Church of England should be moving in the opposite direction, emphasising the importance of the Christian ideal. Nor do I think that the Church should cave in to demands that divorcees be allowed a full wedding service. It is no coincidence that in Roman Catholic Mediterranean countries, where the Church has adhered to traditions, the institution of marriage is stronger than in our largely secular society. The same is true of the strength of the family among Asians in Britain, where religious faith is still a powerful force. Westminster politics can also play a role. Instead of sneering at Tony Blair and John Major for introducing their wives on to political platforms, we should praise them for doing so. If demonstrations of marital affection were more encouraged, we might have less sleaze. When it comes to marital affection, no one has set a worse example than our Royal Family. It is remarkable to think that only forty years ago Princess Margaret felt compelled to reject a union with Group Captain Peter Townsend simply because he was a divorcee. We have travelled a long way since then. After the gruesome antics of the last sixteen years, Townsend would be welcomed as a pillar of stability. But as social commentators are only too keen to point out, in its familial discord, if nothing else, the House of Windsor is truly a reflection of modern Britain.

CHAPTER SEVEN

A Criminal Society

'When they get together they define their own rules. They live by a different set of values – they are totally amoral and have no remorse. The night they raped these girls they could have as easily played football, watched TV or gone bowling. Gang rape had no extra importance to them.' – Detective Inspector Jim Webster, speaking after the Old Bailey convictions of six gang members who abducted and repeatedly raped two fifteen-year-old girls.

'If my son had not been sent on safari to Africa and had money spent on him like water, he might not have thought he could have whatever he wanted. It spoilt him rotten and didn't prepare him for real life at all. Mark was better off in prison than he ever was when he was in the social services' care.' – Mother of Mark Hook, a persistent young offender sent on an eighty-eight-day safari holiday to Egypt and East Africa by Gloucestershire social services.

'We need to reassert adult authority over children and to do so through a compact which entitles them to our generous help in return for orderly and pro-social behaviour. Stressing rights without responsibilities is a recipe for the disorder we increasingly face. Removing responsibility from youngsters who know they are creating mayhem and writing off offences in the interests of diverting people from the judicial process is an abysmal way of promoting such a contract.' – Masud Hoghughi, Director of the Aycliffe Centre for Children and honorary professor of Psychology at the University of Hull, writing in the *Independent*, March 1993.

'Bridlington is not only overwhelmingly white but also overwhelmingly heterosexual in its values and leisure provisions.' – A member of the National Association of Probation Officers explaining its decision to cancel their annual conference in Bridlington in 1993.

'Why should I go straight and earn £100 a week when I can earn over £1,000 a day from crime?' – Jason Rouse, twenty-year-old who has admitted to more than two thousand thefts.

'Support to families where young people are offending is important. There is a need to ensure that the label of "offender" does not preclude the fact that such young people are seen as "children in need".' – *Children's Services Plan 1996–97*, Middlesbrough Council.

'I have become increasingly concerned about fashion in criminal justice being peddled as truth, ideology being clothed as social science, and most of all about the misery of good people in lawless places.' – Professor Ken Peace, Professor of Criminology, the University of Manchester, March 1993.

The growth of crime is one of the most powerful indicators of the crisis in our civic order. If civilisation were advancing in modern Britain, we would not have to endure the rising levels of violence and murder, the sense of lawlessness that exists on some inner-city estates, the loutishness on our streets, the growing incidence of gang warfare, and widespread anxiety over crime, particularly among the elderly. Nor would we have all the paraphernalia associated with a violent society: overflowing prisons, demands for identity cards, closed-circuit television in shops and town centres, record employment in the police and probation service, and record spending on our courts. The more uncivilised a society becomes, the greater the action required of the state to protect its law-abiding citizens. A brutalised penal code, however necessary, is a sign of social decay.

Over the last forty years, crime has risen inexorably in Britain, with only occasional decreases. In 1951 there were 1.2 recorded offences per 100 of the population. In 1994 there were 9.8. In the twelve months from June 1995 to June 1996, a total of 5.1 million crimes were recorded by the police, an increase of 0.4 per cent on the previous year. Research by the British Crime Survey indicated that the real level of crime could be twice as high, since many victims are reluctant to make a report to the police, even in some serious cases. In 1993, only about two fifths of violent assaults were recorded.

On the basis of police figures alone, crime has more than doubled since 1980, despite the tough rhetoric of Conservative ministers. The incidence of robbery has increased threefold. The number of acts of violence against the person has risen from 100,000 to 228,000, a figure which undermines the claims of certain sociologists that rising crime is largely a consequence of poverty and deprivation. Poverty might drive someone to theft, but surely not thuggery. In 1995, the Labour Party argued, with some plausibility, that the total cost of crime to individuals, businesses, local authorities and the Government had reached £20.4 billion. This sum included the £9.5 billion spent on the criminal justice system (£6 billion on the police, £1.6 billion on prisons, £1.4 billion on the courts and Crown Prosecution Service, and £500 million on the Probation Service) – the equivalent of £422 a year for each taxpayer. Labour further estimated that businesses lost £7.5 billion through theft and other offences, while the costs of the private security industry were put at £2 billion. In its report, Labour said that the total value of goods stolen every day in Britain is £10 million, or £3.5 billion a year, an increase of 62 per cent over the previous six years.

Other studies have reinforced the crippling costs of our modern crime wave. The Serious Fraud Office is now investigating fraud thought to be costing £5 billion. In 1993, arson caused £300 million-worth of damage. A senior police officer from Greater Manchester recently warned that juveniles commit some seven million crimes a year at a cost somewhere between £5 and £10 billion. The British Retail Consortium announced in 1994 that crime is costing shops £2 billion a year through direct thefts, write-offs, repairs, and security.

In parts of Britain, fear of crime is now endemic. Opinion polls show that crime is regarded as our most serious social problem, above unemployment. A survey by Exeter University of 24,000 teenagers showed that two thirds of girls and one third of boys live in fear of physical attack. Several MPs have reported growing trends in their constituency cases towards complaints about local criminal behaviour, vandalism, disruptive neighbours, superseding the traditional gripes about housing and social security. As a local councillor in Islington until 1994, I saw on one large estate in my ward the residents reduced to near despair by the violence of a large gang of youths, some aged as young as ten, who terrorised them, vandalised property, set fire to lifts and hurled abuse. When I worked as a constituency assistant to Harriet Harman, the fear that ran through the vast, system-built North Peckham and Gloucester Grove estates was almost palpable. I have always considered myself lucky in having suffered little crime in my adult life, especially as I spent much of it in North London. Yet, even with this good fortune, I have been beaten up twice, threatened with assault on several occasions, had two bicycles stolen, and been burgled once. In 1995, within four months of taking possession of my first car, a battered Metro, it had been stolen. Most thirty-somethings probably have similar or worse tales to tell. The response of most of our cultural leaders to this crisis has been shameful. Some have sought to deny there is a crisis at all, claiming that figures are unreliable or that methods of reporting have changed. We are told that, since only 6 per cent of all crimes involve violence, we should not be unduly anxious, as if burglary and car theft had little impact on our lives. Moreover, we are still talking about almost 330,000 violent incidents a year, hardly a trifling matter. Conservative Home Office Minister, David Maclean, complacently asserted last year that 'those who are often most worried about violent crime are least likely to be a victim of an attack.' Those most at risk are young men aged between sixteen and twenty-nine, he argued. This is a feeble argument. The reason why women and the elderly are apparently more secure is because, as a result of their justified anxieties, they take more precautions and are less likely to go out at night on their own. Did you ever see a drink-crazed granny walking down the street at 2 a.m. or arguing with a bouncer outside a nightclub?

A host of theorists, policy-makers, pressure groups and academics are indulging in a process of 'denial' – to use a therapeutic term – about levels of crime in modern Britain. It is the same approach that has been taken over the dismal standards of schooling or welfare dependency or the breakdown of the family: first deny the existence of a problem; second, when confronted with evidence, either dismiss it with some jargon about the 'unreliable methodology' or argue that the 'real problem' is 'lack of Government support'. It is understandable that our cultural leaders should be so wedded to this process. After all, they helped to create the amoral society. They do not want to admit that it has failed.

It is in this spirit that some argue that the current anxiety over crime is nothing more than one of our periodic 'moral panics', designed purely to whip up popular support for an authoritarian law-and-order policy. Aside from the fact that we might benefit from a little moral panicking, this claim is rarely put forward by those who actually live on crime-ridden estates. It is the poor, not the affluent, who suffer most from crime. And they are the ones with most to lose from theft, because they cannot afford comprehensive insurance policies. For a man earning £150 a week, the theft of his hire-purchased fourth-hand Nissan Bluebird is much more serious than the theft of a P-registered BMW from someone on £1,500 a week.

Another favoured tactic of the high priests of complacency is to claim that the problem is no worse now than it was in the past. Take a look at the studies of Gareth Steadman Jones into the Victorian underclass, they say. The criminal underworld of Bill Sikes and Fagin in *Oliver Twist* was as brutal as anything we have today. The very word yob is Victorian, being boy spelt backwards. Look at the urban gangs of thugs in the first years of this century, and the clashes between mods and rockers in seaside resorts of the fifties. Only thirty years ago, the Kray twins ran their protection racket across swathes of London, while the Metropolitan Police was riddled with corruption. The serial killers of today, like Sutcliffe and Nielsen, have their parallels in the forties through Christie and Heath. The episode on *Juvenile Crime* in the 1994 BBC series *Forbidden Britain* could be seen as part of this effort to explode the 'myth' of a past golden age of law-abiding Britain. The programme quoted from a 1916 report in the *Sunday Chronicle* about the 'terrorist' gangs of Glasgow: 'Each gang outvies the other in savagery and frightfulness. Ladies are held up and robbed; policemen are clubbed or cut with bottles when trying to take some of the ruffians to prison; and old men are beaten and left lying after their pockets have been gone through.' The programme also featured an interview with Larry Rankin, a member of the Beehive gang in Glasgow in the 1930s: 'The Gorbals was a very depressed area. It was rat-infested, bug-infested. You were unemployed. Working was a thing of the past . . . It was lack of money that was the trouble. As you grew older you wanted to get some for yourself. So we took cars and broke into shops and warehouses.'

If crime rates are higher now than in the 1930s, it is merely because we are a wealthier society and there are more goods available to steal. Both Nick Ross of *Crimewatch* fame and Polly Toynbee of the *Independent* have advanced this argument. After all, sixty-five years ago there were no television sets, mobile phones, computers, fax machines, microwave ovens or video-recorders. The average working-class home would have no car or telephone. Fashionable clothes and shoes would be a rarity. So, unlike today, there was little point in Larry Rankin and his friends raiding other homes in the Gorbals. They would have come away empty-handed.

Yet all these denials of a dangerous post-sixties crime explosion are unsustainable. Even if it were true (which it is not) that crime has not greatly worsened compared to earlier this century, this should hardly be a source of pride to our liberal theorists. It is not a test that they would accept in other areas of public life. Would they boast, for instance, that the number of homes with outside toilets is no higher than it was in 1930? Would they dismiss complaints about poverty by claiming that standards of living are no lower than they were during the Jarrow crusade? Would they argue that we should be delighted that rates of infant mortality have shown little increase over the last seventy years? Of course not, so why should crime be any different? If society were progressing, crime would be falling.

It is sometimes claimed by 'experts' that every age is nostalgic about some fictional crime-free era that was said to exist about forty years before its own. People are said, almost by their nature, to think their great-grandparents lived in safer times. Like so many other theories advanced by modernists, this is simply untrue. As I stated in the introduction, many Victorians were struck by declining criminality over the latter half of the nineteenth century. 'We have witnessed a great change in manners: the substitution of words without blows for blows without words; an approximation in the manners of different classes; and a decline in the spirit of lawlessness' reported the *Criminal Register* in 1901 (quoted in Gertrude Himmelfarb, *The Demoralisation of Society*). And here is G. Kitson Clark, in *The Making of Victorian England*, written in 1961: 'I believe that most people feel, possibly unconsciously, that somewhere an invisible line crosses history separating our relatively orderly, relatively humane, relatively well-policed society from the wilder, more savage, if more colourful society of the past.' He is expressing the exact opposite of the nostalgia theory. The present, to him, seemed a safer place than the past. For Kitson Clark was writing at the beginning of the sixties, before our amoral social revolution. He could hardly use such words today.

Crime statistics are the strongest proof that the theorists' complacency is unjustified. However much allowance is made for changes in reporting policy and policing methods, it is indisputable that there has been a staggering increase in all types of crime, including violence, since the late fifties. In the previous century, the crime rate had seen an early, swift decline. In 1857, the rate of indictable offences per 100,000 of the population stood at 480. By 1901 it had fallen to 201, a decrease of almost 50 per cent. As Professor Derek Beales has written:

'This was the period when the lawlessness of the early nineteenth century was effectively tamed. Although the range of indictable offences grew, as legislation invaded new fields, the number of trials in relation to population fell after the early sixties. In 1867 transportation, and in 1868 public executions were abolished, marking a further stage in the advance of humanitarianism and civilisation.'

The Victorian age was followed by a long period of stability. In 1931 the crime rate, at 400 per 100,000 of the population, was still lower than the figure of seventy years earlier. During the Second World War, it shot up to 900 per 100,000 in 1941, partly due to blackout and the stretched resources of the police. In 1955, the rate passed 1,000 for the first time. It was then that the exponential rise began. By 1960, it had reached 1,700 per 100,000. Ten years later it was 3,200 per 100,000. At the beginning of the Thatcher decade, the rate had risen to 5,100. When she left office in 1990, it stood at almost 10,000 crimes per 100,000 of the population – and has stayed at roughly this level over the last six years. It might have been an achievement by Kenneth Clarke and Michael Howard to prevent another increase of the crime rate. But any congratulations must be tempered by the knowledge that the rate of indictable crimes is now forty times higher than it was in 1901. Norman Dennis, in *Rising Crime and the Dismembered Family*, highlights several other statistics which illustrate the criminalisation of our society. In 1900, there was a total of 84,000 recorded crimes in Britain. In 1990, in the West End district of Newcastle-upon-Tyne alone, there were 13,500 recorded crimes, a rate of one for every third person. In 1970, there were 480 armed robberies in Britain. In 1991, there were 5,300.

All the amount of sophistry and weasel words cannot explain away such bald figures. If anything, rising crime levels make it less likely that incidents will be reported to the police, because they will be seen as trivial or impossible to resolve. Moreover, as society becomes more violent and amoral, so the definition of deviant behaviour becomes more narrow. A certain offence which, thirty years ago, might have been seen as a crime (e.g. shoplifting, drug abuse, being drunk and disorderly) might now be treated as a minor misdemeanour.

Such a trend is exacerbated by the growing pressure on the police to keep first-time and young offenders out of the criminal justice system. Cautions are one way to achieve this. In 1994, the police cautioned 210,000 people for indictable offences, some of which were serious. Of those charged with violence against the person, 11 per cent received a caution. In its annual report in June 1996, the West Midlands police admitted that more than 5,000 juveniles were cautioned. These cases had included two rapes and two street robberies at knifepoint. Three other teenagers had been cautioned for arson and 1,004 for wounding offences. In the county of Bedfordshire, near my home, it was reported in 1996 that, in the previous year, 46 per cent of those arrested for indictable offences had been let off with a caution. The unpunished crimes included 290 acts of violence, 12 robberies, 11 cases of indecent assault on girls aged less than sixteen and one case of rape. The use of such cautions puts into perspective the wails we hear from 'progressives' about the supposed harshness of our treatment of offenders. This point about differing attitudes towards deviance was cogently made by Jose Harris in his *Social History of England*, when he observed that, in 1913, a quarter of the males aged between sixteen and twenty-one serving prison sentences in London had committed such offences as gambling, using obscene language, drunkenness, and even riding a bicycle without lights:

'If late twentieth-century standards of policing and sentencing had been applied in Edwardian Britain, then prisons would have been virtually empty; conversely, if Edwardian standards were applied in the 1990s then most of Britain's youth would be in gaol.'

There are some theorists and academics who accept that crime has risen but see it entirely as a result of the deprivation within our society. Indeed, for radicals and sub-Marxists, spiralling crime, like industrial unrest or mass unemployment, can be a reassuring indicator of the failure of capitalism. And for their ideological soul mates, the New Public Servants, high crime becomes yet another excuse for more demands on the public purse – not, of course, to provide more police officers to protect the public but to expand their own payroll of counsellors, community workers, social services staff, welfare rights advisers, addiction co-ordinators, and youth justice workers, all of them geared towards 'addressing the needs' of offenders.

But unemployment and deprivation do not in themselves cause crime. If they did, the 1930s would have been one of the most crime-ridden of the decades, while the 1960s, an age of affluence and near-full employment, would have been almost crime-free. Moreover, the continuing extension of social security, subsidised public housing and free health services since the late forties should have led to a drop in crime. What I believe to be the fundamental cause of crime in our age is the loss of a moral code, and all that has followed from such a loss: the cult of self-gratification, the breakdown of authority, the collapse of the family and the absence of discipline. Unemployment and poverty will only lead to widespread crime when people do not feel constrained by any sense of responsibility to their families or their fellow citizens. The fourteen-year-old boy on an inner-city estate might want a new £60 pair of Nike trainers. If he has been brought up in a disciplined environment and learnt a sense of right and wrong, he would probably be willing to save up to buy them, earning money through a paper round or doing odd jobs for his parents or neighbours. But if he is used to having his every whim gratified and has never learnt the virtues of patience or sacrifice, he is far more likely to go out and steal them. Sadly, in the nineties, the latter scenario is all too common. Our cultural leaders have encouraged this development with their emphasis on victimhood and 'rights'. Since deprivation is seen as the main cause of crime, it logically follows that he who commits crime is one of society's deprived 'victims'. Anyone who feels their 'right' to affluence has been blocked can blame 'society' for not providing them with sufficient benefits or a well-paid job or a three-bedroom flat. They are therefore unlikely to feel much guilt over the theft of a new flat-screen TV. Why should that rich bastard have it when I haven't, goes the reasoning from the burglar, cheered on by the deprivation groupies, despite the fact that the 'rich bastard' might be earning just £250 for 50 hours work a week, while paying more than a third of his income in taxes to keep the burglar on DSS income support.

This cultural agenda is highly destructive to a civilised society. It undermines any sense of right and wrong. It portrays the police and the criminal justice system as 'enemies'. It weakens respect for property. It takes away incentives to work. It promotes the belief that criminals should not be punished, only helped.

The victim approach is seen at its starkest on the issue of race and crime. When Sir Paul Condon, the Commissioner of the Metropolitan Police, announced in June 1995 that, in the inner London area, 80 per cent of those mugged in the street had identified their assailants as Afro-Caribbean, he was subjected to a barrage of abuse. He was accused of racism, of ignoring the economic plight of the black 'community', of stirring up racial hatred, of using flawed data. After years of being told by 'experts' that, since police records are unreliable, we should rely on statements of the victims of crime, we were then informed that in this particular instance the evidence of the (mostly white) victims of muggings was tainted. 'Victims don't always get it right,' warned Professor Bob Reiner of the London School of Economics. Poverty was another predictable exculpation. Professor Jock Young of Middlesex University argued: 'Street robbery is the most amateurish crime and therefore generally committed by the poorest people. While they are likely to be black in inner London, they will almost certainly be white in Newcastle.' This is mathematically illogical. Afro-Caribbeans constitute nothing like 80 per cent of the poor in inner London. In not one inner-London borough does the entire non-white population, including Asians, constitute a majority. Some said that, even if true, the information should have been suppressed for fear of stirring up trouble. This argument could even be heard from anti-racists who usually like to peddle any statistics about the position of blacks in Britain. Others said that the 'most important issue' arising from Condon's figures was 'how British society is failing black people, and in this case black males'. Even some of those who had been mugged took this line. One resident of Hackney, who had been attacked by a twenty-eight-year-old black man, told the *Sunday Telegraph*: 'Since I was mugged I have given a lot of thought to why these crimes are committed by black men. I think they feel they have no opportunities. Part of me felt I deserved to be mugged because I have a decent job and want for nothing, whereas these guys are on the breadline.' Later, when his attacker was arrested and it was revealed that he had a £200-a-day cocaine habit and had spent much of his life in prison, 'I actually began to feel sorry for him. I felt this guy was just as much a victim as me.'

Why was he a 'victim' at all? No one forced him to have an expensive drug habit or rob people in the street. He ended up in prison entirely of his own choice. Yet so powerful is our modern 'victim' culture that an innocent man feels guilty over holding down a job and thinks he 'deserves' to be mugged. Could there be a sadder illustration of the warped values of our times? It is precisely this outlook that encourages criminals to believe they are justified in their actions. Thankfully, not everyone takes such a handwringing approach. Some, like Lord Scarman, author of the famous report into the 1981 Brixton riots, have recognised there is a genuine problem about the level of black street crime. If all the available evidence shows that one social group is responsible for committing 80 per cent of a certain crime in a certain area – far out of their proportion to the local population – then the police can hardly ignore this fact. That is why Sir Paul Condon approached the black community leaders in the first place, seeking their help to find a solution. The words of one of the world's best-known black leaders, the Reverend Jesse Jackson, put the knee-jerk reaction of the anti-racists in its proper context: 'There is nothing more painful for me,' he said in 1994, 'than to walk down the street and hear footsteps and start thinking about street robbery, then to look around and see someone white and feel relieved.' Sadly, few in Britain have shown the same honesty. Our public debates have become so bedevilled by political correctness that we are terrified of speaking openly, whether it be over mass single parenthood, or the treatment of AIDS, or plummeting literacy, or the incidence of street robberies. And some of the very people who should be interested in exposing the truth, academics and sociologists, are the ones waging a campaign to obfuscate it.

While railing about poverty, racial disadvantage, poor housing, and police provocation as sources of crime, the so-called 'progressives' have proved unwilling to address the collapse of universal morality. To do so, of course, would be to fall into the trap of making 'value judgements' about individual behaviour. Crime, they grandly argue, is far too complex a social and economic phenomenon to be subject to simplistic, dated notions about morality. In particular, they have proved reluctant to see any parallel between rising crime and the breakdown of the family, probably the most dangerous consequence of an amoral society. Yet rates of delinquency this century show a far closer correlation with the disintegration of family life than any other single factor. Through the Victorian era, illegitimacy gradually fell, as did the crime rate. The long period of civil order between the Edwardian age and the fifties coincided with a low rate of births outside marriage, rarely above 5 per cent of total births (compared to 32 per cent today) and a negligible number of divorces. As I argued in the last chapter, this is not surprising. The family unit is the means by which males have traditionally been socialised into civilised behaviour. As we are discovering in our fragmented age, it is not a task that can easily be performed by any outside agency, whether it be school or social workers or television. Lack of stability in domestic life also leads to a loss of security and discipline for children. The sense of interdependence that arises from warm familial relationships is missing from so many homes. Dr Swaran Singh elegantly summarised this problem in a letter to the *Independent on Sunday* in March 1993:

'In my two years in Britain I have been increasingly amazed by the futile debate over juvenile crime . . . Parenting has, for centuries, been an act passed across generations by elders who assume new social roles and responsibilities as another generation is born. But the concept of a shared cultural past, extending into a personal present, to ensure continuity with the future, is obsolete in the West, as lives are lived moment to moment, weekend to weekend. It is each for his own, with no relatedness to family, society or the world at large. Why blame children for taking what doesn't belong to them, when all we teach them is that everything exists for our pleasure, ours to exploit and discard?'

In the disordered or irresponsible family, there is often no concept of any boundaries on children's behaviour. Discipline is not something such children react against but something they have never experienced. One teacher told last year's conference of the Professional Association of Teachers that staff 'find children arriving in reception classes who show no indication of ever having been taught how to act like social beings.' Inconsistency is another feature of disordered homes, where children have no idea what reaction their behaviour might provoke. It could be a thrashing, or indifference, or even a reward simply because the parent is feeling guilty. Again, this reinforces the absence of any code of right and wrong. Another characteristic of such households is the way the television and videos can become permanent 'child-minders' in place of a loving mother and father, thus weakening both the ability to communicate with adults and the sense of any internal relationship within the home. Masud Hoghughi, the director of Aycliffe Centre for Children, whom

I quoted in the introduction to this chapter, is especially powerful on this point:

> 'Parents' casual relationships provide children with confused role models. Fatherless families, increasingly common, are particularly prone to producing angry and violent children. This is where video nasties and television come in. Children who have no internal boundaries rely on external stimulation to guide their behaviour to what is and is not acceptable.'

Again, in a similar vein to the earlier argument about unemployment and deprivation, it is not video nasties in themselves that cause crime; rather, it is the absence of any moral boundaries that allows them to exert their influence.

The breakdown of the family over the last forty years might not have had such serious consequences for the crime rate if our cultural leaders had been more willing to uphold the rule of law. But the moral relativism which has weakened family values has also undermined the ability of the criminal justice system to protect our citizens. At the very time when we most needed a morally confident judiciary, and probation service, in order to compensate for the dissolving family structures, we have instead been given equivocation, leniency, and pusillanimity. As the crime wave mounted from the sixties, so policymakers urged more 'understanding' for the criminal, the last thing that was needed. The higher the crime rate, the greater the indulgence. We were told that punishment was counter-productive, that prisons were expensive 'universities of crime' and that criminals needed support, not admonishment. We abandoned the traditional Christian ethic, that a sinner (offender) can only be forgiven (rehabilitated) if he shows repentance (remorse) for his actions. Indeed, since crime was no more than a symptom of society's failure to meet all the material needs of its citizens, it was wrong to make the criminal accountable at all, especially where property crime was involved. In this atmosphere, to explain the cause of a crime was to justify it, thereby destroying the moral force of any punishment.

Over the last three decades, this liberal anti-punishment ethos has been furthered by a band of noisy pressure groups and professional associations, like the Howard League for Penal Reform, the Prison Reform Trust, the National Association for the Care and Resettlement of Offenders, Justice, and the National Council for Civil Liberties, all of them dedicated to explaining the alleged futility of tough sentences for offenders. The pressure groups were joined by the new schools of criminology in universities and polytechnics, who sometimes shared this enthusiasm for sociological explanations (justifications) for most criminal action. As in faculties of sociology, the study of class and race discrimination has often been at the forefront of their work. A number of psychologists and other scientists also signed up to the new ideology, telling us that delinquent behaviour was the result of 'psychiatric disorders' or ill-defined medical conditions. Therapy, counselling and drug treatment were said to be the most effective ways to combat crime. Again, the offender, no matter how brutal his actions, is absolved of responsibility, while the emphasis of the justice system is focused entirely on his supposed 'needs' rather than any duty to protect the public. In an appalling case in 1994, Jason Mitchell, a disturbed twenty-four-year old, was released from mental hospital when a psychiatrist decided he was 'a pleasant young man with no malice' and that 'no useful purpose would be served' by his continued detention. Mitchell had been sent to mental hospital in 1990 after trying to kill a cleaner with a baseball bat. On his release into the community, he immediately strangled an elderly couple, then visited his own father, murdered him, dismembered the body with a hacksaw and hid the head and limbs in bags in an attic. When he was caught by the police three days later, he expressed no remorse, 'other than that he had been arrested, thus ending his ambition to kill again.'

The liberal approach has probably been seen at its worst in probation and social work, where too many practitioners seem more interested in reforming society than criminals, or, in the words of one former senior probation officer, 'regard delinquency as a function of the class struggle'. The indulgent treatment of juvenile offenders by social services departments – in the name of rehabilitation – has rightly become a national scandal. Some of the worst cases, like 'safari boy' Mark Hook and globe-trotting Jason Cooper, have already been mentioned in this book. But they are only part of a nationwide trend. In 1993, for example, Southwark Council decided to send a sixteen-year-old boy to the Caribbean for two weeks while on bail accused of arson. In October of that year, within a month of returning from a £2,000 trip to Portugal organised by Shropshire County Council, a fifteen-year-old boy was convicted of burglary, theft and interfering with a car. In October 1996, Gloucestershire, the council responsible for the Mark Hook outrage, was in trouble again for sending a thirteen-year-old boy, charged with assault, on a month-long canal trip at a cost of £4,400.

Such treatment of offenders ignores one of the basic principles of human behaviour, that people are drawn to activities which give pleasure and avoid those which cause pain. A teenager who finds himself rewarded for committing serious offences has actually been given an incentive to commit them again. The social-work progressives might use therapeutic language about 'building self-esteem' or 'constructing new relationships' but, if there is no concept of punishment or disapproval, such schemes are bound to be counter-productive. Indeed, in one local-authority area, the rewards for delinquency are quite explicit. The Intensive Supervision and Support Programme, started in 1995 and run by Kent County Council and the local police, claims to 'focus more professional help and resources on young offenders than ever before.' Under the scheme, 'social workers devise an individual programme for each young offender and give them quick, preferential treatment.' They are therefore given top priority for housing, for training places, and for drug-rehabilitation. 'It's no good saying to a young person that we'll get you training in six months' time. That's a key theme, immediacy, urgency,' said one of the 'Youth Justice' officials in charge of the programme. Quite so. We cannot expect patience or self-control from our infantilised criminals. There is even a contract 'to avoid complaints of harassment' from offenders. This policy reeks of appeasement of young offenders. As one magistrate and psychologist recently put it: 'I have marvelled at the way those responsible for making the rules have flouted all known and proven learning principles, thus encouraging criminality in our society.'

The probation service is also infused with the social services' ethos. This is because, from 1974 until last year, a social-work qualification – usually a diploma in social work (DipSW) – was an absolute requirement for entry to the service. It would be hard to find a less suitable form of training for the work of probation officers, which includes steering ex-prisoners away from crime, providing courts with advice on sentencing, and overseeing community service orders. Peter Coad, a retired senior officer whose twenty-eight years of service from 1960 to 1988 covered this period of change, has described how, from the seventies, political correctness came to dominate the thinking of social work and probation tutors. 'Responsibility for the public at large was abdicated and probation officers soon became part of the defence advocacy with little regard to the consequences. To many, control was seen as oppression, and the state generally was regarded as the enemy of the criminal classes.'

These are not the views of some lone maverick. Other probation officers shared his dismay. Ronald Lewis, who also joined the service at the beginning of the sixties, felt that 'the fight against the individual's criminality was abandoned and replaced with the fight against punishment.' The probation service adopted other characteristics of social work: the pseudo-professional management jargon of 'action plans' and 'core values'; the politicisation of representative bodies, like the NAPO (National Association of Probation Officers), which became another section of the ululating penal reform chorus (it is telling that Mary Honeyball, the current General Secretary of the Association of Chief Officers of Probation, was previously the head of Gingerbread, the pressure group for one-parent families); the fixation with issues of discrimination (to such an extent that, as the introduction to this chapter showed, innocent Bridlington was dropped as a conference venue in 1993 by NAPO because it was deemed 'racist and heterosexist'). Just as the massive expansion of social services departments failed to reduce the incidence of the social ills they were meant to alleviate, so a growth in the probation payroll coincided with a record increase in crime. Between 1981 and 1994, the number of staff in the service increased from 12,000 to 17,000.

By the early nineties the Government had become increasingly anxious about the anti-punishment culture of the service. In 1994, a major Home Office review was established. This found that some of the social-work training amounted to 'a crusade for social reform which led to courses being more concerned with ideology than with teaching skills for dealing with offending behaviour.' The Review Team also uncovered criticism within the probation service that many courses had 'an unhealthy preoccupation with anti-discriminatory practice which led some recruits to have an unbalanced approach both in their work and their behaviour as employees.' The team was also concerned about the disproportionate number of female, young, unmarried and ethnic minority recruits, a finding mentioned in the chapter on the loss of authority. 'It is becoming unusual for older men to join the service,' the team warned. Acting on the recommendations of the review, the Government abolished the requirement to hold a social-work qualification. Instead, the fifty-five probation services can now recruit directly and provide training through a range of work-related programmes.

This is to be welcomed. But it will take more than a change in entry rules to achieve the cultural shift that is necessary to return the probation service to its former role of protecting society. The 'anti-oppressive' dogma still predominates, as is illustrated by the list of 'core competencies' (jargon for essential knowledge and skills) for probation officers, agreed in 1994 between the Home Office, the Central Probation Council and the Association of Chief Officers of Probation. The list includes the following: 'labelling theory'; 'multi-dimensional nature of individual needs'; 'basic knowledge and understanding of descriptive statistics, including those reflecting discrimination in the criminal justice system'; 'the needs of individuals and groups who experience disadvantage or discrimination'; 'structural, institutional and personal discrimination and its effects'; 'research on discrimination in the criminal justice system'; 'the needs of the vulnerable, disadvantaged and stigmatised groups'; 'cycles of deprivation, loss and change'; 'countering stigmatisation, discrimination, alienation, scape-goating and institutionalisation'; 'identifying learning needs and objectives'; and 'theories and concepts of anti-discrimination and their relevance to supervision'. Where is the idea of controlling crime in the face of this flood of theoretical posturing?

I have gone into some detail about the changing nature of the probation service because I feel it exemplifies the destruction of moral certainties in the criminal justice system. Nowhere on that list of 'core competencies' sent to me by the Association of Chief Officers of Probation did I see any reference to making moral judgements or protecting the public. The world is seen entirely from the viewpoint of the offender.

What needs to change

The 'experts' who dreamt up these competencies adhere to the professional orthodoxy that crime is a deeply complex sociological and economic phenomenon, far too difficult to be understood by the general public. From their redoubts in social-work academe or pressure-group politics, they sneer at 'simplistic' demands that criminals should be held accountable for the damage they cause to society. Dressing up their ideological convictions as 'new research', they cloak their unsubstantiated theories with the status of 'professional' wisdom. Every new Government initiative on crime is dismissed as 'unworkable' or 'reactionary'. Common sense is an irrelevance. They are extreme pessimists, believing that there is nothing we can do to reduce the crime rate until the arrival of a truly 'progressive' Government committed to full employment, a hugely expanded welfare system, and a gargantuan network of New Public Servants.

But their bluff has been called by Michael Howard, the first Home Secretary in more than thirty years to challenge the notion that imprisonment for offenders should always be avoided if possible. And what has been the result of his tough approach? Contrary to the forebodings of the experts and pressure groupies, we have seen the largest fall in the crime rate since 1945. In 1992, 5.6 million offences were recorded by the police – the highest number ever. By 1996, the figures had fallen to 5.1 million, a fall of 10 per cent over four years. Just as the sophists had previously tried to explain away spiralling crime as nothing more than a panic, now, in the face of Howard's comparative success, they try to dismiss this fall as illusory. This does not wash. The methodology of recording crime has remained much the same over the last decade. Moreover, in official police figures, the crimes which have shown the sharpest fall, burglary and vehicle theft, are the ones most likely to be reported, if only for insurance purposes.

The overall rate of crime, particularly of violent offences, still remains far too high, more than ten times that of the mid-fifties. It is therefore vital to continue with the current rigorous approach. Minimum statutory sentences on serious repeat offenders are to be welcomed, as are the new secure training units for juvenile delinquents and the restrictions on automatic parole. We are told by the penal progressives that such a policy is 'inhumane'. But what is 'humane' about failing to punish young thugs who terrorise estates or brutal husbands who beat up their wives? Is it 'caring' to be unconcerned about the savings of pensioners? Moreover, imprisonment need not mean brutal incarceration. Prisons should restrict liberty, not impose cruelty. Rehabilitation should be a vital part of any regime, enhancing the offenders' chances of taking a constructive role in society when released. The new 'boot camps', with their emphasis on training and their classes in developing personal responsibility, show what can be done within confinement. We should be increasing, rather than cutting, prison education programmes. In the longer term they can prove cost-effective. There are two caveats, however. First, for any programme of rehabilitation to work, the prisoner must want to reform. The mistake of too many liberals has been to ignore the motivation of criminals. Second, rehabilitation schemes must never become substitutes for punishment. That is why the wretched 'safari trips' for juvenile offenders have usually been such expensive failures.

We hear much about the dangerous size of the prison population and the poor conditions that result from over-crowding and falling staff-to-prisoner ratios. But the solution is to increase spending to match the number of prisons. It would be the logic of the madhouse to formulate a sentencing policy around the number of prison places that are available at any given moment. It is also foolish to exaggerate the current cost of the prison service. At £1.7 billion, the sum is barely half of our net contribution to the European Union. In a society racked by crime, it is grotesque that we spend almost as much on legal aid as we do on prisons. The administration costs alone of the Department of Social Security, at £4.3 billion, are more than two and a half times as high as the entire prison bill. We employ more officials at the Inland Revenue, 65,000, than staff in the prison service, 38,000. There are six times as many social services employees as prison officers in this country. Nor is our prison population, at 58,000, overly large in comparison to other European states, as is often claimed by the penal reformers. In proportion to the crime rate, which surely must be the determining factor, we are in the middle of the European table. Given the £20 billion annual cost of crime, a large increase in prison expenditure is more than affordable. New prisons need not be expensive. Disused army camps, which already contain an in-built level of security and are usually at a distance from residential areas, could be used for the purpose.

One of the arguments advanced by liberal theorists against prison is that criminals are more deterred by the chances of detection than the harshness of the punishment. It is true that detection and clear-up rates are disappointingly low. According to British Crime Survey, only about one in twenty crimes are cleared up and just under one in thirty results in a conviction. But the liberal theory only holds good if criminals believe they will be punished once caught. If they have nothing to fear from the criminal justice system, the rates of detection are an irrelevance. Sadly, this is still too often the case. I have earlier referred to the absurdity of handing out cautions to serious offenders, even rapists. Giving second and third cautions makes the punishment appear meaningless and the police foolish. Thankfully, this is another liberal policy that the Government has restricted. A look at the overall national crime figures for 1994, published in the latest edition of *Social Trends* by the Central Statistical Office, emphasises the need for a tougher policy. Of the 39,100 offenders sentenced for 'violence against the person', 22 per cent received a discharge, 17 per cent were fined, 32 per cent were given a community sentence, 20 per cent were placed in prison custody for less than five years and just 2 per cent received a prison term of more than five years. Only 11 per cent of 124,500 convicted of 'theft and handling stolen goods' received any prison sentence whatsoever. Only a third of burglars were placed in custody. The need for the new policy of minimum sentences on serious offenders has been further demonstrated by Home Office figures which show that in 1994 the average sentence passed on burglars with seven or more convictions was just eighteen months; a quarter in this category received no prison sentence at all. Spending more on prisons may even be more cost-effective as a deterrent than increasing the numbers of police officers. There is little evidence that a few more 'bobbies on the beat' has any effect on crime levels.

Another myth spread by the anti-prison lobby is that community sentences and probation orders are more effective than prison in stopping re-offending. There is no evidence to back up this claim. Figures released in 1995 showed that 54 per cent of ex-prisoners were reconvicted of a serious offence within two years of their leaving jail, compared to 56 per cent of those given a community service order and 54 per cent of those put on probation. Even the Prison Reform Trust, one of the Tory Government's most vociferous critics, said in its 1993 report *Does Prison Work?*: 'Despite the claims of the probation service, there is little evidence that probation and community service are more effective than prison in preventing re-offending.' The figures mentioned are actually biased against prison, since they compare rates from the **beginning** of a community sentence with those from the

end of a prison sentence. No prisoner, of course, can commit a crime against the public while he is incarcerated. This is not some cheap debating point. The primary aim of any criminal justice system must be the protection of the public. Only prison can achieve this goal with any certainty.

In reality, the figures on the effectiveness of punishment in the community may be even lower than stated. Given that only about 5 per cent of crimes are ever cleared up (the conclusion of the British Crime Survey), a large proportion of those on probation or community service must be reoffending without being detected. Moreover, research has shown how easy it is to evade the requirements of a community or probation sentence. Many offenders simply do not report for work, or disappear to another town. Neither the police nor the probation service have the time or resources to take action against them.

Alternatives to prison for serious offenders have been failures. Too often supposed 'punishment in the community' is no more than a mild inconvenience to the offender, if he can be bothered to complete his sentence. Yes, we should be understanding, but only if the criminal has shown an inclination to reform. Over the last three decades we have demonstrated indiscriminate clemency, without regard to the motivation of the individual or the needs of the public.

The story of the collapse of an ecological village community set up by environmental campaigners, radicals and Utopians on a derelict site in Wandsworth in 1994 is a fascinating example of the way liberal, 'anti-punishment' values can destroy a society from within. Initially the community, called *Pure Genius* after the Guinness company which owned the site, flourished with about 500 people building their own homes, growing their own crops and establishing an education and community centre. But because the site was open to anyone, anti-social elements began to arrive. Vandalism, drunkenness and aggression became problems. 'It is amazing how few pissheads it takes to wreck somewhere,' said one woman who lived on the camp, words that could be echoed by the residents of many an inner-city estate. Yet, because of the deep liberal ethos of the community, there was a reluctance to send anyone violent off the site. Eventually, the community began to implode, riven by discord. George Monbiot, one of Britain's leading environmental campaigners and one of the organisers of *Pure Genius*, was candid about the reasons for its failure:

'The most critical decisions about what behaviour is tolerated and whose actions merit expulsion were fudged. This incapacity was institutional – it is almost impossible to exclude people when exclusion depends upon their consent.' Monbiot further explained that the open-access policy was disastrous: 'As anyone could turn up, exploit goodwill and disturb the peace with little danger of suffering any consequence other than a hangover, the social commons were gradually eroded.' The *Pure Genius* experience could almost serve as a textbook case of what happens when a society refuses to punish wrongdoers.

Just as the eco-organisers should have expelled the destroyers of their community, so we have to take out of society those who would destroy our own civic order. We must therefore stay in the direction the Government has set, handing out prison sentences that actually fit the crime. Thankfully, a change of Government at the next election is unlikely to lead to a change in prison policy. Tony Blair's admirable Shadow Home Secretary, Jack Straw, who grew up on an inner-city estate, has been almost as trenchant as Michael Howard about the need to deal appropriately with hardened criminals. And this is the key point. A tough stance on prisons is not about criminalising huge swathes of the urban poor – as some of its critics claim. Most crime is the responsibility of a few individuals, usually male and young. One estimate is that around half of all crime is committed by just 5 per cent of all males aged between fourteen and twenty-five. In November 1996, police in Northumbria identified fifty-eight youngsters officially responsible for more than 1000 crimes in Newcastle. Between them, there have been 833 arrests. One boy, aged fifteen, has been arrested almost 70 times since 1992 for crimes ranging from car theft to petty vandalism. Commenting in April 1993 on the cases of four teenagers who between them had committed more than 750 offences, Dan Crompton, the Chief Constable of Nottinghamshire warned that 'punishment within the community could become punishment of the community.' Unless they are properly punished, such delinquents will continue to laugh at the law.

While we must be severe with persistent and dangerous criminals, we should also recognise that prison is inappropriate for many offenders, like fine defaulters, or minor tax evaders. The largest single category of female prisoners consists of women who have not paid their TV licences, exactly the sort of offence that merits a community sentence since they represent no threat to the public. Removing the inadequate and the simply impoverished from prisons would create more space for the violent and recalcitrant. It is a perverse system that sends a poll tax protester to prison and lets a rapist off with a caution.

Such contradictions have become part of the process of criminalising society. As our civilisation has become increasingly disordered – as a result of the decriminalisation of recidivists – so our political leaders, in their desire to respond to public anxiety, invent new categories of law-breakers. Unwilling to concentrate the protective arm of the state on the real criminal threat, they propose an ever larger number of offences, and ever more punitive action against harmless malcontents and pleasure seekers. So we have the Criminal Justice Act, criminalising political protesters, environmental activists and New Age travellers. The extravagant action against the Newbury by-pass protesters was especially pointless, given that they were motivated, not by greed, but by their conservative love of the English countryside. We have expensive police clampdowns on raves. We have fathers held for questioning over physically disciplining their sons. The demands for extensions of the law grow louder as confidence in the criminal justice system grows weaker. We are told we need new laws on stalking, on handguns, on motorway speeding, on drug-taking, on noisy neighbours, on drink-driving, on racial harassment, on car boot sales, on censorship of the internet. Name a social problem and you will find some pressure group lobbying for it to be made illegal. All these demands have three things in common. First, they would waste police and court resources without making society more civilised. Second, they would give yet more encouragement to the expansion of litigation. As usual, it would be the pseudo-victims who would benefit most. Third, if they do involve a genuine threat to the social fabric, there will usually be adequate cover in the existing law. Creating a new offence would therefore only be a public relations exercise. For instance, what would a specific criminal offence of racial harassment achieve? We already have laws to deal with any thug who uses physical violence, firebombs a home, or hurls abuse.

We should be moving in the opposite direction, reducing the scope of the criminal law so the police and justice system can better focus their efforts. The possession of drugs, from cocaine through to cannabis, should be decriminalised. At present, as I have said before, we have the most ineffectual schizophrenic position on drugs. On one hand, we demand 'war' against the drug barons and portray dealers as worse than murderers. We speak mournfully of the damage that drugs cause in our society, and demand life sentences for those in the drugs trade. Ecstasy, heroin, and cocaine are seen as killers, despite the tiny number of people who die from their use. On the other hand, we have a pathetic, non-judgemental approach towards drug-takers. We subsidise needle-exchange schemes and detoxification centres. We pay the amoral New Public Servants to act as 'substance misuse co-ordinators' and 'drug project facilitators'. We have 'drug awareness' lessons in schools. This contradictory, twin-track policy should be abandoned. One of its absurdities is the idea of the vicious drug-pushers feeding on innocent users. In reality, a large number of users are also minor dealers. It is one of the ways they fund their habits. Another of its absurdities is its sheer ineffectiveness. Despite all the rhetoric and the Leah Betts 'sorted' campaigns, drug use and drug profits continue to grow. It is time to inject a sense of personal responsibility into the debate. We should no longer legislate against foolishness. After all, the consumption of alcohol and tobacco causes tens of thousands more deaths, and both substances, rightly, remain legal. If people want to take drugs, that should be their own decision. By legalising drugs we would, at a stroke, wipe out one of the most lucrative markets for criminal activity, while reducing the demands on the police. At present, a large proportion of our teenagers are technically criminalised, but there is very little we do about it.

We have the same schizophrenic approach to homosexual activity. There are now two very different types of public servant hanging around gents' toilets. First, there is the undercover police officer, hoping to boost the local station's arrest statistics by enticing some unsuspecting cottager into dropping his trousers and then charging him with gross indecency. Second, there is the 'cottaging and cruising project facilitator', subsidised by the local health authority or district council, dishing out the condoms to the trouser-dropper before his arrest: PC Plod and PC Worker, united in a pointless misuse of public money. Both activities should cease. In another decriminalising move, the age of consent for gay sex should be lowered to sixteen. If you have got this far in the text, you will know I am not an egalitarian. But what is the point of arresting a seventeen-year-old boy for having sex with a twenty-two-year-old man, when he would have committed no offence if the gender of his partner had been different? The police have better things to do with their time.

None of this contradicts the central thrust of this book, an appeal for a return to morality. As I have argued elsewhere, the public's morals are not decided by legislation. When men are restrained from deviant behaviour solely by the law then civilisation is on the verge of breakdown. In the relatively crime-free Britain of the pre-sixties, it was not the fear of police and courts that prevented citizens acting against the criminal law; it was their own internal moral imperatives, based largely on Christian ethics. In our amoral society, we are fast losing any sense of what it is to be a 'good man', or, to use an unjustly discredited term, 'a gentleman'. Our cultural progressives can only think of that word in terms of class and wealth. That is why they despise it. But they are wrong. An unemployed road-sweeper might be a gentleman, whereas a peer of the realm might not. The Marquis of Blandford certainly is not one. It depends on how you treat your fellow citizens, whether you have any empathy with them. The true gentleman will have an innate sense of dignity. Because of his own moral outlook, he will strive to act honourably. He has too much self-respect to descend into anti-social or destructive behaviour, no matter what his circumstances. As Shakespeare wrote in *As You Like It*: 'Let gentleness my strong enforcement be.'

I would say that, in modern Britain, Paul McCartney, Glenn Hoddle and Tony Blair could be classed as gentlemen. Though they are from different backgrounds, they all exude courteousness, and responsibility. Yet it is precisely because of these qualities that they are often derided as bland or overly serious. A recent poll disclosed that many women dislike Blair because they feel he is 'too religious'. So faith has become a defect in our secular world. In place of the gentleman, we have elevated the chancer, the womaniser and the rebel as the new heroes of our age. Even the criminal can enjoy the adulation of celebrity status, as Howard Marks and Ronnie Biggs would testify. They're good lads, really, just having a laugh. At the most local level, in schools and housing estates, the gangster and the juvenile offender are often seen as heroes – one reason why the Government's plans to publish the names of young criminals is doomed. Only by recapturing our sense of right and wrong, of true gentlemanly behaviour, can we break this culture in the long term. It is, after all, men who are responsible for most of the crime in our society.

There are, however, still other steps we can take to reduce criminality, apart from sentencing and actual changes in the law. I have previously mentioned the need to improve the jury system so that it reflects the wisdom of experience, not the whims of those with time on their hands. We also need to speed up the way the courts handle criminal cases. So slow are the present procedures that almost a quarter of the prison population is currently awaiting trial. One method could be to impose strict deadlines on the provision of criminal legal aid; this would give an incentive for the defence team to ensure the case is completed by a certain date, otherwise they would not get paid. The decriminalisation of many offences would also lessen the burden on the Crown Prosecution Service, which would mean they would not have to drop so many actions on cost grounds. We should also divert some of the resources saved from dropping the so-called 'drugs war' into strengthening the CPS, so it attracts a higher calibre of recruit and expands its numbers of lawyers.

Despite some of my earlier reservations about misplaced business jargon and the encroachment of the compensation culture, I believe that the police force has remained one of our more successful public institutions. It is a tribute to their courage that, in the face of much abuse and an unprecedented crime wave, the vast majority of police officers in this country remain unarmed – and, according to the last Police Federation ballot, want to keep it this way. Thankfully, the creed of non-judgementalism does not appear to have yet seriously infected the force. In my dealings with police during my time in local government, I was always impressed with their authority and common sense. As a result of the higher pay scale introduced in the early eighties, the standard of senior police officers is probably higher than it has ever been.

I referred in this chapter to the problems of the probation service. The steps taken to reform the training of probation officers were vital. We need now to recruit more experienced men into the service, for the swelling ranks of juvenile offenders need male models. There are few of our public services where the concept of equality is more inappropriate. Indeed, to borrow the language of the ideologues, the probation service should 'reflect the gender profile of the community it serves'. The reductions in the armed forces and the 'downsizing' of corporations provide a pool of mature labour. Freed from the usual dogma about deprivation, such staff would be more willing to confront offenders and make judgements about their destructive behaviour. We have had a little too much sympathy for offenders in the last two decades. In our morally strengthened culture, the needs of society must be paramount.

CHAPTER EIGHT

An Army of Illiterates

'You can't teach about Standard English without talking about the power structures of society. That's the way to empower kids.' – Ken Jones, lecturer at the University of London's Institute of Education, speaking at an Oxford Conference in 1991.

'Teaching Shakespeare is arse-achingly boring.' – Terry Furlon, Chair of the National Association for the Teaching of English, quoted in the *Guardian*, March 1991.

'As every university teacher knows, the average quality of education that undergraduates receive in all but a handful of universities has declined significantly and this has been disguised by an, albeit unwilling, reduction in degree standards.' – Gordon Graham, Regius Professor of Moral Philosophy at Aberdeen University, writing in the *Daily Telegraph*, 10 July 1996.

'My ten-year-old daughter currently attends a state primary school and I have to say I am appalled at the standards – or lack of them. Because it has a high proportion of Black and Asian children, the school seems to feel it's more important to teach Punjabi, Urdu and – I kid you not – Jamaican Patois than it is to teach Standard English. Teachers admit they are reluctant to correct children when they speak bad English because the school "recognises their multi-cultural diversity" and doesn't want to be élitist.' – Letter from Manchester parent to the black newspaper, *The Voice*, January 1996.

'It is time to question our so-called "progressive" methods. A much more sensible approach is needed to teaching mathematics. We must not be afraid to say a pupil's work is wrong, because it is so difficult to correct misconceptions introduced at an early age.' – Professor David Hughes of Exeter University launching a study into poor standards of mathematics in English schools, March 1996.

'The visibility of lesbians and gay men within the school community greatly enhances the development of all pupils' understanding of equality issues, as

well as the self-esteem of pupils who define themselves as lesbian and gay.'
– Part of a resolution to support gay and lesbian teachers, overwhelmingly
endorsed by the 1996 Conference of the National Union of Teachers.

Our current education system is a disgrace. It has failed to provide
generations of children with either the basic skills of literacy and
numeracy or any appreciation of moral values. Hence, we now have
armies of disaffected, semi-literate, unemployable youths in our inner
cities, whose lives are filled with the inanities of daytime television
or the transient pleasures of drug-taking. Because of hopelessly inadequate schooling, they have been deprived of the equipment to
participate in society. And, as I showed in the last chapter, the worst
of them represent a threat to our social cohesion.

Ironically, 'progressive' education, which has predominated in
schools since the sixties, has achieved the opposite of its objectives.
Condemning grammar schools as exclusive, the 'progressives' created
vast comprehensives in their place, thereby damaging the educational
opportunities of thousands of bright, working-class children. Preaching the creed of multi-culturalism, their teaching methods have failed
to serve the needs of black children. The greatest indictment of
the state system comes from those middle-class Left-wingers who
boast that they send their children to the local comprehensive
but then employ private tutors because the standard of teaching is
so dismal.

The very term 'progressive' has been exposed as a misnomer by
the failure, over the last three decades, of the liberal education
establishment to make any progress on raising academic achievement.
And the inability to reform the culture of our state education system
must rank as one of the greatest failures of the Conservatives since
1979. Despite a raft of measures, from Grant-Maintained status to the
National Curriculum, those who run our schools are still trapped in
their egalitarian mindsets.

Whatever claims the educationists make for their system, there is
now a wealth of evidence to show that standards in schools are
dismally low. In his annual report for 1996, Chris Woodhead, the
reassuringly traditionalist Chief Inspector of Schools, said that 'it is
evident that overall standards of pupil achievement need to be raised
in about half of primary schools and two fifths of secondary schools.'
Other parts of his report are a damning indictment of schooling in

modern Britain. 'There are still too many schools which are failing to give their pupils a satisfactory education,' says one paragraph. 'There is an urgent need to tackle mediocre and poor standards of literacy in many schools,' says another. On mathematics, 'the progress and attainment of pupils remain disappointing.' Other subjects are just as bad. 'In too many schools, teachers base their work on broad topics and give insufficient attention to history. Pupils, as a consequence, gain only a slender grasp of past events.' On science 'pupils achieve well in a little over two fifths of primary and half of secondary schools.'

A pathetic feature of the debate on educational standards has been the attempt by the progressives to portray Chris Woodhead as a 'Tory poodle' simply for performing his duty. It is a sign of their desperation that they have to resort to such puerile abuse. The same desire to conceal the truth about the state of our schools lay behind the fanatical opposition from trade unions and local education authorities to the introduction of assessment tests in primary schools. They would 'damage pupils' self-esteem', we were informed. They were cumbersome and time-consuming. They would tell teachers 'nothing they did not already know'. If that last argument were true, it is an appalling reflection of their complacency. For the primary tests, like OFSTED's reports, have highlighted a worryingly low level of achievement. In 1996, the tests showed that the average eleven-year-old is two years behind the expected standard in mathematics and eighteen months behind in English. According to one analysis of the results, 16 per cent of girls and 19 per cent of boys about to go to secondary schools are at or below the level of arithmetic achievement expected of a seven-year-old. In English, 15 per cent of boys are at this sorry level. In my former borough of Islington, an astonishing 80 per cent of eleven-year-olds failed to reach the required standard for their age in reading. It is perhaps understandable that the educationists wanted to prevent such figures entering the public domain.

Other evidence has pointed to a decline in teaching the basics of English. In 1994, Richard Sheppard, a Fellow in German at Magdalen College, Oxford, complained publicly about students' poor grasp of essential grammatical principles and their lack of general knowledge. 'The system is going badly wrong at the moment,' Sheppard complained. 'People are getting As in modern-language A-levels but know only the rudiments of the language. This is connected with the failure to teach English grammar in schools.' A 1995 report from the Secondary Heads Association argued that basic literacy skills have been falling continuously since 1991. A 1996 study by the University of Cambridge Local Examinations Syndicate concluded that candidates who failed O-level English in 1980 would now be awarded a GCSE Grade C. A comparison of examination scripts showed that, in 1980, there was an average of fifty spelling errors per script. By 1994, this had risen threefold to 149. A 1996 survey, this by the Queen's English Society, highlighted the neglect of English grammar in our classrooms. According to the survey's findings, only a quarter of English teachers thought that grammar should be taught explicitly, while almost half of them did not give spelling tests. A fifth of eleven-year-olds could barely communicate by written word. One A-level teacher told the survey that 'grammar is boring and irrelevant'. Another despaired of the unreliability of examination results: 'We get good GCSE results, but pupils who are very poor at English often get a grade B or even an A.' An analysis of worldwide reading standards by the National Foundation for Educational Research and the Open University – hardly bastions of reaction – published in July 1996, revealed that British primary schoolchildren are in the lower half of international rankings. Of English-speaking countries, only Trinidad and Tobago had worse results. Dr Greg Brooks, of the Research Foundation, said that the analysis 'shows how the bottom quartile of pupils have been let down by the education system. Some are more or less illiterate after four years of schooling.'

Just as the basics of grammar and spelling have disappeared as a result of 'child-centred' discovery methods, so the understanding of essential arithmetic has also been abandoned. Many children cannot even complete simple sums without a calculator. The Royal Statistical Society and the Institute of Mathematics have spoken of their 'unprecedented concern' over the 'crisis' in the teaching of the subject. One international study in 1995 showed that, while more than two thirds of thirteen-year-olds from Singapore could express one eighth as a decimal fraction, only 10 per cent of English pupils could do so. Over fifty universities have now extended their mathematics courses by a year to 'bolster the deficiencies we see among new students coming in from school', in the words of one lecturer from Notting-ham. Dr Tony Gardner, reader in mathematics at Birmingham University, told *The Times* in November 1995 that the curriculum reflected an ethos which said that if some children found a subject hard, it should be made easier for all. 'The result is that children don't do algebra or ratios or proofs any more. When they get to university, it is a bit late to start trying.' Professor David Hughes of Exeter University, whom I quoted in the introduction to this chapter, has been equally appalled at what he sees in British classrooms. 'The discipline of actually writing equations correctly, for example, is not tested in the way it used to be and the way it still is on the Continent.' Hughes has rightly criticised the low entry standards for mathematics teachers, no higher than a GCSE Grade C in the subject: 'I am a Chief Examiner in maths and I know what a grade C means. Not very much.'

When a Chief Examiner is so frank about the quality of public examinations, the educationists should pay heed. Not that they do. In recent years, they have waged an unconvincing campaign to present a remorseless rise in passes at GCSE and A-level as evidence of the increasing success of their system. The Conservative Government have colluded in this discreditable effort, hoping to prove the efficacy of their reforms. Anyone who claims that grades have been devalued is accused of 'undermining' the dedication of children and staff. We should be 'celebrating' pupil achievement instead of questioning standards. This sort of language is partly a reflection of 'child-centred' orthodoxy, where children must always be made to 'feel good' about themselves. We should only praise, never criticise. Such an attitude was encapsulated in a letter to the *Guardian* by David Smetherham, Principal of the South Bristol College, during the row over 1995 A-level results: 'One of the lessons in education is that performance is much enhanced by praise where it is due rather than constant carping and criticism. Should not those responsible for leadership in this country share in this celebration of success?' No, they should not. A more important lesson of education over the last thirty years is that indiscriminate praise, unrelated to real performance, is highly destructive.

The claim that higher GCSE and A-level grades represent rising standards falls down the moment it is scrutinised. On demographic grounds alone, it is unsustainable. Over the last fifteen years, the number of eighteen-year-olds has been falling – due to the sharp decline in the birth rate from 1964 onwards – yet both the number and percentage of A-level passes has increased dramatically. In 1996, the pass rate reached 85.8 per cent, up from 76 per cent in 1989 and the fifteenth year in a row it has risen, while the proportion of students failing is half the level of 1980. Given that more low- and middle-ability students are now sitting the exam than in the past, when it was only the academically able who were entered, we should actually expect a higher percentage of failures if standards had remained constant. To draw an analogy with sport, the organisers of the Olympic 100 metres could not double the number of athletes running under 10 seconds by doubling the number of entrants. They would just have more slow runners. What is as disturbing is the increase in the proportion of pupils receiving A and B grades, up by 25 per cent in the last seven years. In 1996, 34 per cent of those taking the examination received the top two grades, slightly up on the 32.7 per cent of the previous year. Again, given the population decrease and the changing profile of the entrants, we should have expected a reverse of these proportions. The same grade inflation can be seen in GCSEs. In 1996, 54 per cent of GCSE results were graded C or above, compared to 40 per cent of O-level results in 1988, the year when the GCSE replaced O-levels.

If, as progressives claim, standards have not declined, there are only two explanations for this startling progression: either British pupils are becoming more intelligent or they are being taught more effectively. The first scenario is scientifically dubious. How could average IQs be so transformed over such a short timescale? The second is contradicted by all available evidence. If teaching has so radically improved, why has the Chief Inspector expressed such concern about 'serious weaknesses' in the quality of teaching in many schools? Why have independent studies pointed to such low levels of achievement in British schools? Why do so many parents of only moderate incomes feel the need to send their children into the private sector? Why have universities had to institute remedial programmes and lengthen degree courses? In August 1996, in an unequivocal statement, Cambridge University said: 'It is clear that public examinations now offer a substantially lower level of specialised education in mathematics, physics and chemistry, so that the university is faced with students of widely differing attainments.'

It was a recent Government inquiry that provided confirmation that GCSEs and A-levels are now easier than they were twenty years ago. Despite her wish, for political reasons, to join in the progressives' chorus of approval, Education Secretary Gillian Shephard felt she could not ignore the complaints of the realists. In 1995 she therefore ordered an investigation by OFSTED and the Schools Curriculum Assessment Authority. Forty experts examined question papers from 1975, 1985 and 1995. Their conclusion, announced in July 1996, was that, in several core subjects, questions are now simpler, pupils are given more help and there is significant grade inflation, with 'some candidates awarded higher marks than they deserve.' In both mathematics and chemistry, it was felt that the examinations are now 'less demanding'. One mathematics expert, who took part in the review, said 'there is no question about it – standards have declined. Pupils are led through the questions by the hand and as a result have lost the ability to think for themselves.' He was only reinforcing what many already know. The admissions officer of St Mary's College, Twickenham, complained during the 1995 row on standards (which led to the Government inquiry) that 'examination boards are awarding higher grades for lower standards of work.' Referring to students admitted with good A-level grades, he said that 'the quality of the written work of these students did not show any improvement over previous years – in many cases it was worse. Purely subjective observation has led me to question how some had achieved any sort of pass at A-level, let alone C and D grades.' A friend of mine who recently began lecturing at the University of East London was shocked by the academic ineptitude of most of her first-year students, 'some of whom can barely write a sentence, never mind construct an essay.'

There have also been complaints that examiners are encouraged to indulge in what is euphemistically described as 'positive marking'. In typical 'child-centred' fashion, they are told to highlight correct points but not to underline faults. Just as damaging has been the growing popularity of modular A-levels, where students can keep resitting a certain section of the course until they pass it. Even the dimmest can scrape through in such circumstances. Indeed, Margaret Hutchinson, a spokeswoman for the examining boards, gave the game away last year when she expressed the hope that soon there might be a 100 per cent pass rate in A-levels: 'I would like to think we would be moving towards that. Surely we are in the business of trying to provide accessibility.' For enhancing accessibility, read accepting mediocrity. In the egalitarian society, no one must feel academically excluded, no matter what their abilities. But such an approach makes A-levels utterly worthless. Where is the merit in passing an examination which is impossible to fail? When A-levels were established in 1951, they were the gold standard of education. Half a century later, they are fast becoming as debased as the rouble.

The 'progressive' educationists have three types of riposte to accusations of falling standards. The first, of which their lame manoeuvres over A-level and GCSE have been part, is to pretend that the alleged crisis is a fantasy dreamt up by traditionalists and those with a prejudice against their teaching methods. Claims of a decline, they say, amount to nothing more than misplaced nostalgia. As we have seen, this is the same trick that complacent liberal theorists try to pull over crime rates ('no golden age') and the collapse of two-parent families ('changing, not deteriorating'). When the independent National Commission for Education concluded in its report, *Standards in Literacy and Numeracy, 1948 to 1994*, that 'reading standards among 10/11-year-olds and 15/16-year-olds have changed little since 1945', the progressives, far from feeling any shame over this finding, hailed it as evidence of their success. Their house journal, the *Guardian*, claimed it 'contradicted the myth' of a post-war decline in reading standards. The Commission's authors joined the celebration. 'There is certainly no warrant for doom-laden pronouncements of inexorable decline', they wrote. That an admission of immutably low standards can be portrayed as a triumph only reflects the depths to which the education establishment has sunk in its desperate defence of its own failing system. We live in an incomparably richer society than in 1945. We are healthier, better paid, better housed, and more secure. Yet the proudest boast of our educationists is that standards are no lower than they were half a century ago. It is not as if they were high then. The wartime Norwood Committee on 'Curriculum and Examinations in Secondary Schools' warned in 1943: 'From all quarters, we have received strong evidence of the poor quality of English of secondary school pupils. The evidence is such as to leave no doubt in our minds that we are here confronted by a serious failure of the secondary schools.'

The failure of the current education establishment is all the more pathetic, given the substantial fall in pupil/teacher ratios and the large increase in education expenditure since the war. We now spend £29 billion on state education, compared to just £114 million when the war began. Since 1971, education expenditure has more than doubled in real terms. Reductions in class sizes have been almost as dramatic. In 1954, three in five primary schools had classes of more than thirty pupils. Now the figure is only one in four. In secondary schools over the last forty years, the proportion of classes with more than thirty pupils has fallen from nearly one in three to less than one in ten.

As the National Commission's recent report demonstrated, the benefits of smaller classes and record spending have been squandered. Yet the Commission's claim that standards of literacy and numeracy have remained unchanged since 1945 masks the truth – known to most employers and university lecturers who have to cope with ill-taught school leavers – that standards have actually fallen since the late sixties, after decades of improvements. During the fifties and early sixties, there was a heartening rise in reading abilities. In 1963, a Government committee found a 'marked improvement over the last fifteen years' in national reading abilities, and argued that 'today's average boys and girls are better at their books than their predecessors a generation ago.' Since then, we have been on a downward learning curve, thanks to failed egalitarian experiments.

After complacency, we find the second line of defence, social determinism. We are told that poor results reflect the disadvantaged backgrounds of the pupils. In an inner-city school, we should therefore expect a low level of achievement.

I used to listen to this sort of fatuous reasoning when I served on Islington Council's education committee as attempts were made to excuse the worst school examination results in the country. What our education 'experts' could never explain was why Camden, a neighbouring inner-London borough with much the same social profile of deprivation, should have much higher standards. In 1995, only 17.4 per cent of Islington pupils achieved five GCSE passes at Grade C or above, compared to 41.5 per cent in Camden. Even in the poorest areas, a dedicated, well-organised school can be successful. One such school is Sudbourne Primary in Brixton, where almost half the pupils receive free school meals and two thirds of them are from ethnic minority groups. The 'progressives' would no doubt think that such a background would be a recipe for failure. It is not. Of 11-year-olds, 80 per cent reach or exceed the required standard for their age in mathematics, and 64 per cent do the same in English. Both figures are well above the national average of 50 per cent. The reason for the success is simple. The school uses traditional methods, imposes discipline, and has high expectations of the pupils. The headteacher, Susan Scarsbrook, explained in the London *Evening Standard* in January 1996: 'We go for whole-class teaching here because it focuses the children on what they should be doing. We do not believe child-centred learning to be effective.'

Using 'disadvantage' as an excuse for failure becomes a self-fulfilling prophecy, building a climate of low expectations in some inner-city schools. If a teacher thinks that her pupils are bound to fail because of perceived racism or poverty, they almost certainly will. As the 1996 OFSTED report said in its section on schools in *Areas of Urban Disadvantage*: 'Too often these schools have not identified the steps required to combat their particular problems. Their teachers often have unduly low expectations of the pupils. Some schools allow their necessary and understandable preoccupation with pastoral care to distract attention from teaching focused on achievement.' In other words the social worker has replaced the teacher. Providing sympathy is more important than imparting knowledge. In such circumstances, a school is seen purely as a barometer of local deprivation. Rather than providing a means to advancement, it only traps pupils in their backgrounds.

At first glance, it might seem extraordinary that the creed of 'progressive' education, ostensibly devoted to the 'emancipation' of the 'oppressed', should result in the reinforcement of social and economic disadvantage. But through its sub-Marxist determinism, that is exactly what it has achieved. What better way is there to marginalise the poor than to leave them illiterate, innumerate and unemployable? What could be more prejudiced than the stereotyped view that black pupils cannot succeed in a 'racist' British society? Many black parents now send their children to be educated in the Caribbean because they are so dissatisfied with the quality of British teaching. Ironically, Caribbean schools have retained the once-traditional British model – sitting in rows of desks, instilling discipline, wearing uniforms, learning English and mathematics by rote – which the 'progressives' have denounced as 'oppressive', 'hierarchical' and 'inappropriate for the needs of a multi-cultural society'. Black British pupils, studying in the Caribbean for the first time, admit they are sometimes nicknamed 'English dummies'. Could there be a more tart indictment of British schooling? Sadly, for too many children, both black and white, 'multi-cultural, child-centred' education means no education at all.

The cynic might suggest, however, that some noisy egalitarians privately welcome the continuation of inequality in schools. Low standards in the classroom can be portrayed as another symptom of the failings of capitalist society. The chasm between the best independent schools and the worst inner-city schools only serves as confirmation of the 'apartheid' of British society. Appalling examination results are a campaigning tool, not a source of shame. Just as the professional anti-racist delights in evidence of racial disharmony in Britain, so the Left-wing educationist feels nothing but pleasure at evidence of the weaknesses of inner-city schools. A whole industry of New Public Servants – academics, local authority bureaucrats, education social workers, equal opportunities training consultants, race advisers, gender inspectors, policy researchers – has been founded on the premiss that education is riddled with inequalities. Where would they go if all 'socially deprived' schools showed a sudden improvement?

A third, more commonly used, defence of poor standards is the argument that 'lack of resources' is to blame. Indeed, this claim is used not only by the professional educationists, but also by parents, pressure groups, councillors, even Tory MPs. It has become one of the most widely-held beliefs of the nineties that education is grossly 'under-funded' because of an uncaring Tory Government. Listen to any news item about schools and you will hear a complaint about 'cash shortages'. In the audience of most editions of BBC TV *Question Time*, we have some loudly self-announced 'parent', quivering with indignation about 'Tory education cuts'. In both of the last two years, we have had rallies, protest marches, and petitions. The Liberal Democrats, hoping to exploit the public's altruistic fury, promise an extra penny on income tax to provide more revenue for schools. In 1995, the party's education spokesman, Don Foster MP, warned that 'Education has been cut to the bone. The Government is now forcing cuts into the bone.'

His language was both grotesque and inappropriate. The truth is, as in most of the public sector, spending on education has increased heavily in recent years. Between 1980 and 1995, spending on primary schools rose in real terms from £6.2 billion to £8.6 billion. In secondary schools it went up from £7.9 billion to £8.9 billion. In terms of spending per pupil, the rises are even more dramatic, up from £1,100 in 1981 to £1,650 for each primary pupil last year, and from £1,540 to £2,310 for each secondary one. We spend a higher proportion of our Gross Domestic Product on education than Germany and Japan. Class sizes and pupil/teacher ratios are no higher than they were fifteen years ago and far lower than at the beginning of the seventies.

Contrary to the propaganda about 'Tory cuts', there is no direct correlation between success and expenditure. Many of the highest spending local education authorities achieve the worst examination results. According to 1996 Audit Commission figures, Lambeth spent £4,113 on every secondary pupil, yet only 23.2 per cent of them received five GCSE passes graded C or above the previous year. My own former borough of Islington was the fifth biggest spender on schools yet had the lowest proportion of top GCSE grades. Again, urban disadvantage cannot explain such figures. Councils like Sheffield, North Tyneside, and Kirklees spent lower than average yet achieved much more creditable results. Much of the debate on 'resources' has concentrated on class sizes. 'Over-crowded classrooms' is a phrase that has joined 'crumbling schools' in the lexicon of 'underfunding'. But, here too, there is no proven link between the size of classes and the quality of teaching. Hackney Downs in East London had to be closed down in 1996 after a string of disturbing reports on its chaotic standards. Yet the school had a ratio of one teacher to every eight pupils, better than the most expensive public school in the land. Expenditure per pupil was more than three times the national average. The whine of 'lack of resources' – used at the time of closure by local MP Diane Abbott – was never less justified. Too many parents, sadly, have swallowed this line, encouraged by the teaching trade unions which want to increase their membership rolls. 'Smaller classes' are now seen as the holy grail of modern education. A few more teachers in every school will lead to a miraculous transformation in standards, say the campaigners.

This is so much nonsense. What is wrong with our schools is not lack of funding but the 'progressive' culture of non-achievement. More expenditure on propping up the present system, without changing the culture, would be a criminal waste of public money. Indeed, the flood of demands for more 'resources' for schools only serves to disguise the enormity of the failure of the progressive educationists.

If we are going to spend more on education, let us not reward those who have presided over this betrayal of generations of British children.

Since the Plowden report of 1967, the progressive 'child-centred' approach to education has become the orthodoxy of primary schooling. In Britain this century, few more discreditable theories have held such sway in their field. At its heart is the belief that the child learns best when he 'discovers' information and concepts for himself, rather than having them 'imposed' by the teacher. The traditional apparatus of education is therefore redundant. Teaching staff become no more than 'facilitators' of learning, supporting the child through his own scholastic journey, but never instructing or correcting. The opinions of the child are no less valuable than those of the adult, even if they are based on ignorance. Indeed, children are just as likely to learn from each other as from a teacher (hence the devotion to collaborative group work rather than whole-class teaching). Because the child 'owns' (to use the politically correct jargon) the process, he is therefore supposed to learn more quickly. In this context, education becomes a means of personal development. The aim is to acquire 'skills' rather than knowledge. The emphasis is entirely on the process, not the content. In history, the child should be able to interpret source materials; it is unnecessary to remember events or dates or historical figures. In maths, the child need only look at the theory of multiplication or division; the actual tables are an irrelevance, especially as calculators can be used from the earliest possible age. In English, expression is all; grammar, spelling, and punctuation have no significance. Indeed, subject boundaries can disappear altogether, replaced by the 'topic-based' approach. As one Islington parent complained to me, her child spent a year allegedly learning about 'water' but could not name any of the rivers in Britain and looked blank when asked about the qualities of H_2O.

The characteristics of the progressive classroom have become all too familiar: pupils chattering together in groups or wandering aimlessly from one table to another, with a din echoing permanently in the background. It would be difficult to invent a less suitable environment for learning. Not that there is always much attempt made at learning. Colouring in books and asking to go the toilet seem to be the main activities of some primaries I have visited. We hear much about the 'stress' that teachers now suffer, but it is the chaos and disorder of progressive education which is a major cause.

This is why I find it extraordinary that the National Union of Teachers should continue to support progressive methods. A return to whole-class teaching would lift a burden off their members, as well as giving them a renewed authority.

Even in the most well-resourced education system, child-centred education could never work since it is founded on a preposterous theory. The idea that, left to their own devices, children will somehow absorb information and gain understanding is plainly absurd. The 'real books' mode of studying English represents the nemesis of this thinking: give some books to an untutored child, without a grasp of the alphabet, and he will learn to read as the sentences 'jump out at him' from the page. This bizarre practice is deemed preferable to the traditional 'phonics' system, through which children used to learn English. OFSTED has summarised the importance of phonics like this:

'Phonics provides pupils with the knowledge to decode and build words, upon which success in early reading and writing depends, and gives pupils the confidence they need to tackle new texts. Moreover, because phonics is a set of culturally determined conventions, it cannot be left to be "discovered".'

Would you expect someone to learn to drive a car on their own without any handbook or instruction? Of course not. In reality, learning is a highly complex process. Literacy and numeracy have to be taught. They cannot be gained through a process of osmosis. Once again, we see the paradox of a system designed to encourage 'creative expression' achieving the very opposite. Without a mastery of the English language, self-expression is impossible.

One of the most insidious features of 'child-centredness' is the reluctance to criticise children's work, no matter how poor it is. Judgements cannot be imposed. Corrections only hinder the process of self-learning. A wrong answer should be described as 'nearly right'. This is another symptom of the relativist creed of our age, where there are no absolutes, either morally or intellectually. Chris Woodhead, the Chief Inspector, has despaired of this attitude: 'It is no good just walking the corridors muttering about the empowerment of children. You've got to evaluate, analyse, understand what is happening and face up to the strengths and weaknesses of children's work,' he told me in an interview last year. The reluctance to criticise any child creates a suspicion of the usual methods of assessment, like marking and tests, for that leads to the 'labelling' of children, and the creation of intellectual 'élites' and 'ghettoes'. Where public examinations cannot be avoided, they should be on a modular or coursework basis. Children should not be compelled to endure the 'pressure' of a single test without access to other material. Besides, such examinations, in the eyes of progressives, do nothing more than probe the remembered facts. They do not test the application of 'skills'. (Untrue, as usual. Answering a scientific question or writing an essay under pressurised conditions is the most rigorous way to test the application of knowledge.) This enfeebled mentality has been disastrous for the teaching of the curriculum; it has also undermined discipline and destroyed the authority of the teacher. Correction of poor behaviour is as prohibited as that of poor work. We must always attempt to empathise with the unruly child.

An in-depth study in 1991 led by Professor Robin Alexander of Leeds University into primary school practice in the city shows the folly of increased expenditure on an education system dominated by 'progressive' teaching. Worried by criticism of its primary schools in the mid-eighties, Leeds City Council initiated a special 'Primary Needs Programme' under which an extra £14 million was invested in additional teachers, books, classroom furniture, support staff and equipment. But, because of modernist teaching methods, the money was wasted. The research by Professor Alexander's team exposed the progressive system at its worst. There was a 'taboo on didacticism', with teachers discouraged from giving information directly to pupils. Indiscriminate praise led to children becoming 'confused and cynical'. While great emphasis was placed on the needs of ethnic minority and socially disadvantaged children, discussion of the needs of the most able children was often 'bogged down with talk of élitism and privilege'. It is not surprising that the inquiry found that, after all this extra investment, reading standards were actually deteriorating. In his dispassionate but damning conclusion, Professor Alexander said that his project

'highlighted the prevalence and power of certain orthodoxies about primary teaching methods and the extent to which many teachers feel obliged to conform to these while in some cases being all too conscious of the problems they may pose. It is likely that this conformist culture has elevated particular classroom practices into ends in themselves.'

Another study, this in 1994, by Professor Maurice Galton, demonstrated how rare whole-class teaching has become. He estimated that in 'the typical primary classroom', only '15 per cent of time is devoted to whole-class teaching'. Yet his research concluded that this was easily the most effective method, enabling pupils to 'pay more attention and concentrate more on their work'. In 1996, OFSTED produced the results of an investigation into *The Teaching of Reading* in primary schools in three London boroughs, Islington, Southwark and Tower Hamlets, which illustrated the sorry consequences of the 'child-centred' approach. The OFSTED report found a 'serious and unacceptable' gulf in pupils' reading performance – only 20 per cent of seven-year-olds 'achieved a reading age at or above their chronological age. Almost one in five achieved no score at all.' The report's authors felt that 'at the heart of the problem is a commitment to methods and approaches to the teaching of reading that were self-evidently not working when judged by the outcomes of pupils' progress and attainment.' OFSTED inspectors saw 'many sessions devoted to free reading with little or no intervention by the teacher which did not contribute much, if anything, to pupils' progress.' Much of the work lacked 'any systematic teaching of an effective programme of phonic knowledge and skills.' Other criticisms included a lack of demanding texts, poor knowledge and skills of teaching staff, tolerance of indiscipline, little direct teaching of grammar, the low quality of topic work, 'aimless lessons' and ineffective group working; all this in schools belonging to three of the highest-spending local education authorities in the country.

One of the many absurdities uncovered by OFSTED is that, on 'Reading Recovery Programmes' (designed for pupils with special reading difficulties), and in support for bi-lingual students, the three boroughs are willing to use the despised, heterodox methods of phonics and direct teaching, thereby admitting that they are actually more effective. But why should this be an approach of the last resort? Would we need these grandly-titled Reading Recovery Programmes at all if children were taught properly in the first place? I had a similar feeling about a local education centre for children suffering from the fashionable ailment, Attention Deficit Disorder (ADD). The centre was presented as a radical breakthrough in treatment, yet it seemed to me that it only provided 'sufferers' (all of them adolescent boys, of course) with the disciplined, rigorous environments which had been so conspicuously lacking from their school lives.

Fear of so-called élitism dominates 'progressive' educational thinking. It is reflected, not only in the teaching methods outlined above, but in educational structures. Anti-élitist thinking lay behind the grandiose experiment in comprehensive secondary schooling – or as Labour's education secretary of the sixties, Tony Crosland, put it, 'the closure of every fucking grammar school in the land'. Once grammar schools were seen, even by Left-wingers, as a means of providing opportunities for bright, working-class pupils to realise their potential. When the egalitarians came to power they were turned into symbols of privilege, which drained away resources from other secondaries and reinforced the sense of exclusion felt by the vast majority of lower-income families. There certainly was some truth in this. Labour's Deputy Leader, John Prescott, has recounted his feelings of grievance at failing his 11-plus and being sent to a secondary modern. But the solution, the abolition of selection and the merger of grammar and secondary schools in vast comprehensives, has proved disastrous. Standards have been lowered. Morale and discipline have fallen. Tens of thousands of children have been denied the chance of a quality education in the state system. The continued existence of a flourishing private sector is a tribute to the failings of the comprehensive experiment. The private sector in British medical treatment has never taken off because of the loyalty the public feels towards the NHS. The mood is very different with secondary schools. To the egalitarians none of this matters. The destruction of privilege is what counts. It is better that all should fail than only some succeed. And how does one define success anyway? For the true progressive, the school is not a place of learning but an instrument of social change. Altering the élitist assumptions of the middle class (and aspirant working class) is more important than pandering to the 'cultural or knowledge monopolies' (as the *Dictionary of Marxist Thought* puts it).

Anti-élitism also runs through the curriculum. Throughout this book, I have referred to the ideologically correct reluctance to impose 'white, heterosexist, Christian values' on schoolchildren, for fear of upsetting certain regional and racial minorities. It is an outlook that has infected history (studying post-war immigration instead of the Industrial Revolution), geography (learning about squatter camps rather than the capitals of Europe), and English (analysing rap poetry).

The anti-élitist spirit was captured in a letter sent to *The Times* in 1995 signed by over 500 English academics, attacking the idea of a reading list for English literature. Condemning the Government for its alleged prejudice against 'regional and working-class forms of speech', the correspondents warn that the study of Shakespeare may 'risk permanently alienating a large number of children from the pleasurable classical literary works'. It might, but why deprive all children of Shakespeare because of the ignorant objections of the few, who wouldn't be happy anyway unless they were watching the latest episode of *Baywatch* or reading the last edition of *Viz*? Perhaps most disturbingly of all, the academics wailed about the 'dictatorially-imposed canon of supposedly great works'. This is a classic piece of modernist relativism, questioning the very idea that some books might be more worthwhile than others. At the extreme of educational relativism, even the purpose of studying books is under attack. We should learn to appreciate children's understanding of 'non-literary texts', that is videos and computer games. One writer has even regretted the fact that education seems 'fixated on book culture'. Such attitudes can only undermine attempts to teach English. In the introduction, I quoted from a letter to the black newspaper *The Voice* by a mother who complained that egalitarian multi-culturalism had destroyed the teaching of Standard English in her daughter's school. Here is the conclusion of her letter: 'This sort of nonsense invariably comes from white, middle-class teachers foisting half-baked ideas on working-class black kids, who then leave school with no qualifications but a headful of sociological rubbish. That is why I am trying now to get my daughter into a grammar school.' Those words should make all the egalitarians hang their heads in shame.

Teacher training has also suffered from the progressive orthodoxy. Instead of providing trainees with the skills to perform in the class-room, too many training colleges subject their students to irrelevant egalitarian dogma. As in social-services training, there is a grossly misplaced emphasis on social disadvantage and discrimination. The best way to combat disadvantage, of course, is to provide a quality education, one thing that so many training establishments fail to do. The course in *The Teaching of Reading* at the University College of Ripon and York St. John, for instance, aims to provide students 'with an awareness of political differences in chosen approaches to the teaching of reading'. Why should the teaching of reading be political?

The college also boasts that the content of this course includes a study of 'the reading process and the development of literacy', and 'appropriate organisational strategies within the classroom' (whatever they are). We are back again with the world of child-centred learning, where process is all. According to the 1996 prospectus for De Montfort University, 'the structure of the PGCE (Postgraduate Certificate of Education) course is progressive and allows students to find their own way into the business of teaching at their own rate without undue pressure for immediate performance.' Sounds like one of the dismal, low-achieving progressive classrooms. Imagine if doctors or civil engineers were allowed to carry on like this, 'finding their own way' into performing operations or building bridges. Half the population would be dead or lying under rubble. It is astonishing that we still tolerate such gross negligence in the vital profession of teaching. It is no use being merely informed of various academic theories, while the practice remains a mystery. An OFSTED survey in 1992 found that 'fewer than a third of teachers felt well prepared to teach reading.' In the report on Islington, Southwark and Tower Hamlets mentioned earlier, several teachers were highly critical of the 'doctrinaire narrowness' of the training they had received.

Fear of élitism has also driven the spectacular expansion of higher education in recent years. In the early seventies, only one in ten eighteen-year-olds went into this sector; now the figure is one in three. In 1971 there were 414,000 full-time undergraduates on degree courses. In 1994, there were almost 1 million. Over this period, total enrolments, including part-time and post-graduate students, have risen from 640,000 to 1,700,000. The upgrading of the former polytechnics in 1992 created an additional forty-one 'new' universities, a near-revolutionary change in our educational landscape.

The Conservative Government has hailed this development as an unalloyed triumph. No longer the preserve of the élites, the universities are now opening up opportunities for all young people. A university degree is now within the reach of almost anyone who wants one. And that is precisely the problem. By presiding over this unprecedented growth in higher education, the Conservatives have debased the value of a university degree. Where all are honoured, the honour becomes worthless. Once graduate status represented genuine academic achievement; now it is a routine part of growing up. Where is the pride in having a BA in 'Public Sector Studies' from Sheffield Hallam (former polytechnic) University? Or a degree in 'Contemporary Cultural Studies' at Middlesex (former polytechnic) University?

No doubt the egalitarians would dismiss such talk as unadulterated snobbery. Perhaps it is. But as I argued earlier, snobbery is one of the unfortunate results of having a system of values. In academia, if there is no hierarchy of attainment, there can be no standards. It appears that we are no longer willing to accept the reality, understood through centuries of civilisation, that some people are more intelligent or diligent than others. To the dogmatic egalitarians, everyone can reach the same standard provided they are given the right support. I once attended an Equal Opportunities course at which the trainer told us we were all equally talented and equally capable of reaching the position of Chief Executive. In the same way, we have the pretence that all British degrees are equally good, whether they be in Natural Sciences from Cambridge or in Sports Studies from Warrington. Dr Ted Nield, of the Committee of Vice-Chancellors and Principals, has dismissed criticism of a devalued currency: 'We like to think different university degrees are different but no worse.' It is this sort of wishful thinking that has contributed to the dumbing down of our education system. As A-levels are taken by most pupils, so their standard slips towards that of the former O-levels. In turn, degrees begin to take the place of A-levels and universities become glorified sixth forms. In order to signify academic ability, the bright student has therefore to acquire a postgraduate qualification like an MA. The honours degree no longer suffices. The 'myth of increased success' in our universities was subject to a withering attack in July 1996 by Gordon Graham, Regius Professor of Moral Philosophy at Aberdeen University (part of it quoted in the introduction):

'The official story is that a far higher proportion of the population, including many with what are euphemistically called "non-standard" educational backgrounds, have been given access to the advanced education that was formerly the preserve of the few. The truth is that, while vastly more are enrolled at "university" courses, what they receive is a shadow of what was once on offer.'

Whatever the noises from the anti-élitists, growth in the university sector has coincided with a decline in entry requirements. Two

A-level passes used to be the absolute minimum for acceptance on to a degree course, hardly demanding in itself. Even that has now disappeared. Some universities are accepting students with no passes at all on to so-called 'foundation' courses, which were originally designed for mature students or those who wanted to change subjects. They were certainly never envisaged as an entry route to university for A-level failures. In August 1995, an investigation by *Sunday Times* reporters revealed that nine of the 'new' universities were willing to accept those who had failed their A-levels. Reassuringly, none of the 'old' universities contacted by the paper would consider students without A-levels.

As well as lowering entry requirements, there have been complaints that some universities now indulge in 'grade inflation' – the same process we have seen in A-levels – where students are awarded higher marks than they deserve. In the last ten years, the number of students awarded first-class honours has risen by 50 per cent. There have been charges of 'positive marking' and wide variations in standards. The increasing replacement of formal examinations by modular assessments (again like A-levels) has caused concern about a lax approach to assessment. On some courses, students are allowed continual resits if they fail a certain module. Above all, there has been the disturbing trend away from the study of difficult intellectual subjects (engineering, physics, mathematics, languages, classics) to the more fashionable, 'relevant' ones (media studies, sociology, women's studies, leisure and tourism). In the last decade, the number of admissions to 'design studies' has increased by 1,787 per cent while those for 'media studies' have gone up by 1,538 per cent. Both subjects now enrol more than 1,500 students a year. The number of sociology students over the same period has quadrupled, while enrolments for physics have risen by only 8 per cent. Leisure and tourism studies has seen a 600 per cent increase since 1986, drama a 780 per cent one (contrary to the whines of the arts lobby about a crisis in drama training). Degree awards in French, engineering, and German have seen declines or only marginal increases. Like degree standards, these courses reflect the 'dumbing down' of our society. Nothing should be made too demanding for students. Give them what they want. Turn their leisure interests into academic studies. As one academic has said, the logical conclusion of this approach is to 'offer students courses in beer drinking. I'm sure that would be popular.'

Already students can read for a BA in 'Popular Music Studies' at Bretton College or a similar qualification in 'Screen Studies' at Liverpool John Moores University. In this age of political correctness, there are a host of courses for the discrimination ideologues, like 'Race and Ethnic Studies' at Central Lancashire University. In one guide to higher education, I counted thirty-six undergraduate courses which covered 'women and gender studies'. The BA at East London University offers such options as 'women and the visual media' and 'lesbian and gay cultures'. The women's studies programme at Birkbeck College includes 'lesbian culture and gay politics', while at Kent students can examine 'contemporary issues for black women'. At Worcester College of Higher Education, women's studies 'explain the intersections of sexuality, ethnicity, class and age'. So many of these courses seem geared towards Leftist propaganda, rather than the pursuit of knowledge. They are a contradiction of the goal of higher education, the promotion of rigorous independent thinking. One feminist academic has actually admitted that their objective is to 'serve direct action'. So why not send the students to a collective for a few months rather than using up public money?

Ideological correctness is now infecting other more traditional courses. One prospectus I read for 'English Literature' included, amongst a limited number of options, the following: 'Women's autobiography'; 'Jeanette Winterson'; 'twentieth-century women's poetry'; 'feminist literary perspectives'; 'Black American women writers'; 'Women's writing and modernism'; 'Representations of Women in Early Modern England', 'nineteenth-century Single American author study – Emily Dickinson'; 'twentieth-century single American author study – Sylvia Plath'. In this travesty of a literature course, it appears that the student could reach graduation without reading a single work by a man. To many of us, this is nonsensical, since most great works have been written by men. To cultural radicals, who see literature only in its relativist social or political context, this is justifiable, for there is no such thing as a 'great work', merely a work that reflects 'cultural norms'. The so-called 'canon' is thus a catalogue of the writings of 'Dead White Males'. What such radicals want is to see literary criticism giving way to sociology. Last year, when I complained in an article about the uselessness of degrees in 'race relations' and 'women's studies', I received a letter from an aggrieved academic, asking me how else I expected race and women's equality workers to receive training for their work. But that is just the point. Joining the ranks of the New Public Servants is about the only employment open to the graduates of these ideologically correct courses. What call is there for qualifications in 'gender studies' outside pressure groups and local authority women's units?

This brings us to a central difficulty raised by the expansion of higher education. The award of a flood of degrees in undemanding subjects to mediocre students creates a climate of expectations that cannot be met by employers. The graduate with one E at A-level and a degree in Modern Studies from the University of Humberside might feel he deserves professional status and the salary to go with it, but most employers would disagree. I remember listening to a whine from a former student in 'environmental studies' from the University of North London about the injustice of having to work as a customs officer. She felt, with her degree, that she deserved something better. Our discredited education system is churning out thousands of graduates with unwanted qualifications from second-rate institutions. Sixteen per cent of 'leisure and tourism' students are still without work six months after graduation, compared to 0.1 per cent of medical students. Twenty-one per cent of design studies and 15 per cent of media studies graduates are unemployed six months after they receive their BAs. One of the remarkable concomitants of the expansion of higher education has been the complaint from business leaders that shortages of effective skills, literacy and numeracy, have actually become worse. Far from meeting the demands of the economy – a task which the more vocational polytechnics used to perform quite effectively – the new universities are making thousands less equipped for the workplace. Meanwhile, to the chagrin of the egalitarians, leading firms will only trust graduates from the traditional universities, like Oxford, Cambridge, Durham, Bristol, Exeter, Leeds, Southampton, Liverpool, Manchester, and Birmingham. The anti-élitist experiment has failed.

Further education is also in a poor state. This sector, like the universities, has enjoyed phenomenal recent growth. In 1970 there were just over 1 million full- and part-time FE students. Now there are 2.5 million, based in 450 colleges costing almost £3 billion a year. FE colleges cover a wide range of teaching, from GCSEs and A-levels, to General National Vocational Qualifications (GNVQs), NVQs and tests for the Royal Society of Arts (RSA) and City and

Guilds. But again, the system is failing to meet the needs of employers. In a 1996 report, the Chief Inspector of the Further Education Funding Council warned that a third of teaching in colleges 'has more weaknesses than strengths' while 30 per cent of students were absent at any one time. Much worse has been the NVQ catastrophe. NVQs, introduced at a cost of some £100 million ten years ago, were meant to provide reliable vocational qualifications, while GNVQs were supposed to be a work-orientated alternative to GCSEs for less academic pupils. None of these aims has been met. A report by Dr John Marks, of the Educational Research Trust, published in July 1996, argued that many NVQs are awarded at such a low grade that 'they would scarcely be recognised as worthy of certification' in other countries. Most of the NVQs are riddled with jargon, and fail to test adequately specific skills compared to traditional qualifications, warned Dr Marks's report. Few employers, apart from hairdressers, regarded them as reliable – one quarter of all the NVQs awarded over the last five years have been in hairdressing. Dr Marks has been joined in his criticisms by Professor Alan Smithers of Brunel University, who explained that 'employers have shunned NVQs because they don't lay down what skills are to be taught or how they are to be tested. That is their basic flaw.' GNVQs have fared just as badly. An OFSTED report in June 1996 found that 'marking schemes were unreliable, standards inconsistent and the qualifications devalued.' One leaked GNVQ paper carried questions so simple that they could have been answered by an average seven-year-old. Here is one example: 'If seeds are planted and watered, which will grow best: a) those in a dark cupboard; b) those under a bench; c) those inside a cardboard box; d) those on a sunny windowsill.' And this is part of the test for the equivalent of a GCSE in 'intermediate science'. Dumbing down has reached rock bottom.

What needs to change

NVQs are just one example of the changes introduced by the Conservative Government in an attempt to alter the fabric of our tertiary education system. We have also had the end of the binary division between polytechnics and universities, reductions in student grants, the introduction of student loans, the establishment of Training and Enterprise Councils, the removal of Further Education colleges from local authority control, and, above all, the vast increase in student numbers. But, as I have shown, these reforms have singularly failed to produce a generation of well-motivated, highly skilled young people. Instead, we have an army of graduates with undemanding and undemanded qualifications. In one respect, it is the Conservative philosophy of the free market that has led to this decline. Universities and colleges have been compelled to compete with each other to grab as many students as possible, thus driving down quality. The same applies to the class of degrees: the more firsts and upper seconds, the better the university looks, and the more money and applications it attracts.

The present crisis in higher education funding presents an opportunity for reform. It is widely recognised that the growth in student numbers has become financially unsustainable. The limited scheme of student loans has not proved a successful means of providing more funds without placing an intolerable burden on the taxpayer. The Tories, Labour, the National Union of Students and the Committee of Vice-Chancellors and Principals are all considering new ideas on university finance: top-up fees, extended student loans, a graduate tax, payment of fees through national insurance, and private sector partnerships.

All of these proposals are worthy, but none address the fundamental problem: the loss of standards in our universities. It is no use pouring more money, private or public, into a system which is failing to deliver quality. If any new scheme is to work, we must first be honest about the poor standards of much of higher education. We should not pretend that the overnight switch from polytechnics to universities led to a sudden revolution in achievement. The 'polite myth' (a term coined by the Higher Education Funding Council) that all universities are equal should be exploded. We still have a binary system in practice, if not in theory. Second, we should stop pretending that all degree subjects are equally worthy, that media studies is just as intellectually demanding as physics.

What we must do, therefore, is to rebuild a hierarchy of both subjects and institutions. Rather than shying away from the creation of an academic élite, we should welcome it. Such a move would strengthen our civilisation. What successful modern society has existed without an élite group of thinkers, engineers, scientists, and writers? There is one simple way to help achieve this, using the £3 billion lever of student finance. The Government could introduce a system whereby the amount of funding that students receive is dependent on their degree subjects and the university they attend. Since the most drastic shortages of high-calibre undergraduates are in engineering, technology, mathematics and the three sciences, these subjects would attract the highest level of support. Medicine, because of its vital importance to the nation's health, would also fall into this category, though it has not experienced the same recruitment problems. At a lower level, there would be the demanding but less vocationally necessary subjects, like law, history, classics, languages, and geography. The third category, carrying the least finance, would be those without a firm knowledge base or intellectual discipline. (The culprits have been named too often to bear repetition.) Under this proposal, students in the first category would have all their tuition fees paid, and receive an annual grant top. In the second group, they would have their fees paid but have no grant: in the third, they would have to pay 50 per cent of their tuition fees. In addition, the Higher Education Funding Council, which would oversee and review the categories, could provide additional funds to high-achieving universities to provide scholarships, based on their entry requirements. Before the anti-élitists utter their howls of outrage, they should remember that, on a small scale, such a system already operates to encourage able recruits in certain occupations. The armed forces offer substantial bursaries, while individual institutions often provide scholarships in certain subjects. At the other extreme, many drama and dance students receive no support from the state at all.

Yes, this would amount to a form of social engineering, but that is what we need if we are to restore a sense of purpose and rigour to higher education. At present, as the former Vice-Chancellor of the University of Manchester's Institute of Science and Technology, Sir John Mason, says, students 'can follow any course they like without regard to the intellectual or vocational quality, utility, social or economic needs, and at the taxpayers' expense.' At a stroke, my proposed scheme would elevate the status of science and engineering, which for too long have been ignored by our liberal education establishment. The effect would soon start to be felt in schools, as students would have a financial incentive to abandon soft A-levels. As more able students were recruited, so the standard of teaching would be raised at both A-level and university, and we would enjoy a virtuous circle of attainment. If this idea sounds the death knell of some of the more ideological or modish courses, then so much the better.

Reform is also needed at the other end of tertiary education. At present, there is a tangled mass of different qualifications for young people, the purpose of which is not always clear. Simplification is needed. NVQs have proved an expensive failure. They should be abandoned. In their place, the scheme of 'Modern Apprenticeships' should be expanded, since they are based on the practical needs of employers. It is usually better for businesses to arrange their own training than for the state to dictate it. That is one of the reasons for the lack of credibility of NVQs. To encourage the expansion of the scheme, major companies could be provided with limited subsidies to take on a certain number of trainees. The TECS and Further Education Quality Council should monitor apprenticeships to ensure that such subsidies are not used to recruit cheap young labour at the expense of long-serving employees. (This is one of the problems with direct job subsidies.) The other advantage of apprenticeships, mentioned in a previous chapter, is that they help to speed the transition from adolescence to adulthood by taking teenagers away from their closed peer groups and putting them in the workplace.

The most vital task of education reform lies in schools. Here again, the Conservatives have introduced a wide range of measures: the National Curriculum, Standard Assessment Tests, Grant-Maintained status, local management of schools (LMS), the assisted places scheme, and the creation of OFSTED. Yet all these steps have failed to change the fundamental culture of progressive schooling. The reason is clear. The education establishment remains firmly entrenched in its redoubts of the local authorities, the trade unions, and the training colleges. Fortified by their numbers, they have turned almost every reform to their own advantage. As we have seen, the National Curriculum has been used to further the relativist creed of the progressives, with facts ditched from history and grammar from English. Curriculum bodies have been packed with supporters of the 'child-centred' orthodoxy. Simple primary tests became incomprehensible bureaucratic exercises, thereby heightening the opposition they incurred. Governing bodies were encouraged to focus all their energies on 'resources', thereby distracting attention from academic non-achievement. Within the education field, those who stood up to the orthodoxy could find themselves out of a job. That is what happened to Chris McGovern, a history teacher at a secondary school in Sussex. When he protested in the late eighties at the weakness of the history curriculum and offered his pupils an alternative syllabus, he was made redundant.

The continuing strength of the progressive establishment makes New Labour's promises to raise standards utterly unconvincing. For Labour is an integral part of the establishment. The vast majority of local education authorities are Labour-controlled. It is the Labour Party, not the Government, which is in charge of most of our schools. Tony Blair might be a trenchant critic of the 'child-centred' creed, but his political followers have been foisting it on schools for the last two decades. Socialist egalitarianism lay behind the comprehensive experiment. The same anti-élitist ideology has encouraged 'discovery' teaching, the removal of discipline from the classroom and non-achieving multi-culturalism. For Labour to wail about falling standards is like an architect lambasting his own building.

To break this establishment we must destroy the control of the local education authorities. We should have universal grant-maintained status. The LEAs would become redundant, while schools would receive more funds as 100 per cent of all local budgets would be delegated. Schools would be free to choose their own selection policies. The best would be over-subscribed, while the worst would have to improve if they were to avoid closure. Money would cease to be wasted on the tiers of LEA bureaucracy, the policy advisers, inspectors (who duplicate the work of OFSTED at present), race officers, accountants, directors, deputy directors and curriculum planners. None of them would be needed any more. If some LEA service is deemed vital (like meals or payroll administration) then the schools can still contract to buy it. Democracy would be enhanced, for governing bodies would no longer be constrained by Town Halls. In fact, the influence of LEAs can be highly undemocratic. As a Labour activist, I was thrust on a governing body at the behest of my local LEA without having any connection with or interest in the school.

Having broken the power base of the progressive establishment, we could then move to other changes. The most important of these is a return to whole-class teaching and the renunciation of 'child-centredness'. Phonics must be the chief method of teaching

English, not one amongst a 'number of different approaches'. In maths, calculators should be banned from the classroom until second-ary school. Teachers must exchange their current 'facilitating roles' for didactic ones. Group work should disappear and children should face the front of the class seated at desks. School uniforms should be compulsory. I have already referred to the need to restore discipline, through a graded system of punishments leading to the restoration of the cane. Schools should be encouraged to have more single-sex classes. New research shows that both boys and girls do better when they learn in their own sex groups. Boys no longer want to show off, while girls do not feel so distracted or intimidated. In an experiment at the Cotswold School in Bourton-on-the-Water, when the GCSE English course was divided into two single-sex classes, four times as many boys as expected achieved grades A to C. Of course, the progressives will condemn such a move as unnatural but we should remember schools are meant to be places of learning, not 'social interaction'.

The return to traditional teaching should also be reflected in the curriculum and examinations. Pupils should be tested on the application of knowledge. The fashion for testing by modules and coursework must end. It is quite absurd that, at present, class teachers can act as supposedly independent assessors. We should also have one national examination body for both GCSEs and A-levels. The system of competing boards leads to doubts about parity of standards. Is a grade C in chemistry from one board the same as a grade C from another? To the cynic, the different boards have a market-led interest in devaluing standards: easier papers mean more entrants and hence more revenue. One national board would end such criticisms.

If teachers are to restore their roles as pedagogues, the status of the profession has to be raised. I have argued that salaries should be substantially increased in order to attract higher-calibre recruits. A special allowance could be introduced, on top of higher salaries, to provide an additional incentive to bright teachers to take up posts in the toughest inner-city schools. One of the occupation's other drawbacks has been its high degree of politicisation – as illustrated by boycotts, strikes, marches, and ranting conferences. Few actions can have damaged the authority of teachers more than the abuse meted out to David Blunkett, Labour's then Shadow Education Secretary, at the 1995 NUT Conference. At present, too many teachers appear to want the trappings of professionalism (higher salaries, public respect) without its consequences. They demand the status of members of the British Medical Association but the rights of members of the Transport and General Workers Union. They should no longer have it both ways. If they wish to be treated like professionals, they should act like professionals. The six teaching trade unions should abandon their quarrels and unite to form a professional body, called the General Teaching Council. The Council, the education equivalent of the General Medical Council, would set professional standards and ensure that those who become teachers have the correct qualifications and will maintain a high standard throughout their careers. The worst action that can be taken against a doctor is to be 'struck off' by his own professional body. The same should be true of a teacher. With this new professional ethos, strikes and boycotts could become unthinkable. It has been estimated that there are fifteen thousand incompetent teachers in our schools, an intolerable number. One reason they have been allowed to continue working is the vigorous defence the trade unions have made of low standards, always blaming them on 'lack of resources'. The new professional body would not tolerate such nonsense.

A key step towards this new professionalism is the reform of teacher training. Half of new teachers say that they feel ill-equipped by their training. This is partly because the colleges often appear more interested in political theories about disadvantage than in teaching classroom skills. One recent graduate of a training college has recounted how some of his instruction 'was almost a caricature in political correctness. Certain lecturers were preoccupied with anti-sexist and anti-racist teaching.' This trainee also complained about the casual attitude of staff, the inadequacy of their lectures and the lack 'of any grounding in practicalities'. The absence of instruction in maintaining discipline has been another complaint from teaching students. Training colleges should therefore abandon theorising in favour of practice. The new National Curriculum for teacher trainees, which requires them to reach certain standards before qualifying, is welcome. No one should be allowed on a training course without good A-level and degree results. Those with one E and a third should be shown the door. Someone who has proved incapable of learning can hardly be expected to teach successfully.

All these changes build into a process of re-establishing basic standards in our schools. In this way, education could serve as the metaphor for the wider societal change we need: the recapture of a sense of right and wrong.

CHAPTER NINE

A Welfare Society

'I don't like living off the state. I've known no other life but I want to be part of society, a good part. I want to run my own business one day. I start a year's course in hair and beauty in September. I hope that I'm learning to handle myself and my kids better. I want to break the cycle.' – Single mother from London, living on benefit, who has five children by four different men.

'The plan is not one for giving to everybody something for nothing and without trouble, or something that will free the recipients for ever thereafter from personal responsibilities. The plan is one to secure income for subsistence on condition of service and contribution.' – Sir William Beveridge, *Report on Social Insurance and Allied Services*, 1942.

'Income support now helps create the very long-term welfare dependency which the Government says it is out to destroy. Those who work lose benefit, savings are confiscated and honesty is taxed. Hence many people remain on benefit rather than take work opportunities.' – Frank Field, MP, article in the *Daily Telegraph*, July 1995.

'Welfare rights advice is the most positive thing social services can do to help their clients.' – Andy Campbell, benefits officer for Kent Social Services.

'I have always felt that a big rite of passage is leaving school and entering work and that is how you define becoming an adult. But a whole generation of young people now are not making that transfer and are stuck in a kind of limbo.' – Bob Aynsley, probation officer, Newport, South Wales.

'The Council's first priority is to maximise the incomes of local people and for many this means claiming their full entitlement to benefit. Over the past year Anti-Poverty Unit staff have carried out a number of activities to ensure people receive all their benefits.' – Cllr Aslam, Chair of Community Affairs, London Borough of Newham.

'If your live-in partner is in paid employment you can still receive the same level of benefit because he won't be expected to support you in the way that partners are in a heterosexual couple.' – Advice for gay men from Kate Gray, 'welfare rights' officer at the Scottish AIDS Monitor.

That last comment from Ms Gray exemplifies the morally degraded nature of our benefits system. While the cultural revolutionaries complain of alleged 'homophobia', the Department of Social Security is actually discriminating against straight couples. In the inverted universe of the British welfare state in the nineties, a transient homosexual relationship is financially more attractive than marriage. Ms Gray's advice is also a further illustration of the irresponsible 'rights' agenda. Gay campaigners demand equal recognition of their relationships in terms of state support, but not the same obligations for the care of their partners.

The bloated modern welfare system is one of the prices we pay for our infantilised society. In its relentless growth, it has both encouraged and reflected the breakdown of our moral values. Welfare dependency is now rife. A generation of people are growing up without any connection to the world of work. Many individuals no longer feel a responsibility to themselves, never mind their children and relatives. They look instead to the Government to care for every aspect of their lives, from providing a home to paying all the bills. In many families, the state has taken over the roles of breadwinner, father, rent-payer, and childminder. The dependency culture saps initiative and self-respect. For the long-term welfare claimant, no event need have any consequences. As life becomes a series of empty moments, the traditional rhythms of human existence are lost. There can be little sense of progress; no movement towards building a career or a family or a home. Relationships may fall apart, jobs come and go, children may be born or leave school, but the benefits keep flowing. If any proposal is put forward to restrict entitlement it is met with a wave of protest from the 'rights' lobby. Yet social security does not free its 'clients' from poverty. In fact, it traps them in it. By a combination of benefit withdrawals and low tax thresholds, our welfare state discourages people from taking jobs. And so the dependency increases. It is worth quoting again from Alexis de Tocqueville's prescient *Democracy in America* in which he foresaw the debilitating results of an overarching state:

'Having thus taken each citizen in turn in its powerful grasp and shaped him to its will, government then extends its embrace to the whole of society . . . It does not break men's will, but softens, bends and guides it; it seldom enjoins, but often inhibits action; it does not destroy anything, but prevents much being born.'

Like other features of the infantilised society – crime, illegitimacy, and state bureaucracy – welfare spending has risen spectacularly in the last two decades, more than doubling in real terms. Using 1996 prices, expenditure has gone up from £42 million in 1977 to £92 million now, the equivalent of a third of all state spending. When the Conservatives came to power social security was little more than a quarter of Government spending. In the last five years alone the funds taken by the DSS have risen by 35 per cent. Even after the measures the Government has introduced to restrict the size of the budget (Jobseekers' allowance; limits on income support and housing benefit for young people; withdrawal of support for asylum seekers; and tightening of invalidity rules) it is still expected to rise, at today's prices, to £95 billion by the year 2000. Looking at the longer historical trend, the expansion of welfare has been just as dramatic. Since 1949/50 – the first year when the new Beveridge scheme was fully operational – spending on benefits has risen eightfold in real terms. In that less fragmented age, social security represented just 13.5 per cent of public expenditure, costing £597 million.

The grasp of the welfare state is comprehensive. It is estimated that 46 million people – or 76 per cent of all households in Great Britain – receive some form of benefit. A system originally designed to help the poorest now extends to a large proportion of our citizenry, no matter what their wealth. The richest families in the land are entitled to their weekly cash payout for child benefit, though the sums involved would barely make the smallest dent in their school fees. Child benefit now reaches some 12.7 million children in 7 million families. Other beneficiaries (in some cases overlapping) include 10.1 million elderly people on retirement pensions, 1.8 million on incapacity benefit, nearly 1 million on single-parent benefit, 4.8 million receiving housing benefits, 5.7 million getting council tax and community charge rebates, 2 million on disability allowance, 5.8 million on income support, and 1 million on attendance allowance. It is also forecast that in the first year of its operation, the jobseekers' allowance will be paid to almost 2 million people.

While many of these benefits are means-tested, others, like pensions and child benefit (which together cost more than £35 billion a year), carry universal entitlement. This universality has been a major source of controversy. When the Shadow Chancellor, Gordon Brown, proposed last year that child benefit for sixteen- to nineteen-year-olds in higher-income families should be abolished and replaced by an education allowance, he encountered criticism from both sides of the political divide. The poverty campaigners indulged in their usual hysterical scare-mongering, as if the goal of social justice rested on the distribution of a £10-a-week benefit to millions of affluent households. So sacred do they regard the present sprawling welfare structure that the only change they can ever contemplate is the uprating of benefits. Indeed, the near-universal scope of social security is one of its attractions to such ideologues, for it is said to lock the middle class into the system and give them a (small) return on their investment in taxes. Welfare thus becomes a means of emphasising social interdependence. Without universality, it is argued, the middle class would not support the system, the poor would be increasingly marginalised, and savage cuts in benefits would become expedient. Will Hutton, in his revamped Keynesian best-seller, *The State We're In*, has cloaked this argument with the 'stakeholder' rhetoric of New Labour:

'The middle class and the top third of the income parade must have good reasons for accepting the progressive taxation upon which the welfare system depends. They need to get enough out of the system directly in terms of provision and indirectly in terms of social cohesion to make them support the principle of universal welfare to which they are disproportionately heavy contributors. This requires well-designed and high-quality welfare services that meet their needs as well.'

For good measure, Hutton adds that 'universal participation is the only moral basis' for welfare, since such an arrangement stresses 'the mutuality of rights and obligations'.

There are several problems with this outlook. First, in the world beyond socialist theorising, a sense of 'obligations' to others appears to be largely one-way traffic. 'We have not had any help from anyone really,' a Berkshire mother, who had nine children from three failed marriages, told the press in August 1996. This lack of help consisted of receiving benefits of £220 a week and being provided with local authority accommodation for nineteen years. In the hundreds of social-security and housing cases I dealt with as a councillor and as Harriet Harman's constituency assistant, I rarely encountered any recognition of duties from younger welfare recipients. For too many, the only duty they understood was that of the state (i.e. the taxpayer) to provide, whether they had made any contribution or not. This is the weakness of Hutton's claims about the 'moral basis' of a vast, state-run welfare system. Where is the morality in providing disincentives to work, in absolving individuals of responsibility, in making no judgements about personal behaviour? As Melanie Philips, the *Observer*'s brilliantly trenchant columnist wrote in June 1994: 'In welfare, the original community ideals of the left have been subverted by the rights agenda. Making benefits conditional upon behaviour is a taboo because benefits are seen as rights and claimants have no responsibilities.' Contrary to Hutton's view, the current system reinforces the amorality of our age.

The second problem with the Hutton thesis is that the cost of maintaining his 'high-quality' welfare services leads to punitive burdens of taxation. Far from building 'mutuality', such a process only breeds resentment from those in low-paid jobs, who may have to pay almost a third of their earnings in tax to sustain the (sometimes better) living standards of benefit claimants; hence the understandable, if not justifiable, complaints of 'scroungers'. To a guilt-ridden local-government anti-poverty research officer, with a salary of £28,000 a year and a substantial property, the welfare state might look like 'the badge of a healthy society' (to use Hutton's phrase). To a catering worker earning £9,000 a year for a forty-hour week, paying out £2,800 a year in income tax, national insurance and council tax, while living next to a young single mother on benefits worth £11,000 a year, it looks like a state-organised racket. Third, universality means that too much welfare is spread too thinly across too many recipients. Despite having paid contributions throughout their working lives, many of our ten million pensioners are living in poverty. Nor do contributory unemployment benefits (now the jobseekers' allowance) provide anything beyond the bare necessities of life. Fourth, through the quirks of the system, it can actually result in a transfer of wealth from the working poor to the idle rich. A single man with lower than average earnings, in private rented accommodation, may receive nothing from the state. But an unmarried man with three children, living with his 'partner' on a private income of over £100,000, receives at least £1,500 a year in child benefit.

When the Left talk about 'social renewal', 'rebuilding communities' or a 'new crusade against poverty', so often this is no more than code for an extension of welfare services. Behind such language is the belief that the Conservatives have inflicted massive cuts in benefits over the last seventeen years, and torn up the post-war Beveridge welfare state. A look at the resolutions submitted to the 1995 Labour Conference provides a flavour of such views. There were demands that an incoming Labour Government: 'reverse the rundown of the welfare state'; 'restore the cuts in services to the elderly made by successive Tory Governments'; 'maintain and improve the welfare state on the basis of universality of provision, available at the point and time of need', and 'overhaul the benefits system to enable claimants to understand and maximise benefits, and introduce benefits for all sixteen- to eighteen-year-olds who are unable to claim benefits under the present system.' Other constituency parties 'condemned the damage done by Conservative Governments since 1979 to the fabric of the welfare state' including 'the relentless removal of rights and their replacement with discretion'. The Transport and General Workers Union, never slow at devising new methods of swallowing public money, wanted to see an uprated universal child benefit; 'support for women's rights through tax and benefit provision, and comprehensive childcare'; and the provision of 'affordable, decent housing, through public investment and the benefit system'. As the statistics proved earlier, however, the idea of a Tory destruction of the welfare state is so much nonsense. But it is one of the most pervasive myths of our time, along with the idea of 'cuts' in the NHS, local government and schools. Its widespread acceptance is due largely to the infantilisation of our society. For me, the real mistake of the Conservative Government has been its failure to enhance the livelihoods of those in work but on low incomes, particularly families. Here is yet more evidence to back up the earlier point made about tax burdens on the family. Recent research by the independent Institute of Fiscal Studies revealed that in 1979 a single-earner couple on half of average earnings were paying 16 per cent of their income in direct taxes. In 1996 the figure was 19 per cent. Paul Johnson, the programme director of the Institute, has summarised the Tory tax policy as follows: 'Big tax cuts for those at the top of the income distribution, relatively little change for those in the middle and small increases for those at the bottom.' That is the real disgrace of eighteen years of Tory rule, not the fantastical cuts in welfare spending. Such a pattern has occurred for one shameful partisan reason: low-income groups are less inclined to be Tory supporters. What has been remarkable, however, is the way the Left has colluded with the heavy taxation of the poor. All talk of 'tax cuts', at whatever level, is seen as anti-socialist. The entire focus of most 'anti-poverty strategies' is towards increased benefits and higher take-up rather than lower taxes. Taxation is seen as something virtuous in itself, the expression of the redistributive powers of the state, the enactment of the progressive ideal to shift wealth from the rich. Yet it is the working poor who have to pay for it.

Other voices on the Left admit that welfare expenditure has risen dramatically over the last decade and a half. They claim, however, that this is entirely due the Conservatives' mishandling of the econ-omy, which had created two recessions and driven millions on to the dole queues. This is another myth from the voluminous box of flawed socialist theories. It is true that unemployment remains unacceptably high, having reached levels that must horrify those who grew up in the era of full employment just after the war. Joblessness is one of the great social evils of our age, bringing despair and poverty to millions of families. But the Conservatives have a much better record on employment than most of the other European Govern-ments, especially the socialist-led administrations of the late President Mitterrand in France and González in Spain. At the time of writ-ing less than 8 per cent of the workforce is unemployed in Britain, compared to more than 11 per cent in France. 'Fiddled figures', cry the Left, pointing to the twenty changes the Government has made in the unemployment count since 1979. But this will not wash. There are not greatly significant differences between the official Department for Education and Employment figures and those of the Left-leaning International Labour Organisation (ILO). The ILO definition of unemployment counts 'all those aged sixteen and over who are without a job, are available to start work in the next two weeks, who have been seeking a job in the last four weeks or are waiting to start a job already obtained.' Since 1992, the ILO figures have shown the same powerful downward trend. Yet the social security budget has continued to rise. This is the anomalous

Tory legacy of the nineties: falling unemployment and a growing welfarism.

It is societal change, not unemployment, which is largely responsible for the increase in demand for benefits. The unemployed only account for about 10 per cent of all welfare spending, compared to 45 per cent on the elderly and 24 per cent on the sick and disabled. Between the financial years 1991/92 and 1995/96, expenditure by the DSS on unemployed people increased by only £500 million, while the total benefits bill went up by £14.4 billion. Most of this increase is accounted for by more funds going to pensioners (up to £3 billion) and the long-term sick and disabled (up £7.5 billion). The latter is explained by both an increased number of recipients (up by 500,000 over the last five years) and, according to the DSS, 'people staying on benefit longer'. Again, this contradicts the myth of a cruel Tory Government hitting the most vulnerable in society. Apart from these two groups of beneficiaries, the other major changes in welfare spending have been the growing costs of lone-parent benefit and housing benefit.

Both are partly the result of the breakdown of the family. Total DSS spending on lone parents has more than doubled in the last five years, from £4.7 billion to 1990/91 to £9.5 billion in 1995/96 (more than DSS spending on the unemployed). Single, never-married mothers aged twenty to twenty-nine account for a third of the increase in the number of recipients over these years. In another reflection of our irresponsible society, the proportion of single parents receiving maintenance has declined heavily since the Conservatives came to power. In 1979, around half of lone-parent families on benefit also received maintenance. Now less than 20 per cent do so. It can only be hoped that the long-term influence of the Child Support Agency will start to reverse these figures. Housing benefit (which covers a wide range of claimants, pensioners, the unemployed, lone parents) has seen its spending rise from £5.1 million in 1990/91 to £10.8 million in 1995/96. Over this period, the number of claimants has risen by 800,000 to 4.8 million. A large proportion of the group will have been people leaving the family home as a result of divorce, separation, or rows between young people and their parents. What I find disturbing is the attitude from too many young people that the state should provide them with their own accommodation the moment they decide to live on their own, even when they do not have a modicum of economic independence – or the intention of acquiring any. The *bien pensants* support this view. They encapsulate it in that ruinously expensive slogan, 'decent and affordable housing for all'. The idea that everyone, no matter what their age, diligence, marital status or personal behaviour should have their own home has been elevated into 'a fundamental human right'. When the Government last year introduced mild restrictions on the right of young people under the age of twenty-five to claim housing benefit, limiting payments to the average cost of shared accommodation in the area, Ministers were denounced by Labour MPs and welfare groups for their callousness. The impact would be 'devastating' on young people, said one charity. Yet why should a low-income taxpayer, struggling with his own mortgage, have to pay the rent of an out-of-work seventeen-year-old who decides he would like his own expensive apartment, a move that was certainly possible under the old arrangements? We can see again that in the infantilised society the traditional process for males of maturing into adulthood – apprenticeship, job, save, leave home, rent, save, marry – is being destroyed. I doubt that the founders of the welfare state intended that the public should subsidise the aspirations of teenagers to have 'me own spice'.

On top of paying out all these benefits, the DSS has another burden: the huge cost of running the welfare system. In 1995/96 the Government spent £4.3 billion on the administration of social security – the equivalent of the entire budget for higher education. The total number of staff working for the DSS and its agencies rose from 85,700 in 1989/90 to 99,500 in 1995/96, a growing army of bureaucrats employed partly to shift wealth from one impoverished group (the low-earning taxpayer) to another (the non-taxpayer). Any attempt to reduce this payroll through greater productivity is characterised by the 'progressives' as 'another assault on the poor'. Because of the complexity of means-testing, some benefits carry a ludicrous administrative charge. The Social Fund, for instance, costs £209 million a year to run, the equivalent of 46 per cent of the £451 million total benefits given out by the Fund. Would any organisation outside the public sector contemplate spending this proportion of its money on bureaucracy? Income support cost an incredible £1.7 billion to run, equal to 10 per cent of the total benefits paid out in this category. One administrative bill that falls on the local authorities rather than the DSS is housing benefit, which last year cost £285 million. Even with this high level of bureaucracy, fraud is rife within the system. The Government estimates that it is losing £900 million a year through fraudulent housing-benefit claims. In one recent operation in Oxford, investigators found that no less than 254 people, all registered as living in one four-bedroom house, were making separate claims. In 1994, the Benefits Agency admitted that fraud in income support could be costing £1.4 billion a year. Like most other crime, benefit fraud has not been taken seriously by some on the Left because they feel that the perpetrators are necessarily the poorest members of society. Demanding action amounts to a politically incorrect attack on the 'victims' of society, especially if the fraudsters are from ethnic minorities. Such a view was vividly demonstrated in the Crofton scandal in the London Borough of Hackney. When he became Director of Housing in Hackney, Bernard Crofton, a former GLC housing official with impeccable anti-racist credentials, began to investigate allegations of fraud within the council's housing depart-ment, including the misuse of housing-benefit funds. Suddenly, he was sacked for alleged racism. It was only when the Labour leadership of the council changed – partly as a consequence of revulsion at the Crofton sacking – that he was reinstated. To the shame of the PC ideologues, most of Crofton's loudest supporters were tenants from Hackney's housing estates, who had welcomed his anti-fraud drive. What they recognised, and the liberal theorists ignored, was the way that money gained by fraudsters can be money lost to genuine welfare claimants. That is why the greatest resentment against fraud often comes from the working class, not the middle class. I have never met anyone who felt more passionately about benefit cheating than the chairman of a large tenants association in my former ward in Islington. But that is because he had a powerful sense of moral values, as he constantly proved by his work for charity and the concern he showed for his members.

The costs of welfare bureaucracy extend beyond direct adminis-tration. We now have a host of individuals employed indirectly by the welfare state. There are the DSS landlords, bed-and-breakfast proprietors, and small-hotel owners providing (often wretched) accommodation to social security claimants. In some of our seaside resorts, like Margate and Hastings, the DSS is now easily the largest client. In their own way, these landlords are as much part of the dependency culture as their residents. Then there are the professional pressure-group campaigners who earn their (not insubstantial) salaries by demanding the requisition of more taxpayers' money for welfare services. Here are just a few of such groups: Shelter, the National Unemployed Centres Combine, the National Council for One Parent Families, the National Childcare Campaign, Gingerbread (action for single-parent families), the Low Pay Unit, the Child Poverty Action Group, Campaign for the Single Homeless, Rights of Women, the Joint Council for the Welfare of Immigrants, the Campaign for Non-Racist Benefits, Church Action on Poverty, the Strathclyde Poverty Alliance, the Law Centres Federation, and the Campaign Against the Child Support Act. This last mentioned opposes the Act because 'it denies the state's responsibility for children', a perfect summary of the collectivist position of most welfare campaigners. And this denial of parental responsibility is one reason why our society is in crisis.

The pressure groupies are joined by the New Public Servants employed by the local authorities, like welfare rights advisers and anti-poverty workers. The Borough of Crewe and Nantwich, for instance, has a prestigious new post entitled the *Tackling Disadvantage Co-Ordinator*. When Enfield went Labour in 1994, one of the Council's first acts was to recruit two *Anti-Poverty Information Officers* on the distinctly comfortable salary of £25,000. Such a move has become the rather unambitious symbol of the advance of socialism in the nineties. Hertfordshire has a *Take Up Campaigns Worker* who 'initiates and contributes to welfare-benefit take-up campaigns' throughout the county, while Nottinghamshire has a special *HIV Welfare Rights Officer*. During my time at Islington, each of our twenty-four neighbourhood offices had a 'welfare rights' team, supported at the centre by researchers, social services officers, project leaders, and a central anti-poverty information unit. Their work was duplicated by a number of publicly-funded voluntary groups and community projects devoted to welfare advice, like 'Islington People's Rights', North Islington Law Centre and the Pakistan Women's Welfare Association, as well as the Citizens' Advice Bureau. If you want your income-support form completed, Islington is the place to go. Then there are the EU bureaucrats based in this country, overseeing the distribution of regional funds, social funds, and 'action-programme' funds to tackle poverty, with yet more duplication and administration. The pressure groupies have not one but two Euro-organisations: the European Anti-Poverty Network and the strangely-named Observatory of Policies for Combating Social Exclusion, 'an independent group of experts appointed to study poverty-related problems'. What all these groups and employees have in common is their interest in the expansion of the welfare state. More welfare means more advice, campaigns, briefings, counselling, research, lobbying, consultancy, advocacy, conferences, documents, committees, liaison, casework, representation, publicity, monitoring and 'policy development' – all activity geared towards exposing the 'inadequacy' of current spending. The beauty of this arrangement is that more welfare also means more 'poverty' – for, by definition, anyone who is in receipt of benefit must be poor. As the welfare state grows, so does the 'client base' of the poor, thus extending the scope for action by welfare professionals and poverty campaigners.

It is this perverse process that results in the ever-changing definition of poverty. Because of our extensive benefits system, no one in this country, thankfully, has to live in absolute poverty, defined by Robert McNamara, former President of the World Bank as 'a condition so limited by malnutrition, illiteracy, disease, squalid surroundings, high infant mortality and low life expectancy as to be beneath any reasonable definition of human decency.' Whatever the lurid imaginings of certain radicals, Tory rule has not reduced Britain to this state. If anyone has to live in such environments, it is usually the result of their own tragic mental illness or their extreme irresponsibility, a word we rarely hear from the welfarists. (I mentioned earlier the case in Islington of a baby left to die in his own urine after monstrous neglect by his parents. More than sixty-seven professionals from thirty departments of various welfare agencies were involved in the case. Despite all this attention, the child lived in 'some of the filthiest conditions that are likely to be imagined' said an independent inquiry report. The inquiry also found that the family was given 'considerable' sums by social services and charities to buy furnishings and equipment.) In the absence of 'absolute poverty' and with living standards continuing to rise – real household disposable income per head was 80 per cent higher in 1994 than in 1971 – the welfare lobby has to fall back on using the term 'relative' poverty. 'Relative poverty', like relative morality, is a flexible concept. J. K. Galbraith, the guru of 'progressive' economists, has said that 'people are poverty-stricken when their income, even if adequate, falls markedly behind that of the community.' But what does 'markedly' mean? Can anyone with an 'adequate' income be meaningfully classified as poor? And who is included in this community? One pressure group recently claimed that anyone without a video-recorder could be defined as living in poverty, a patently ludicrous benchmark. The most widely used definition is less than 'half of average income'. This has the great advantage that, as the nation's wealth rises, so does the standard of 'relative' poverty. Even in Dubai or Liechtenstein, there must be some people living on less than half average incomes. The Government can never win, no matter how much prosperity it brings to the nation. And the poverty lobby can never be out of work.

The most frequent demand of the welfarists is for an improvement in the levels of benefit. The problem is that the system already acts, especially for young people, as a disincentive to work and responsibility. Because of the benefits structure – and the high levels of direct taxation required to sustain it – thousands are better off remaining idle than taking jobs, the scenario that has become known as the 'poverty trap'. As soon as the new jobholder starts to receive his wages, so personal taxes increase, benefits are withdrawn, and thus he sees only a fractional rise in his real earnings. Labour's Commission on Social Justice, set up by the late John Smith to come up with ideas on reforming the welfare state (which it singularly failed to do) summarised the problem as follows: 'The combination of National Insurance contributions, income tax and the withdrawal of means-tested benefits means that half a million of the poorest people are effectively paying marginal tax rates of 70 per cent or even higher.' In such circumstances, it is astonishing that half a million people still have the self-respect to go out to work. To put more detailed figures on the 'poverty trap', analysts use a measure called the 'marginal deduction rate'. A marginal deduction rate of 90 per cent means that, for every extra £1 in the wage packet, 90p is lost through the payment of tax and National Insurance and the withdrawal of benefits. Despite several reforms by the Government to eliminate the problem – such as reducing National Insurance contributions for low earners and calculating means-tested benefits on net rather than gross income – the effects of the trap are still felt by too many. Incredibly, 10,000 people still face marginal deduction rates above 100 per cent, making welfare literally more desirable than work.

Another 100,000 face rates of 90 per cent and above, while 630,000 have rates of over 70 per cent. Closely related to the poverty trap is the 'unemployment trap' whereby the costs of working are higher than the costs of unemployment. The measure often used here is a replacement ratio in which, according to the Department of Social Security, 'income out of work is expressed as a percentage of income in work. The higher the ratio, the less is the financial incentive to work.' Again, the Government has tried to tackle the problem, most importantly through the introduction of Family Credit. Yet, replacement ratios above 70 per cent are still prevalent, affecting 510,000 in 1995/96. No less than 15,000 have a ratio above 100 per cent.

Such figures highlight the corrosive effects of an all-enveloping welfare system. Despite eighteen years of Tory rule, we are trapped in a downward spiral. Costly benefits require high taxes. High taxes reduce income, encouraging more to claim benefits. More claimants mean an increased welfare bill and higher taxes, driving more into the embrace of the welfare state. The cost is not just felt in financial terms. We are destroying the sense of responsibility and dignity in thousands of young men and women. More than a fifth of sixteen- to nineteen-year-old men are unemployed. The longer they are unemployed, the more unemployable they become. Living off benefit, marginalised from the adult world, many turn to drugs and crime. The Home Office study of January 1996 (mentioned in the previous chapter) about a new generation of 'perpetual adolescents' warned of the damaging consequences of youth unemployment, since work 'provides a sense of direction and security and bestows the status of manhood upon young males.' From the American political Right, the sociologist Charles Murray has called this group of jobless male youth The New Rabble, existing beyond the normal restraining influences of civilisation: the family, the workplace, marriage. From the British Left, the feminist Bea Campbell, in a not dissimilar analysis, has warned that unemployment has removed the traditional controls on aggressive masculinity, with the resulting crime and thuggishness on rundown housing estates. The rise of the disaffected, idle and unemployable young man is one of the most serious social problems of our time, far more serious than all the excited attention that is devoted by our cultural leaders to spurious gender problems in the police, the fire brigade and the armed forces.

In the creation of our social security leviathan, we have also lost the connection which used to exist between contributions and benefits. Until the second half of this century, the amount of benefit was related – at least in part – to contributions paid. The welfare state was seen not as an open-ended arrangement but a scheme of nationalised social insurance. The contributory principle lay at the heart of the first modern welfare system built by the great reforming Liberal Government of the Edwardian era. Churchill, who, as President of the Board of Trade, played a leading role in the introduction of old-age pensions, labour exchanges and unemployment assistance, argued that insurance 'would promote the self-reliance of the individual'. In the words of the historian Paul Addison, 'Churchill, Asquith and Lloyd George conceived of their reforms as creating a strictly limited safety net. It was not intended to provide social security for all, but to assist families in the struggle to avoid the worst extremes of poverty.' Contributory insurance was also central to the Beveridge plan. 'It is first and foremost, a plan of insurance,' wrote Beveridge in his 1942 report, 'of giving in return for contributions benefits up to subsistence level, as of right and without means tests, so that individuals may build freely upon it.' Yet even in the forties, this principle was under threat. To the Left, insurance was wrong because it contravened the egalitarian belief that wealth from the 'rich' should be redistributed to help the 'poor'. As the darling of Labour Left-wingers, Aneurin Bevan, put it: 'A strictly socialist approach would condemn the whole idea of contributory insurance.' In line with such thinking, the Labour Government made benefits immediately available to all, depleting the National Insurance fund, and breaking for ever the contributory basis to the welfare state. We are living with the consequences. The inverted values of our infantilised age are captured in a system that pays out 'something for nothing', the approach that Beveridge expressly warned against. To the doped-out jobless youth in his rent-rebated bedsit in Hastings or the twenty-something single parent in her housing association flat, the term National Insurance probably sounds like a finance company based in the Midlands. This is another way that welfare weakens moral responsibility. If an individual knows that he will receive support from the state regardless of his contributory record, then he has little incentive to make any contributions. What need is there to build up savings, be thrifty or think of the future when the state can provide permanent protection?

The destruction of the contributory principle makes it odd that, in our society, widespread disgust should always be expressed at the thought of anyone having to live off 'charity handouts'. For a claimant who has never paid anything in tax or national insurance, the chief difference between charity and benefits is that the revenue for the former has been freely given while the revenue for the latter has been compulsorily taken by the state. I am not suggesting for a moment that we should abolish welfare and go back to the Victorian philanthropic tradition, a move which would drive millions of families into the most terrible destitution. It was precisely the hopeless inadequacy of Victorian charity that led to the creation of a primitive form of welfare at the turn of the century. But what I am questioning is the assumption that welfare is somehow more 'moral' than charity. The high taxation required to provide social security actually removes any moral imperative from the individual to care about poverty. Take two employees, both on salaries of £30,000. One might feel delighted at the £10,000 a year he pays in tax, treating it as evidence of his concern for those less fortunate than himself. The other might bitterly resent the sum, denouncing all claimants as 'scroungers'. But both are compelled to pay the same. And if the more 'caring' individual felt that the money going to the poor was inadequate, his reaction would probably not be to pay more into charity, but to demand that the Government increase taxes on everyone. So the welfare system weakens the moral responsibilities, not just of its 'clients' but also of its financial providers. The duty of care towards others has been subsumed by the state. In the same spirit, middle-aged, prosperous families demand that welfare services look after their elderly relatives – and still expect to inherit their properties. The nadir of this attitude was reached last year, when the BMA asserted that families were 'saving' the state £34 billion a year by looking after their own disabled or elderly dependants, as if the state should have the primary responsibility for them. I suppose, in the BMA's view, millions of mothers have 'saved' the state billions by bringing up their own children instead of passing them on to local-authority care.

For many radicals and Marxists, the whole concept of charity is a repugnant one, for it conflicts with the role of the all-embracing state. Charity is dangerous because, by mitigating the effects of social 'dislocation' and 'oppression', it reduces the demand for political change. In 'filling the gaps' left by the absence of state provision, charities have committed the crime of helping to prop up the status quo. Sadly, some charity leaders appear to have taken on this attitude, aping the pressure groups in their demands for more state cash, in producing 'research' documents, and running highly political campaigns attacking Government policy. When the Government last year introduced its benefit changes for asylum seekers, both charities and the Church joined in loud protests, complaining that they would have to meet the needs of refugees awaiting verdicts on their asylum applications. But surely that is exactly what such bodies should be doing, rather than indulging in political protests? I have also heard third world charity activists criticise Mother Teresa and Albert Schweitzer for failing to campaign against social injustice and racism, as if they would have achieved more as members of the Socialist Workers Party than as devout Christians. A recent feature in the *Guardian* also criticised Mother Teresa for praying too much, which is an odd accusation to make about a nun. Presumably, instead of giving physical and spiritual assistance to the sick and dying, she ought to have been campaigning for their 'rights'. Many other charities, while not descending to these levels, have become locked into the contract culture of the welfare state, either through the provision of services to local authorities (running old people's homes, residential care, social services, childcare) or through the bidding arrangements for National Lottery funds. In the longer term, both these developments could inhibit the freedom of those charities involved, reducing them to no more than arms of the institutionalised welfare system. Again, one of the more ridiculous accusations made against Mother Teresa is that her organisation 'lacks a professional management structure', as if she were the Director of Social Services in the borough of Calcutta.

But it would be wrong to exaggerate this movement. The long British tradition of charitable work continues to flourish beyond the rants of political theorists. Thankfully, the vast majority of charitable expenditure goes on health, welfare and housing rather than campaigning. Donations to charity remain strong, despite the scaremongering over the effects of the National Lottery. A quarter of women and a fifth of men in Britain participate in some form of voluntary activity. Institutions like the RNIB, St John Ambulance,

Save the Children Fund, the NSPCC, and the Hospice Movement continue to command the affection of the British people. Our task is to ensure that the spirit of moral responsibility which runs through voluntary work is extended to a wider plane.

What needs to change

In spite of record spending, an army of 100,000 bureaucrats, and tentacles in every sector of life in Britain, our welfare system is a failure. It has encouraged fecklessness, undermined personal responsibility, damaged the family and increased unemployment. Worst of all, by spreading its resources too thinly and requiring high levels of taxation, it has done little to raise the living standards of the poorest groups in society.

The traditional answer to this failure from the welfarists, the political Left and pressure groups is to demand an increase in all benefits, paid for out of higher taxation. Such foolishness would be mind-boggling were it not for the fact that these are the same breed of *bien pensants* who think that the solution to crime is the closure of prisons, that 'child-centred learning' increases literacy, that family breakdown has no effect on children, and that anti-racism campaigning promotes racial harmony. More spending on benefits will only create more poverty and unemployment traps, leading to higher joblessness, more resentment from taxpayers (especially at the lower end of the scale) and greater social friction.

Equally fallacious is the solution of some nihilists from the political Right. They propose that all welfare be abolished and its place taken by private philanthropy. This follows the view expressed by Frederick Hayek in *The Mirage of Social Justice* where he wrote: 'We can choose to whom we are benevolent and this requires that welfare provision should be privately based.' Such a policy would be a disaster, inflicting Third-World-style impoverishment on most of our cities, reducing housing estates to ghettoes of abject squalor and destitution. Starvation could become a reality, social unrest a probability. A less brutal approach has been outlined by Alan Duncan and Dominic Hobson in their book, *Saturn's Children*, where they advocate the replacement of social security with a 'basic income for all', which has the attraction of simplicity while also removing the disincentives to work. The problem is that, to provide a subsistence standard of living, the scheme would require exorbitant levels of taxation. Worse, it would leave very few people better off, as Duncan and Hobson, with refreshing candour, admit: 'A computer analysis of a Basic Income payment of £53 a week suggests that, although the poorest tenth of the population will be considerably better off, five out of the six poorest deciles will actually be worse off. Three out of the four richest deciles gain, and only the richest tenth stand to lose.' To overcome such distributional problems, the authors say that some form of means testing might be necessary, which would reintroduce the bureaucratic complexities of means testing that the scheme was meant to avoid.

The problem with all welfare reform is that we are dealing with some of the vulnerable groups in society. As I have pointed out, 70 per cent of all welfare expenditure is geared towards the elderly, the sick and the disabled. However, given that the other 30 per cent amounts to the equivalent of £33 billion, there is certainly wide scope for action. What is vital is to have a clear objective as the basis for change. Many would-be reformers talk airily of 'targeting benefits at those in real need' without giving any definition of 'real need'. Almost everyone in receipt of non-universal benefits is in 'real need' in the sense that they have no alternative income. Another vapid favourite is the phrase 'a hand up, not a handout', a rhetorical device used by moderates to avoid any hard decisions on the subject. What is a hand up to one claimant might be regarded as a handout to another.

The goals I would place at the centre of reform are those that have been running throughout this book: strengthened moral confidence, greater personal responsibility, support for the family and respect for the elderly. These can be achieved in four ways: first, by new pension arrangements; second, by changes to the tax and benefit system; third, by guiding young people from welfare into work; and fourth, by creating more employment opportunities. I will deal with each in turn.

First, on respect for the elderly, I have already argued that there should be an immediate increase in the basic pension. It is quite wrong that, through the recent decline in its value, we should be penalising those people who went through their careers believing they were paying for security in retirement by their National Insurance contributions. It is not their fault that the contributory principle has been so devalued by the bloated expansion of social security in the last twenty years. As I have said, such an increase should be disregarded for the purposes of calculating income support. This can only be a temporary measure for the present generation of the elderly. In the longer term, the state pension cannot be regarded as anything more than the most limited safety net. With an ageing population – it is estimated that by 2031, 23 per cent of the population will be over sixty-five, compared to 12 per cent in 1961 and 16 per cent now – the costs to taxpayers of providing a comfortable retirement for all are simply unsustainable. Moreover, if the safety net is too luxurious – 'a hammock rather than a net', as one American politician has described it – there will be no incentive to save. Those in work should be required to make alternative arrangements for their old age. I believe that the present system of National Insurance should be gradually phased out and replaced with a compulsory private levy that would cover both pensions and unemployment. Contributions would be paid into private funds, as happens now, but a much stricter regulatory regime must be introduced to ensure that they are protected. Much tougher powers should be given to the Pensions Investment Authority to check that a fair rate of return on the investment is provided and that administrative charges are dropped from their current absurd levels, in many cases over 25 per cent. The practice of front-loading charges, whereby a pensions company tries to recoup all its costs within the first few years of the operation of a scheme, should be ended. Sir Norman Fowler, who as Social Security secretary in the eighties helped to build the modern private pensions industry, has joined calls for more supervision, admitting there should be 'an agreed system of regulations which gives proper assurance to the public.' Utility regulators, which have proved quite effective in achieving reduced charges, could be the model for a new interventionist PIA. The authority, in liaison with the Inland Revenue, could also set the minimum levels for contributions. It would also be the duty of pension companies to provide some form of cover to contributors for set periods of unemployment – in the way that many self-employed now buy income-protection plans.

The advantages of compulsory private pensions, regulated by the Government, are obvious. They enhance personal responsibility by making explicit the link between contributions and benefits. Contributors will feel more in control of schemes they have built with their own money, as opposed to the bureaucratic black hole of welfare into which their NI contributions now disappear.

Through the expansion of pension funds, they create new sources of revenue for investment in the economy. The political Right might object to the compulsory element as another piece of state intervention in personal salaries. But the state already takes a portion of income through National Insurance. And all the libertarian theorising cannot disguise the fact that, if people do not make pension contributions, other taxpayers have to pick up the bill. As one pensions analyst said last year, 'Unless people have to save, all the evidence is that they won't.' From the Left will come the usual objections to privatisation. If people are compelled to make contributions, then why not pay them into a Government fund? We have tried that one. It is called National Insurance and it has not worked. As the contributory principle has disappeared, so NI has become just another form of direct taxation. Moreover, the NI fund provides a pot of money which no Government has proved able to resist, especially not in this age of whining about 'lack of resources'. As the fund declines, so taxes have had to replenish it, thus further destroying the point of the insurance principle. It is better that the Government regulates, rather than owns, pension schemes. A third, more coherent, objection is that low earners will not be able to make the contributions necessary for a decent pension. Under the present absurd tax arrangements, this may be true. That is one reason why reform of the tax and benefit system is so urgent.

Tony Blair says in his collection of essays, *New Britain: My Vision of a Young Country*, 'the best way to ensure everyone has the means to a decent life is not to boost benefits but instead to help people into work.' But, as I have shown, the welfare system acts as a powerful disincentive to work through the creation of poverty and employment traps. One measure, proposed above, the phasing out of National Insurance for employees, would marginally reduce the costs of entering a new job. More fundamentally, tax thresholds have to be raised substantially. It is quite ridiculous that, at present, employees can have such low wages that they are eligible for benefit, yet they still have to pay tax on their income. I argued in the chapter on the family that the tax threshold for an earner in a married couple should be raised to £10,000 at the lower 20 per cent rate, with an additional allowance of £500 for each child, up to a maximum of four. I believe we should also raise the threshold to around £7,500 for unmarried earners. What about the lost revenue, cry the fiscally prudent? There would be some, but there would also be substantial savings made by encouraging people off welfare and into work. Nor should we exaggerate the amount of revenue the Government currently gains from taxing the working poor. According to 1995/96 Inland Revenue figures, 1.8 million people have to pay the lower-rate tax on salaries below £5,000, yet the Government 'take' is a measly £230 million. Just £1.6 billion is raised from those earning between £5,000 and £7,500, and another £3.3 billion from those earning between £7,500 and £10,000. Compare these figures to the massive £8.1 billion taken from the 100,000 taxpayers who earn over £100,000 or the £8.2 billion from the 400,000 with incomes between £50,000 and £100,000. This takes me to another proposal: introduce two new 'super' tax rates of 45 per cent on incomes over £50,000 and 50 per cent on incomes over £75,000. It seems odd that at present there should be three rates of tax on incomes below £30,000 yet no gradations on the taxation of far greater wealth. This would not only raise substantial funds to cover the tax cuts on the poor, but would also reverse, in a minor way, some of the extravagant gains that the rich have made under the eighteen years of Conservative rule. There has been too much hot air expended about the 'unleashing of enterprise' through low tax rates on the rich. What spirit of enterprise have the overpaid utility bosses, legal-aid lawyers, management consultants and two-days-a-week boardroom directors brought to Britain? Another argument used against a tax rise on the wealthy is that they would merely use devious accounting to avoid paying it. Such an attitude only shows the depths of the amoral society. Because some selfish people ignore their responsibilities is hardly a reason to avoid action. Do we stop requiring absent fathers to pay maintenance because of the difficulties in collecting it from some of them? Such objections can only be used with the wealthy. The security guard on £2.80 an hour is unlikely to have an accountant.

Even with such tax changes, very low earners will still not have greatly increased incomes, particularly those with family responsibilities. The reason child benefit was introduced by the Labour Government in the seventies was because child tax allowances brought no financial rewards to the poor who did not pay tax. Two further changes are therefore necessary. First, we should extend family credit, both to provide a greater incentive for married people to look for work and to make up for the loss of child benefit, whose abolition I proposed in the chapter on family breakdown. Second, to prevent employers abusing family credit, we should introduce a minimum wage of around £3.50 an hour. Though family credit has helped to reduce some of the worst of the poverty traps, it has also acted as a perverse subsidy of poverty wages. More than one million people in Britain today are earning less than £2.50 an hour and 300,000 earn less than £1.50 an hour, while the DSS has to pay out £2.5 billion in benefits because such wages are obviously too low to provide a decent living. The state should stop subsidising such a racket. The Conservatives say that a minimum wage would destroy jobs, but do we really want to protect jobs that pay less than subsistence levels? Even Republicans in the USA support the concept of a minimum wage. There would be a cost to some employers, though to few who had any sense of social responsibility. The phase-out of employers' national insurance on salaries of less than £10,000 might be one way to offset their increased pay bill. Progressive in theory, employers' NI contributions have in practice acted as another tax on jobs.

The people who most urgently need jobs are the young unemployed. At present, the benefits system is encouraging too many of them to follow lives of 'voluntary idleness', to use Charles Murray's phrase. Some would be attracted into employment by the abolition of poverty traps but many would not: £50 a week, a few splifs and a bedsit is all they seek. Work sounds, well, too much like hard work. Returning to the contributory insurance principle, we should remove all benefits, including housing benefit, to young people aged sixteen to twenty-one. They should be either in full-time education or training, or in work. As I argued in the previous chapter, firms could be provided with subsidies to provide training places and apprenticeships. Lounging around at the taxpayers' expense can no longer be an option. But we could not let those who have left home starve on the streets. Therefore, instead of paying out housing benefit and bed and breakfast bills, the money should be used to run young persons' hostels. These should not be intimidating institutions but places where they would have a room of their own, where there would be mature adults to give support and careers advice. Indeed, these hostels could be a key part of breaking the cycle of nihilism. It is vital that those working in these places are responsible, preferably married, men who can provide role models to the youths. The introduction of a Voluntary National Service, under which young people would be required to perform regular 'unpaid' work in society, will also help to reduce the irresponsibility of some of these adolescent males. A hostel network could be a physical base for organising some of these voluntary activities, again emphasising their positive role.

The idea of hostels for young single mothers is usually greeted with derision, but, again, these could be of great benefit to their users. They could provide support networks, communal subsidised laundry and eating facilities, and clean, secure accommodation. Above all, they could have a reliable, on-site crèche, enabling the mothers to go out to work if they wanted. Would such a supportive environment not be preferable to a poorly furnished council flat on an estate? Of course, it can be seen as a restriction of 'freedom' but having a child is the greatest restriction on freedom imaginable. Far from treating young adults as children, both types of hostel could inspire greater maturity through the guidance of experienced adults. It is the instant gratification of young people's desire to 'have their own space' which is the greatest catalyst of infantilism.

Incentives to leave the dole queue depend on the existence of jobs. Some of the changes already outlined, like apprenticeships and youth training, will help people into them. The long-standing Labour proposal to release capital receipts from the sales of council property will create a sizeable number of jobs in the construction industry. It has also been estimated that capital grants from the National Lottery have injected £1 billion into construction. This is excellent and I believe the Lottery charities should spend even more on capital projects rather than subsidising anti-poverty campaigns and politically correct projects. Direct job creation is the best way to help the impoverished. The Government can act in other pro-active ways to reduce unemployment. Local authorities and voluntary agencies could have ring-fenced grants to create more jobs in social care, like home helps and residential assistants, or manual jobs in parks, cleaning and sports centres. What they must definitely not do is expand the army of New Public Servants. In fact, the reduction in the New Public Service, envisaged in almost every chapter of this book, would actually provide funds for more useful public employees. For every £30,000 'Needs Assessment Manager' we could have two £15,000 care assistants. The new scheme of Voluntary National Service will also create jobs for supervisors and organisers throughout the country. The expansion of the prison service will lead to more employment for prison officers and construction workers.

Ultimately, though, it is the macro-economic climate that leads to long-lasting reductions in joblessness. The one way to guarantee high levels of unemployment is to lock ourselves in the strait-jacket of European Monetary Union. We would be denied the chance of reducing interest rates or devaluing our currency to boost industry. It is telling that unemployment in this country has fallen by more than one million since the day we left the ERM, while much of the Continent remains plagued by rising dole queues. That is one reason why we cannot continue to be involved with the disastrous European project. More than any of the tax and benefit changes I have outlined, withdrawal from the European Union would secure the employment prospects of millions of Britons.

Conclusion

'He abhorred plastics, Picasso, sunbathing and jazz – everything, in fact, that had happened in his own lifetime.' – Evelyn Waugh, *The Ordeal of Gilbert Pinfold*.

Some might feel, after reading the previous nine chapters, that I am of the same ilk. I would deny it. I have little time for the querulous attitude that sees every technological innovation as a threat. Almost every such development of my lifetime – computers, space travel, the Internet, medical treatment, video recorders, pharmaceuticals, compact discs – has brought enormous benefits to mankind.

What I do abhor is the change in moral and social attitudes that has occurred in my lifetime. The decline of religion, the loss of belief in our cultural heritage, the breakdown of the family, the growth of the welfare state, the destruction of education, and the rise in crime have led to a revolution in British society far greater than anything that could have been dreamt up by a white-coated laboratory technician.

Over the last three decades we have, to an extent, been living through a vast social experiment in which our cultural leaders have been testing a number of theories. The most important of these has been the *laissez faire* theory. Through a (literally) unholy alliance of free-marketeers, libertarians, progressives and egalitarians, the state and its institutions have been compelled to abandon their role in upholding the traditional, Christian-based, morality of our civilis-ation. In the name of 'freedom' or 'rights' or 'equality', individuals have been encouraged to pursue their own immediate needs at the expense of wider responsibilities. A number of corrosive ideas have been spawned by this approach. The obsession with equality, for instance, has brought us the notion of 'cultural diversity', the strange idea that we are brought closer by emphasising our racial differences. Similar to this is the European federalists' belief that Britain's national interests lie in the destruction of our own independence. We have attachment to intellectual relativism, which has destroyed the authority of teachers, academics, and the Western canon. The supremacy of a bastardised notion of the market has brought rampant greed to the boardroom and sprawling bureaucracy to the public sector.

Above all, the modernist *laissez faire* outlook has robbed us of our judgement, our values, our common sense. 'Now heaven knows, anything goes,' Cole Porter wrote in 1934 (just to show I do not 'abhor jazz'). Anything really does go, now: incest on a TV soap at peak viewing times, legal aid for millionaires, gay orgies organised by public employees at the taxpayers' expense, MPs taking bribes and not realising they have done anything wrong, men having nine children by four different women and expecting the public to pay maintenance, young serial offenders sent on trips to Florida to 'raise their self-esteem', wage-earners having to pay tax on incomes of less than £5,000 a year, and teachers refusing to correct work for fear of 'oppressing the child'.

This book is an appeal for a return to common sense. The experiment in amoral non-judgementalism has failed. If you give a child what it wants all the time, impose no values, and instil no sense of right and wrong, you will create a monster. We are fast creating a monstrous society. But we are not there yet. This book has set out a wide range of proposals for trying to re-create the sense of morality, responsibility and authority that we need.

Many of the ideas, apart from European withdrawal, could be supported by both major political parties. The Tories have challenged the anti-punishment ethos of the criminal justice system and the anti-élitism orthodoxy of the education establishment. New Labour has spoken powerfully about family values. The problem is that both parties have presided over the continuing destruction of a morally-confident society. The Tory record on crime, the family, welfare, education and ethics in public life is a shameful one. As I write, the Government's apparently corrupt behaviour in the 'cash for questions' scandal is coming to light. Labour is equally untrustworthy, through its dominant role in the 'progressive alliance' of pressure groups, New Public Servants, local authorities, voluntary agencies, academics, professional experts, and trade unions. These people, holding positions of power throughout the country, have promoted the infantilised culture of 'rights' and 'equality'. On 'child-centred learning', bureaucracy, the family, prisons, and religion, Tony Blair's rhetoric is badly at odds with the record of his political supporters. What any incoming Government must do, at the very least, is to halt the continuation of the disastrous *laissez faire* experiment. Some of the theorists recognise its failure, but their solution is to demand more of the same. As crime goes up, we must have **more** rehabilitation of criminals. As families collapse, we must have **more** childcare, **more** divorce counselling. As the dependency culture deepens, we must spend **more** on benefits. As literacy and numeracy decline, we must provide **more** resources for child-centred learning. As employers are subject to a tide of 'discrimination' claims, we must have **more** race- and sex-equality laws.

This is not the road that a future Government should take. Rather than expanding state bureaucracy and regulation to deal with the problems of a fragmented Britain, they should put their energies into rebuilding the moral authority of those institutions that, only forty years ago, lay at the heart of a peaceful, well-ordered, cohesive society: the family, marriage, the police, the Church, the courts, Parliament and schools.

In 1966, it would have been utterly unthinkable for the Church of England to demand an apology from the BBC for broadcasting a comment from a vicar's wife, criticising a celebration of 'gay lifestyles' at Southwark Cathedral. This is what happens in the Britain of 1996. The Anglican Church, like the rest of society, has lost its sense of moral purpose in the space of just three decades. Yet, in the sheer speed of that revolution, lie the seeds of hope. If society can be transformed so quickly, is it not possible that a similar change can occur over the next thirty or forty years, given the will of our cultural leaders?

There is a parallel in British history for the speed of such a social revolution: the reign of Henry VIII. In his thirty-eight years on the throne, he destroyed the abbeys, closed hospitals, executed More and Fisher, cold-shouldered Erasmus, and left the universities and grammar schools withered. The historian A. F. Pollard wrote that during his time 'the English spirit of independence burned low in its socket, and love of freedom grew cold' while 'the finer feelings seem to have been lost in the pursuit of wealth.'

Yet soon after his death came the revival of England under Elizabeth. So there is still hope for our nation. The roots of the amoralists' project cannot have grown so strong in so short a period. All we need is the courage to turn the tide.

Index